Praise for *Finally Out*

"*Finally Out* is a timely and prescient exploration of aging and sexuality. Dr. Olson has the rare ability to combine the personal with the analytical, providing a fascinating glimpse of the advantages as well as the challenges of maturity for gay men."

—*Dean Hamer, PhD, Scientist Emeritus,*
National Institutes of Health

"*Finally Out* is a book that everyone who cares about supporting diversity should read."

—*Julie K. Silver, MD, Associate Professor,*
Department of Physical Medicine and Rehabilitation,
Harvard Medical School

"Dr. Olson eloquently provides insight into the physical and emotional roller coaster ride that LGBTQ people face when addressing their sexuality. As a sixty-year-old lesbian, I can attest that his personal experiences are not too different from what women also experience in the coming out and acceptance process. It is helpful and comforting to read and understand his medical analysis and reasoning as it gives validity to the feelings that one experiences during this uncharted journey to acceptance and peace."

—*Sharon Malheiro, attorney*

"Dr. Olson's book is a comprehensive covering of the wide range of issues relevant to gay men's experiences of coming out beyond young adulthood. Ultimately every man's experiences will be uniquely individual to them and their context—though many are likely like the experiences of the author. I strongly recommend this book for anyone with an interest in making sense of the complex factors that impact the lives of hundreds of thousands of men."

—*Craig White, Professor,*
College of Medical, Veterinary and Life Sciences,
University of Glasgow

"*Finally Out* goes far beyond a coming out story of a married, middle-age gay man. It represents a carefully reasoned book about all human sexuality. Dr. Olson is so honest and direct that any reader will soon get the impression that he knows what he writes about. Lay readers, both gay and straight, will relate his ideas to their own lives, and professionals in social work, religion, psychology, and sociology will find this book invaluable."
—*Bernard J. Brommel, PhD, Professor Emeritus,*
Northeastern Illinois University,
and coauthor of Family Communication

"*Finally Out* is a must-have book for men recovering from conversion therapy and navigating life after heterosexual marriage. Dr. Olson's work is smart, scientific, and personal."
—*Tim Rymel, MEd, speaker, educator, and author of* Going Gay

"*Finally Out* is a much-needed book that fills out our picture of how gay men come to terms with the apparent dichotomy between their rational assumptions about the two sexes and their own set of sexual attractions that do not fit that norm. An insightful read."
—*Amity P. Buxton, PhD, author of* The Other Side of the Closet
and founder of the Straight Spouse Network

"A must-read. Provides insight into a hidden population of men who have sex with other men but may not wish to identify themselves as gay."
—*Abraham Morgentaler, MD, FACS,*
author of Testosterone for Life; *Director, Men's Health Boston;*
and Associate Professor, Harvard Medical School

"Dr. Loren Olson's book is highly readable, well researched, and wise. It comprehensively details the political and social setbacks and successes of the LGBTQ community. It is also autobiographical. *Finally Out* will be of value to people with an academic interest in the topic but also to the individual who is seeking private revelation."
—*Saxby Pridmore, Professor, Department of Psychiatry,*
University of Tasmania

"Dr. Olson lays out a complex process for coming out and prepares the reader for a journey. The relevant questions are answered in *Finally Out*. I was curious about baby boomers since statistics on coming out are not documented in national surveys, and I discovered several specific examples and referents identified in the index."

—*Graham J. McDougall Jr.,*
Professor and Martha Saxon Endowed Chair, Capstone College of Nursing,
Alabama Research Institute on Aging, University of Alabama

"Coming out was a deeply personal experience for me growing up on a farm in rural, northwest Iowa. Every LGBTQ person's journey is unique and should be shared. *Finally Out* adds to the breadth of coming out stories and helps put a face and voice to coming out later in life for many individuals who are still struggling with their own sexual orientation or gender identity."

—*Daniel Hoffman-Zinnel, EdD, Executive Director, One Iowa*

"Dr. Olson is a compassionate professional and a well-informed LGBTQ activist. His updated version of *Finally Out* recognizes the enormous strides that LGBTQ people have made in the last ten years. He updates, as well, his understanding of bisexuality and of transgender people. Dr. Olson's new book is a must-read, particularly for older LGBTQ men and those close to them."

—*Rob Howard, former President, Prime Timers Worldwide*

"I knew I was gay from my early college days. I wondered why other men found it so difficult to come out. Now, after reading *Finally Out*, I understand."

—*Larry Jacobson, motivational speaker*
and author of The Boy behind the Gate

"Until recently, gay men over forty seemingly didn't exist. In *Finally Out*, Dr. Olson debunks such ignorance and lends insight into the hearts of mature men who can be gay, sexy, and respectable. It's high time."

—*Tim Turner, playwright and journalist*

"Dr. Olson's book is a must-read for anyone who's personally dealt with coming out or experienced it within the family. His book is a well-written and enjoyable read. It offers hope and compassion."
—*Matt McCoy, Iowa Senator and author of* McCoy, You're Going Straight to Hell

"Today's LGBT seniors grew up in a system that not only threatened to jail them but also labeled them as mentally ill. Dr. Olson provides an excellent portrayal of the struggles and joys that LGBT seniors and their caregivers face, and he guides both gay and straight readers in the importance of being finally out."
—*Christopher MacLellan, MA, Certified Caregiving Consultant, CEO, Whole Care Network Inc., author, radio show host, and speaker*

"In this excellent book, Dr. Olson has applied his skills to a more rational understanding of male sexuality. He proposes a more complete view of male sexual behavior than that accepted by most clinicians. *Finally Out* will help professionals, patients, and other men better understand and accept gay and bisexual men."
—*Allan F. Demorest, MA, clinical psychologist (retired) and former Clinical Director, United Behavior Clinic*

"I was impressed with your erudition and refreshing honesty. Your discussion of priorities as we navigate our seventies rang true as did the questions on social justice. Nice work!"
—*George McNeil, MD, psychiatrist (retired), Maine Medical Center*

"The new edition of *Finally Out* is that rarest of books: jam-packed with scholarship and up-to-date information but so well written it is hard to put down. Wise and friendly, as valuable as it would have been when I came out at forty, it's worth its weight in gold to me at sixty-one. Loren Olson makes a powerful case that at the age many believe life is winding down, it is just starting to get interesting."
—*Lindsay Thompson, owner of Henry Bemis Books*

Finally Out

Letting Go of Living Straight

LOREN A. OLSON, MD

*For the community at Bethlehem
Lutheran Church.*

*Thanks for your accepting
those of us with
differences*

OAK LANE PRESS

L Olson

To my husband, Doug,
for enriching my life in countless ways
and for his sense of humor that forces me to tip generously

And to Whitney, Krista, and Lynn
for their continuing love and support
and for accepting me as good enough

Oak Lane Press
2815 100th Street #274
Urbandale, Iowa 50322

Quantity sales. Special discounts are available on quantity purchases by corporations, associations, and others. For details, contact the "Special Sales Department" at the address above.

Orders by US trade bookstores and wholesalers. Please contact Independent Publishers Group, 814 North Franklin Street, Chicago, IL 60610. Tel: (312) 337-0747; Fax: (312) 337-5985, www.ipgbook.com.

Printed in the United States of America

Cataloging-in-Publication Data
Olson, Loren A., author.
  Finally out : letting go of living straight :
  / Loren A. Olson.—Revised edition.
    pages cm
    Includes bibliographical references and index.
  LCCN 2016917427
  ISBN 978-0-9979614-3-0 (pbk)
  ISBN 978-0-9979614-4-7 (ebook)

  1. Olson, Loren A. 2. Middle-aged gay men—United States—Biography. 3. Coming out (Sexual orientation) 4. Coming out (Sexual orientation)—United States—Case studies. 5. Autobiographies. I. Title.

HQ75.8.O589A3 2017   306.76'6092
QBI16-900075

Second Edition

21 20 19 18 17   10 9 8 7 6 5 4 3 2 1

Contents

Foreword

JACK DRESCHER, MD

What does it mean to come out as gay? In the mid-1990s, I wrote a professional book to answer that question. My goal was to explain the psychology of homosexuality and provide an alternative to the rigid dogma that used to inform psychiatric and psychoanalytic discussions of lesbian, gay, bisexual, transgender, and queer (LGBTQ) lives. In that book, *Psychoanalytic Therapy and the Gay Man*, I offered a range of stories that define some gay men's identities without offering any singular definition of what it means to be gay. I knew from both personal and professional experiences that gay men of my generation were not like those of previous ones and that the sensibilities of gay men younger than me differed in other ways. To paraphrase the anthropologist Gilbert Herdt, gay identities are not static and vary according to time, place, and culture.

Loren A. Olson's *Finally Out*, the story of a psychiatrist and self-described late-blooming gay man, is a welcome addition to our understanding of gay identities. Coming out late in life has its own special set of challenges, and Dr. Olson's book, part memoir and part self-help, poignantly addresses many of them. He speaks to older men who are struggling to come out, to those who already have done so, and to those who know and love such individuals. He recounts his own coming out process, draws from his own psychiatric experiences with gay men he's treated, and offers helpful professional advice to individuals and families engaged in similar midlife struggles. All of this practical help is sprinkled with his far-ranging and insightful thoughts about neuroscience, sex research, psychopharmacology, psychiatry, issues of aging, literature, philosophy, politics, religion, gay culture, and human relationships.

As Dr. Olson's story illustrates, the decision to call oneself gay is not just about one's sexual orientation but also about creating a social identity, not just about sex but about learning to develop intimate relationships with other men. While developing intimate relationships may seem perfectly natural to some heterosexuals, for many gay men same-sex intimacy is a process that requires practice. Numerous socially sanctioned outlets are available for heterosexual youngsters that serve the purpose of modeling or role playing the part of future heterosexual adults. Teenage dating, high school dances, and adult supervision of coed activities help preteens and teens develop interpersonal skills required for later life and relationships. If and when they manage these interactions successfully, an adolescent's confidence may grow.

Yet those same rituals intended for heterosexual adolescents can generate confusion, shame, and anxiety in kids who grow up to be gay. The closet, which requires that gay people pretend to be straight, imposes a heavy burden. Not only does being in the closet interfere with learning necessary social skills, for many it may lead to the development of hiding and other coping mechanisms that make it difficult to develop relationships after coming out.

Ironically, younger gay men who come out during their late teens and twenties can appear adolescent. They form social cliques characterized by in-groups and out-groups. They place a strong emphasis on style, conformity to standards of dress, a hierarchy of popularity based on looks, and athleticism and affability, and they take advantage of opportunities for experimentation with sex, alcohol, and drugs. For many younger men, this "delayed gay adolescence" is a chance to catch up, in a manner of speaking, with the social skills of heterosexual peers who engaged in similar behaviors years earlier.

The person who comes out later in life faces different challenges. Common points of entry into the open gay community, like gay bars and dance clubs, are usually designed for the pleasure of younger people. Gay men who come out in midlife, having lived in an inauthentic way for a long time and often in need of interpersonal skill building, may not be welcome in venues mainly catering to younger men. As a result, a preexisting sensation of alienation from the straight community sometimes can turn into feelings of alienation from the more visible younger gay community, which some mistakenly believe to be the *entire* gay community.

For these and other reasons, coming out is not always easy for older gay men. Yet the courage to come out is best defined as choosing to do the right thing, not because one has no fear and anxiety but *despite* having fear and anxiety. In fact, those who come out late do so regardless of the difficulties of making a new gay life for themselves because the painful inauthenticity of the closet is more unbearable. Fortunately, as social acceptance of homosexuality has increased and as more people come out, a growing gay infrastructure has become available for older people. These include LGBTQ community centers and national organizations like Services and Advocacy for GLBT Elders (SAGE). Of course, not everyone is fortunate to live close enough to a supportive gay infrastructure, but the Internet has eased the isolation of many gay people who rightly or wrongly believe they are the only gay person in a five-hundred-mile radius.

Finally Out is full of helpful advice for gay men coming out late in life and should be counted among the resources for those men who feel they are alone, their families, and their counselors. Dr. Olson has written an invaluable survival guide for older gay men with a clarity that is both highly accessible and greatly appreciated.

Preface to the Second Edition

In the few years since the original publication of *Finally Out: Letting Go of Living Straight, a Psychiatrist's Own Story,* the world for gay men and women has changed more than in the sixty-seven years of my life before I wrote it, and the rate of change seems to be accelerating. When I first learned that Massachusetts on May 17, 2004, became the first US state and the sixth jurisdiction in the world to legalize same-sex marriage, I was not only surprised—I was skeptical. *How can two men or two women get married; marriage is one man and one woman, isn't it?* My mind was not quite ready to grasp the concept. When I originally wrote this book, Iowa, where Doug and I live, was but one of a very few states that had legalized same-sex marriage.

Few could imagine back then that on June 26, 2015, the United States Supreme Court would hand down its landmark ruling in the case of *Obergefell v. Hodges* declaring that same-sex couples could legally be married in all fifty states. In a 5–4 decision the US Supreme Court ruled that states cannot prevent same-sex couples from marrying and must recognize their unions wherever their marriages take place. Justice Kennedy wrote, "They ask for equal dignity in the eyes of the law. The Constitution grants them that right."[1]

These developments come with increasing acceptance of LGBTQ people in American society. The Pew Research Center reported that as of June 8, 2015, just two weeks before the US Supreme Court announced its decision to legalize same-sex marriage, support for same-sex marriage had reached a record high. In polling done by Pew Research, in 2001 Americans opposed same-sex marriage by a margin of 57 percent to

35 percent; in 2016 those percentages were reversed with 55 percent supporting same sex marriage and only 37 percent opposing it.[2]

Support has increased among nearly all segments of the public, although some groups remain broadly opposed; while support has increased among both Republicans and Democrats, the differences between the two political parties are as wide as they were a decade ago. Greater opposition also comes from older people, people of color, religious conservatives, geographic region, and people who have limited contact with those in the LGBTQ community. The South is the only region where same-sex marriage support falls below 50 percent.[3]

When the Iowa Supreme Court ruled in *Varnum v. Brien* (2009) to allow same-sex marriage in Iowa, I often heard from friends in other parts of the country, "Iowa? Of all places."[4] Because the decision surprised so many people, Iowa played a key role in making marriage equality a national conversation. Support for same-sex marriage was no longer seen only as a liberal issue supported primarily on the coasts of the United States but an issue for all LGBTQ people, even in the heart of America.

In December 2010, the US House and Senate passed a bill repealing Don't Ask, Don't Tell that ended the restriction of gay, lesbian, and bisexual personnel from serving in the US military. On June 30, 2016, the military lifted its ban on transgender men and women as well.

One other important change in this book from its previous edition relates to the use of the word *homosexual*, which many in the LGBTQ community now find pejorative. Not only was it used historically in a clinical sense, implying pathology, but it has also been used aggressively by antigay extremists to suggest that gay people are psychologically and spiritually damaged. This word remains in this book many times, but I have tried to use it only when it has historical or clinical significance or in the context of discussions involving religious conservatives where homosexuality is used to denigrate gay men and women. I have tried to avoid its use where *gay* or *same-sex* is preferred.

Nothing that I've ever written has provoked as much controversy as an essay published on the *Psychology Today* website on July 5, 2015, called "The Messy Realities of Bisexuality." My point in writing it was primarily to suggest that bisexuality lacks clarity in definition between attraction, behavior, and identity, but apparently not everyone shares my lack of clarity. According to GLAAD in its report *In Focus: Reporting on the Bisexual Community*, the definition of bisexuality is "A person who has the capacity to form enduring physical, romantic, and/or emotional attractions to those of the same gender and to those of another gender."[5]

In Focus goes on to say that people may experience bisexuality in differing ways across their life span. While I accept the legitimacy of the definition and I recognize that the B in LGBTQ is often overlooked, bisexuality is a very huge umbrella. It appears from that definition that I would be included since I have had enduring physical, romantic, and emotional attractions to both genders, but I am far more comfortable defining myself as gay. As one of my interviewees said, "I see a woman and nothing happens, but when I see a man, something happens." But I also understand that many others are far more comfortable defining themselves as bisexual or something else. Possibly my comfort with the label gay comes from my current life circumstances, and I can accept that under different circumstances that might change. In my small sample nearly 28 percent of the respondents to my survey, all men having sex with men, preferred some label other than gay.

Biphobia is defined as a fear of bisexuals and is often based on stereotypes including inaccurate associations with infidelity, promiscuity, and sexually transmitted diseases. I was roundly criticized in the essay for being biphobic. While I have no fear of bisexuals, I understand why some made that interpretation from what I wrote. While I don't argue that bisexuality does not exist, I continue to believe that this label is so broadly applied—and probably misapplied—that it lacks consistency. I have tried in this edition of my book to be more sensitive to the issues facing bisexuals, and I hope that nothing in this book suggests that I am being dismissive of bisexuals.

Those 30 percent or so of Americans who resist acceptance of gay people have accelerated their pushback against the advances in LGBTQ freedoms under the rubric of religious freedom. This has generated a raft of proposed laws related to bathrooms for transgender men and women with spurious charges that the use of bathrooms according to gender identity rather than birth gender will increase sexual assaults on women and children. Although acceptance has increased, those who resist acceptance in some cases are violently intolerant. Hate and terror joined forces and collided with a culture of increasing violence on June 12, 2016, in Orlando, Florida, with the largest mass shooting and the deadliest attack on a gay target in United States history.

In a post about GLAAD's *Accelerating Acceptance* report, Matt Goodman wrote that over 50 percent of non-LGBTQ Americans now believe that gay people have all the same rights as everyone else, a false and potentially dangerous impression that with marriage equality the law of the land, all the work for LGBTQ equality is now done.[6] While the majority of non-LGBTQ Americans are increasingly comfortable with gay people, at the state and federal level, gay people are still discriminated against in employment, housing, and public accommodation, and these problems are compounded for aging LGBTQ. They face many consequences because of continuing negative social attitudes, including homelessness, mental illness, and violence.

Many challenges lie ahead. More than two hundred pieces of anti-LGBTQ legislation have been introduced on the state level. Many states are using the religious freedom argument to support denying services to LGBTQ people. In many places, you can marry your same-sex partner on the weekend and be fired the next week for being openly gay. Twenty-eight states lack antidiscrimination laws that include sexual orientation or gender identity, and no federal law protects access to employment, housing, and public accommodations like hotels or restaurants.

Violence continues to be a big problem in our community. In some places people believe that committing acts of violence against LGBTQ is okay, and the number of bias-motivated killings rose by 20 percent from 2014 to 2015.[7] All LGBTQ people know that their safety is not guaranteed. As visibility of transgenders has increased, so has the violence directed at them, and trans people are more likely than gay men, lesbians, and bisexuals to experience poverty, discrimination, and violence.

In terms of healthcare, LGBTQ people are more likely to be uninsured, but the Affordable Care Act, known as Obamacare, prohibits anti-LGBTQ discrimination. HIV continues to ravage our community, particularly people of color and transgender people. Pre-Exposure Prophylaxis (PrEP) is a promising treatment that produces high levels of immunity in people not yet affected by HIV, but the prohibitive cost of prescriptions limits access to this option. About one-third of the estimated nine hundred thousand LGBTQ immigrants are undocumented, and they have even greater challenges in accessing adequate medical care [8]

An estimated one billion people now live in countries where marriage of same-sex couples is legal, but that means that about one in seven LGBTQ people live in countries that don't allow same-sex marriage and in many cases continue to allow people to be put to death for being gay.[9] Even in those countries where there exists an increased acceptance of being gay, many men and women, for a wide variety of reasons, live deeply closeted, often lonely, and sometimes desperate lives.

For this book to remain relevant, I needed to address all of these issues.

Introduction

I didn't intend to write a book. After all, I was just your average gay, close-to-retirement psychiatrist, living with my husband on a farm in rural Iowa. All I wanted were some answers. An essay by Jane Gross in the *New York Times*, "Aging and Gay, and Facing Prejudice in Twilight," published October 9, 2007, had attached itself to my brain like a barnacle. She wrote that older gay men and women were being forced to go back in the closet because geriatric social-service agencies were discriminating against them.[1] Having not come out until I was forty, I was flooded with anxiety. When I read the article I was in my sixth decade, and I imagined that I would need those services before long. I did not want to let go of the feeling of freedom that first surged through me when, in the middle of my life, I recognized and accepted that I am gay.

So I did what any physician would do. I researched medical literature to see what I could find about mature gay men and women. But my search of both the medical and lay presses frustrated me; research almost entirely ignored the subject of coming out in midlife, and what little information I found didn't resonate with my own experience or the experiences of most of the mature gay men I know. Most of the research I did find had been done on young, urban, self-identified gay men. I noticed a striking absence of information about those I saw as my cohorts. The absence of answers led to more questions. I grew increasingly concerned about men who have sex with men (MSM), particularly rural and minority MSM who are at high risk for HIV/ AIDS because their conservative environments make them feel isolated, leading them to seek partners in public sex environments, through the Internet, through travel to places with a high prevalence of HIV, and with the use of drugs and alcohol. People aged fifty and older have many of the same HIV risk factors as younger people but may be less aware of their risk.

I am frequently asked—sometimes quite angrily—two questions: "How could you not know you were gay until you were forty years old?" and "Wasn't your first marriage just a sham designed to protect yourself, and at your wife and children's expense?" The second question is easier to answer. Although I know that my sexual orientation and my decision to come out hurt my wife and children deeply, I never intended to use them as a shield to protect me. As a psychiatrist, I focus on relieving pain, not causing it. Before I was forty, there was never a time in my life when I was committed to anything more than to being a good husband and a devoted father.

My decision to leave my family came about because I was losing the battle to control the feelings that raged inside me. I worried that my secret life would be exposed. Right or wrong, my judgment was that if I were outed while still married, the potential for humiliating my family and of bringing shame on myself loomed larger than the pain I would inflict by leaving. Cheating on my wife, whether with a man or a woman, was wrong, and recognizing I was gay did not absolve me from the guilt I felt about it. Perhaps my reasoning was twisted rationalization, but I absolutely believed that I faced a choice between only two unacceptable outcomes: either break a deeply held commitment to marriage and family or inflict shame and embarrassment on the people I love.

The other question, "How could you not know?" is much more difficult to answer. Probing for an answer is ultimately what led to this book. All memories are but reconstructions, but what I can affirm without qualification or reservation is that until I was forty, I had no idea I was gay. Before that, I suffered from a sense that things weren't right inside me. It seemed that I had to work harder to feel like a man than other men appeared to, but I could never speak of my confused feelings to anyone. I believed that my father's death when I was three years old had crippled me. It was as if his death created negative space around me, like the optical illusion of Rubin's vase. Was I really a man or just the illusion of one, defined by that negative space surrounding me?

Our minds contain two distinct systems of thought: rational thought and feeling thought. Although we prefer to believe that as humans we operate exclusively through rational thought, our feeling thought makes up the majority of our thinking and operates continuously and usually unconsciously. The conflict between our rational thought and our feeling thought creates within us a great sense of dissonance characterized by considerable anxiety. We try to control that anxiety by repressing this inner contradiction to bring our mind into unity.

That need for harmony in our thinking is why men like me who experience a significant conflict between our rational thought (men should love women) and our feeling thought (I am attracted to men) search for a way to find accord, deceiving ourselves about our sexual attractions. To protect ourselves from unacceptable feelings, we instinctively erect barricades in our brains so that we may hoodwink ourselves into absolute assurance that we are heterosexual. In the process, we unknowingly perpetrate a hoax on our spouses, our children, and everyone else we know. If that partition develops even a small crack, that breach is not a fissure that enlightens our conscious minds, but rather a fault line in the darkening lens we've constructed that blocks the blinding light of unwanted feelings. As I look back on my life now, I can see that the unconscious operations of my mind pushed me to burst through the divide created by my traditional upbringing to explore a world that lay beyond Nebraska's prairies.

Inquisitiveness about how the mind works and why people become who they are, including a curiosity about understanding myself, drew me into psychiatry. As I finished medical school, the unconscious forces in my brain were pushing me to consider continuing my training in New York, Chicago, or New Orleans, but my rational brain told me to get married and remain in Nebraska. Instead of choosing to be young and single in a world where gay men congregated, I chose instead to become a young doctor with a beautiful and educated wife from a similar background and with similar values. It should have been a perfect match.

During medical school and my psychiatric residency, I read—with what I thought was only intellectual curiosity—everything I could find about the "psychopathic deviancy" of homosexuality. Very early in my practice, I displayed too much interest in the life of one of my gay patients. He came into my office one day and, before I could sit down, stripped off all his clothes. Stunned, I said, "Put your clothes on again, then sit down, and we'll talk about what just happened." The implications were obvious; unchecked empathy creates what psychiatrists call countertransference, something I should have worked out with a supervisor in training. My asking this patient for details about his same-sex experience was driven by my own curiosity more than by a need for information that was necessary for his treatment. I used his answers to try to understand myself more than to understand him. All of this he interpreted as an invitation to satisfy my curiosity with him. What led to my earlier study of homosexuality proved to be driven far more by the forces of my unconscious mind than I ever imagined. This incident with my patient served as a wake-up call to me; my interest in homosexuality was much more than just an intellectual curiosity.

Children's belief in Santa Claus might shed some light on the question of "How could you not know?" Very young children have no difficulty accepting the fantasy of Santa Claus no matter how improbable that fantasy is. As children age, they begin to suspect that the fantasy isn't true but want so badly to believe in Santa Claus that they dismiss all evidence to the contrary. As they grow even older, the evidence becomes overwhelming and they must forfeit the belief in the magic of Santa Claus. Children's continued belief in Santa Claus despite the evidence is an example of how dissociation works.

Dissociation is a ubiquitous defense central to everyone's growth, and it was certainly a part of my own. The hysteria around sexual abuse during the 1980s and '90s, however, has tainted the concept of dissociation. During this time, in an effort to assuage their guilt about having paid little attention to sexual abuse for so long, mental health professionals began to go to the opposite extreme. If patients couldn't remember a part of their childhood, it was assumed that dissociation was at work and that the most likely explanation was sexual abuse. This led to the false- or pseudomemory syndrome where patients seemingly remembered vivid and emotionally charged events that in many cases never actually occurred. Memories can be confusing mixtures of fragments of real and dreamed events, a montage of happenings from different times and places that are remembered as if they were one. All memories are distortions of actual experiences—reconstructions filled with factual errors—and in some cases they may be entirely imagined. When emotions are attached to memories, the memories are intensified.

Abuse is not a part of my life experience. I never considered myself pathological, so I did not identify with gay men whom psychiatrists and society as a whole considered sick. I briefly questioned whether my intensifying attractions to men meant I might be bisexual, but at a psychiatry conference, one of the speakers proclaimed, "Bisexuality is nothing more than a state of transition." I immediately dismissed the possibility that I was bisexual because I was not willing to loosen my grasp on heterosexuality if it meant I was going to slip right past bisexuality into being gay. I was heterosexual—with a little quirk.

In 1985, when I learned of a gay fathers' support group, I went to that first meeting with Roberto, the Argentine man I had secretly been seeing while I was married. For the first time in my life, within that small group of men I felt a sense of sanctuary, a feeling of being at peace with myself among men who accepted me without the pretenses that by then had become so automatic. It was like being welcomed home for a holiday. Our common experiences created an immediate sense of intimacy, an insurgent connection with other men that I had never before experienced. After forty years, I had finally found a group of men with whom I felt I belonged. It transformed me from wondering if I might be gay to knowing without ambivalence or reservation that I was gay. Next I had to figure out what I was going to do about it. I knew that coming out was going to be a long and complicated process.

There were moments during the years I was transitioning from living a heterosexual life to being an openly gay man that I began to wonder, What have I done to my life? It was a frightening time to be coming out.

Harvey Milk, the first openly gay man elected to any significant political office, was murdered on November 27, 1978. In June 1981 the Centers for Disease Control and Prevention (CDC) reported an outbreak of a fatal disease subsequently named acquired immunodeficiency syndrome (AIDS).[2] In 1988, Ken Eaton was murdered, the victim of a hate crime. Ken was one of my friends in the gay fathers' support group. Although socially coming out now is easier, on an individual basis it often remains a frightening experience.

But in spite of these events, I never seriously questioned the legitimacy of my decision to leave my family and begin my new life as a gay man. I saw a video clip on television of Harvey Milk saying, "If every man who is gay would just come out, we would win this battle." My mind was beginning to find a peace and unity that I had never before known, and to come out in more and more areas of my life began to feel like a moral obligation.

As my circle of gay friends expanded, I learned that many of them had been married, and all of them took their roles as fathers very seriously. None had abandoned their families in pursuit of a stereotypical hedonistic gay lifestyle. For some time, I thought that my experience as a gay father was uniquely Midwestern and that men who knew they were gay early in their lives would have moved to the urban coastal areas, leaving those of us who were more tightly bound to traditional values behind, married and with families.

Any envy I felt toward those who had come out as young men and had become a part of the gay community was offset by the incredible joy I felt at being a father. I also discovered that many men who enjoyed sex exclusively with other men found it impossible to identify with the out-and-proud values of the activist gay community. Many of them who, like me, lived in a heterosexual world and passed as straight were sheltered from the diversity of the gay community, and our prejudices toward gay people persisted unchallenged.

I discovered that there is no universal pathway to accepting that you are gay and coming out, and traditional values are not the exclusive property of heterosexuals. Many men who truly honored their strong religious and cultural experiences believed that the losses they would experience if they came out were far greater than continuing to lead a duplicitous life. They chose to maintain their struggle against the undertow of their attraction to men.

Despite the comfort I felt in finding a community, I still believed that, at forty years of age, I was over the hill as a gay man, clueless about what being gay meant, and suddenly alone. It seemed I had all the prerequisites for clinical depression. A lecture in a class for physician-executives at the University of Arizona given by Dr. Harry Levinson, an emeritus professor of psychology in the Department of Psychiatry at Harvard, dispelled that idea. As I studied his remarks, I realized that I would never achieve lasting self-esteem if the person I wanted to be was so far removed from the person I considered myself to be. I had to let go of pretending to be straight and work toward becoming the best gay man I could be. Dr. Levinson pointed out that lasting self-esteem never comes through seeking approval from others.[3] In other words, the only way to improve the way you feel about yourself is to take charge of the person you want to be—make it your own, actively attempt to reach that ideal, and be realistic about the progress you are making toward it. You also need to stop beating yourself up for not being the person someone else wants you to be.

As Anna Freud, daughter of Sigmund Freud and a psychoanalyst herself, said, "I was always looking outside myself for strength and confidence, but it comes from within. It is there all the time." Dr. Levinson's remarks provided a moment of tremendous insight for me. Letting go of the need for approval allows the coming out process to begin.

Over the years, as I spoke to more and more men who were attracted to other men, I found that each had resolved his inner contradictions in his own way. Those who had resolved this conflict successfully had done so by developing a moral integrity—an authentic relationship between who they want to be and who they think they are. They had let go of being preoccupied with trying to please others. Many men had only begun to deal with their same-sex attractions later in life, and many others had no idea how or where to begin to find that congruence.

As I spoke about my ideas of writing a book, I heard over and over again, "I wish your book had been written when I was trying to find myself." That is the force that drove me to write this book. This book is not only for those men who are still engaged in the struggle but for all of those who love them or want to understand them. Too often what has been written about sexual orientation suggests that every person must be either gay or straight; no allowance is made for those who are struggling in a state of confusion, a kind of sexual purgatory. In fact, some gay activists appear to have forgotten their own experience of locking horns with this issue and have suggested that gay people don't want to include "those hypocrites" as a part of the gay community. Have they grown insensitive to the fact that attempting to resolve conflicts about sexual orientation is a process that can go on for many years and for some never ends?

I was drawn to psychiatry because I wanted to know people's stories. But doctors are first and foremost scientists, and our training teaches us to be objective, to question, to look for data. Medicine teaches doctors how to cure illness. It doesn't teach them how to heal people. Healing involves much more than data. For men and women coming out, healing often comes through hearing the stories of others who have crossed the bridge successfully.

I began the research that led to this work to see if there was evidence to support what I believed to be true of MSM. My hypothesis was that the coming-out process for men who come out in midlife or later is distinctly different from the coming-out process for young men as described in the literature. My research conducted in 2008–09 was composed of two parts: (1) an online convenience survey of mature MSM, and (2) biographical interviews to add depth to the survey findings. Convenience sampling is done by recruiting respondents from people known to the researcher and then asking them to recruit others. A convenience sampling is not scientific; it reveals correlations but not causes. The conclusions cannot be generalized to a larger population, but convenience sampling still can be useful. I initially recruited personal friends and contacts through Internet social networks; my connections then recruited others.

To test my hypotheses, I conducted an online survey of 132 of these men. I promoted the survey by requesting respondents from mature MSM, specifically avoiding the word *gay* because I believed then, as I do even more now, that many MSM for a variety of reasons do not wish to be labeled gay. I was interested in reaching men who might still be living a heterosexual life but who felt an irresistible pull toward sexual relationships with men. I chose to have people self-define *mature men*. Although some of the men in the survey and that I interviewed had been involved in counseling or psychiatric treatment, none of them were patients I had treated.

I conducted some of the interviews face to face and others via the Internet. Through social media, I was able to interview men from a wide variety of cultures, both within and outside the United States. The face-to-face biographical interviews are not psychiatric examinations; they followed a structured list of questions, although the answers I received frequently departed from the structured questions. Many of the online interviews were with men who had contacted me on a now-defunct blog called *MagneticFire* that I wrote while doing my research. The online interviews were more free-flowing, and I introduced myself by my saying, "I'm a psychiatrist doing research on a book about men who have sex with men. Do you mind if I ask you a few questions?" Many of them were eager to talk with someone about parts of their lives that until then had been deeply hidden; many times I had to remind them, "I am not your doctor. I cannot give you medical advice."

Through this series of formal biographical interviews and informal conversations in person and online, I found that each of the men I interviewed had a "rational" explanation for why he felt different from other men, and usually he attributed it to some historical event in his life, often one over which he had no control. Just as I had used my father's death to explain my feelings of difference, the men I interviewed found experiences in their own lives that helped them accept their feeling of being different.

Respondents to my survey ranged from twenty-four to ninety-one years of age, with a median age of sixty. Purely by chance, the respondents broke nearly evenly between men who were twenty years old or younger at the time of the Stonewall riots in 1969 and those who were older than twenty at that time. The respondents were also almost equally divided between those who are or have been married and those who have not.

Respondents came from twenty-two states and three countries outside of the United States. They were both urban and rural. The vast majority of respondents to the survey were Caucasian. From all the respondents, I chose the most diverse set possible to interview.

Table 1 shows the breakdown of survey respondents' answers. Any attempt at interpreting the data or comparing the findings to previous studies goes beyond the scope of this book.

Table 1: Results of convenience sampling survey

	Percent of Respondents
Relationship Status	
Have you been married to a woman?	
Yes	53.4
No	46.6
Of those previously married	
Average times married: 1.02	
Range of times married: 1 to 4	
Median times married: 1	
Do you have children?	
Yes	43.5
No	56.5
Do you have a partner or lover?	
Yes	70.2
No	29.8
How many previous relationships have you had?	
Average number of previous relationships: 2.23	
Range of previous relationships: 0 to 12	
Median number of previous relationships: 2	

With whom do you currently live?

I live alone	42.7
I live with a partner or lover	32.1
I live with a roommate	6.1
I live with family (spouse, children, relatives)	14.5
Other	4.6

Comfort with Sexual Orientation

At the present time, how would you rate your
sexual orientation?

Exclusively heterosexual	0.0
Primarily heterosexual, only slightly homosexual	0.0
Primarily heterosexual, but more than slightly homosexual	0.8
Just about equally homosexual and heterosexual	5.3
Primarily homosexual, but more than slightly heterosexual	4.6
Primarily homosexual, only slightly heterosexual	16.0
Exclusively homosexual	71.8
Other	1.5

I wish I were not homosexual.

Strongly agree	4.6
Agree	6.1
Not Sure	10.7
Disagree	33.6
Strongly disagree	45.0

I would not want to give up my sexual attraction for men, even if I
could.

Strongly agree	52.7
Agree	26.7
Not Sure	12.2
Disagree	6.9
Strongly disagree	1.5

Who knows about your homosexuality? (Check all that apply.)

Family	91.8
Work	52.7
Straight friends	62.6
Gay friends	84.0

I don't care who knows about my homosexuality.

Strongly agree	26.7
Agree	26.0
Not Sure	13.0
Disagree	19.1
Strongly disagree	15.3

Physical Health, Mental Health, and Sexual Health

In general, how would you describe your health?

Excellent	25.2
Very good	38.9
Good	22.1
Fair	12.2
Poor	1.5

In the past, have you ever consulted a counselor or mental health professional?

Yes	56.5
No	43.5

Are you now or have you in the past taken medication for anxiety or depression on a regular basis?

Yes	32.1
No	67.9

Over the past six months, how satisfied have you been with your sex life?

Very dissatisfied	9.9
Mostly dissatisfied	23.7
Neither satisfied nor dissatisfied	16.8
Mostly satisfied	35.9
Very satisfied	13.7

Socioeconomic Status	
How would you describe your political views?	
Very liberal	32.8
Somewhat liberal	30.5
Progressive	13.0
Moderate	15.3
Somewhat conservative	6.1
Very conservative	2.3
What was your work status during the past twelve months?*	
Retired	32.1
Work full-time	50.4
Work part-time	14.5
Disabled	3.1
What is your current household income from all sources?*	
Less than $25,000 per year	11.5
$25,000–50,000	35.9
$50,000–100,000	35.1
More than $100,000	17.6

* In some instances, totals are slightly more than or less than 100 percent because of the effect of rounding

Attention is appropriately being focused on the mental-health crisis of gay American teens who often experience bullying, rejection, and depression. They have a nearly twofold increase in the likelihood of successful suicide over their nongay cohorts. Gay, bisexual, and other men who have sex with men are at even greater risk for suicide attempts, especially before the age of twenty-five.[4] According to the CDC's *Morbidity and Mortality Weekly Report* of May 3, 2013, during the first decade of this century, suicide rates for both men and women between the ages of thirty-five and sixty-four have increased nearly 30 percent with the highest increase between fifty and fifty-nine.[5] The secretive nature of the lives of MSM creates logistical, financial, and ethical issues in attempts to study them and makes such research very difficult, and perhaps society lacks motivation to find the answers. Many of the men

I have studied turned to alcohol and other drugs as a solution, but the number of men receiving counseling appears to be increasing.

This book is not intended as a directive of what must be done. My thoughts and experiences are presented only as an example of what has worked for me. I hope that sharing my story will help men like me, the families who love us, and the people who counsel us to have a better understanding about the lives of men who delay their coming out or perhaps choose not to come out at all.

In *Prescriptions for the Mind*, Dr. Joel Paris wrote, "Memories of the past are rarely factually accurate. We tell old stories in new ways, re-creating and reinterpreting the past in light of the present."[6] In this book, I have reconstructed my memories to create with as much accuracy as possible a narrative of my past. I could not have written -this book earlier in my career; the stories are far too personal.

Because many of the men whose stories I have related are not yet open about their sexual orientation in every area of their lives, most of their names have been changed. I have not made any attempt to write about this experience as it relates to women. Some of the same principles may apply to them, but I found it necessary to limit the scope of this project. Since it began with a search for my own answers, I have focused on mature gay men. Mature women will surely wish to define themselves.

No universal blueprint exists for coming out; each individual must work out his own solution. My hope is that some of the answers I have found will offer others insights into why some men who love other men might marry and have families, choose to come out or not, or delay coming out until midlife or beyond. My primary message is one of hope, encouraging others to discover who they want to be. I'd like to help them take responsibility for working out their own solutions so that they and the families and friends who love them will believe that happiness is attainable, although perhaps in a different way than they had once expected.

1

I Am Not Gay, but I Might Be a Little Bit Queer

That fear had been inside him for many years, if it lived with him,
it had been another shadow cast over his own shadow
ever since the night he awoke, shaken by a bad dream,
and realized that that was not only a permanent probability,
as he had always believed, but an immediate reality.

—GABRIEL GARCÍA MÁRQUEZ, *LOVE IN THE TIME OF CHOLERA*

I know precisely the moment I became gay. As Cary Grant said in the role of Dr. David Huxley in the 1938 movie *Bringing Up Baby*, "I just went gay all of a sudden!"[1]

Of course, my transformation did not occur suddenly. Nothing much about my life had changed, at least not yet. But at the precise moment after I turned forty years old, things shifted inside my head. I went from thinking of myself as straight to knowing that I am gay. Only then did I begin to realize how my gayness had cast a shadow over me my entire life.

On August 28, 2007, after having been arrested for making sexual advances in a men's bathroom at a Minneapolis airport, US senator Larry Craig stood before the microphones of the national media with his wife, Suzanne, at his side and declared, "I am not gay! I never have been gay!" What he did not say overshadowed what he did say. He did not say "I have never had sex with a man." Senator Craig's voting record had earned

15

him top ratings from social-conservative groups. He had voted in favor of the Defense of Marriage Act (DOMA), and he had supported a federal constitutional amendment banning same-sex marriage.[2]

Reactions to Senator Craig's announcement varied. Some gay activists smiled smugly, believing that one more hypocritical, closeted gay man had just been exposed. Religious conservatives, often intolerant of any same-sex behavior, countered that gay activists proved their own hypocrisy; the conservatives said gay people support the separation of a person's public and private lives only when it benefits their community and that gay activists now were viciously smearing someone's private behavior. They claimed that the senator had supported legislation as a matter of public policy and he had not targeted anyone's personal behavior. Other people thought police had wasted their time entrapping otherwise honorable male citizens. Some felt that Senator Craig should resign; as a married man, he had cheated on his wife, lied to his family and constituents, and broke the law.

But a considerable number of men were frightened and thought, "Man, that could have been me!" Countless numbers of ordinary men live with the fear of being exposed and discredited, humiliating themselves and their families, friends, and coworkers. The exposure of the underground sexual activity of celebrities and politicians like Senator Craig briefly generates a commotion in the media, which typically refer to men who are exposed for having sex with other men in public places as gay. However, a significant portion of these men, like Senator Craig, would not define themselves as gay. Many of them are married to women. Why would anyone choose to risk so much and behave in potentially destructive ways?

First of all, does anyone really behave rationally when they are having sex? Sexual desire operates within the primitive levels of our brains, and truthfully the scientific community knows very little about how sexual desire affects our judgment. Perhaps more powerfully, the use of psychological defense mechanisms like denial, repression, and rationalization protects the conscious mind from awareness of unacceptable desires. Sex is not rational, but it is rationalizing. Sexual desire arises from parts of our brain outside of rational thought, but sometimes we call upon the higher, cortical portions of the brain in an attempt to offer a rational justification for our sometimes-irrational sexual behavior.

Senator Craig's situation became fodder for late-night television comedians until the next scandal bumped it aside. Meanwhile, a much larger issue was emerging: according to a 2006 study of men in New York City published in *Annals of Internal Medicine*, nearly 10 percent of working-class and immigrant men who labeled themselves as heterosexual have sex only with other men. The study also found that almost 10 percent of all married men have had sex with another man in the previous year. Although the study describes a limited population in New York City and cannot be generalized to an entire country's population, it suggests that the number of men who have sex with men (MSM) is much greater than most imagine.[3]

Sex is not rational, but it is rationalizing.

A study of thirty thousand men and women in the United States found that the number of adult men and women having sex with members of their own gender has doubled between 1990 and 2014 as modern culture has begun to embrace same-sex relationships.[4] It appears likely that more men who label themselves as straight are having sex with other men than are gay men.

MSM come from all communities, all ethnicities, and all socioeconomic levels. Whether single or married, they lead hidden lives. Society colludes to lock these men inside its collective closet by ignoring, denying, or repressing the fact that men have sex with other men.

Several forces operate in our culture to sustain the misperception that men are not having sex with men. Many people believe that same-sex behavior is sinful and undermines traditional family values. They believe the behavior would go away if we returned to the natural and timeless values of 1950s small-town America. Oddly, many older MSM were raised in—and many still live in—these mythic small towns, particularly in the Midwest and the South. They remain there, believing that if they go away they will be changed in ways that will never allow them to return.

In 2013, the CDC estimated that in the United States, gay, bisexual, and other MSM represented 2 percent of the population but accounted for 55 percent of people living with HIV.[5] Since many of these men do not use condoms, women justifiably fear that MSM serve as a bridge for the transmission of HIV and other sexually transmitted diseases (STDs); this fear is supported by CDC statistics.[6] In the 1980s, the CDC sought to expand its education to all men at risk for transmitting HIV and other sexually transmitted diseases, and it began using the term *MSM* to incorporate men who are straight-identified but still have sex with men, not just those who are gay-identified. Initially the gay community reacted negatively to the term. Although the position of the gay community has changed in recent years, they originally felt it was too broad and that it rejected their hard-fought, self-affirming label of gay.[7]

It appears likely that more men who label themselves as straight are having sex with other men than gay men are having sex with men.

Many in both the gay and straight worlds believe that only gay men have sex with men. It turns out, however, that MSM are much more diverse than the gay community. MSM are more diverse as to ethnicity, geography, age, current or prior opposite-sex marital status, and children. Many have discovered their same-sex attractions buried deep within themselves and want to expel themselves from the life they have led thus far. In the survey that I conducted, as well as in conversations and correspondence with other mature men, I found that some experience no sense of shame about their hidden same-sex activities, while others live with significant conflict about their sexuality. Many MSM never consider the possibility of publicly disclosing their same-sex behavior and refuse to identify themselves as gay. In fact, many of these men are repelled by the idea of being called gay and have barricaded themselves in a heterosexual world because they have incorporated an inaccurate and stereotypic view of gay men. Many of them see the gay community as a radical counterculture defined primarily by sexual behavior, the same way much of the heterosexual community sees it, and these men don't want to be part of such a community.

Some men seek only casual man-on-man sex—an impersonal orgasm such as they might have with a female prostitute—and have no interest in any emotional connection with their sexual partner. They consider it an easy, no-strings way of obtaining sexual gratification, as if their sexual partner is nothing more than a genderless sex organ. They believe that soliciting sex from another man does not make them gay— that only feminine, deviant, and abnormal men who respond to the solicitation are gay. Even though they may be having sex exclusively with men, they do not consider themselves to be gay or bisexual because they claim, and often firmly believe, that their interest in men is secondary to their primary affection-based interest in women. In his response to my survey, one man said, "My wife is a wonderful woman. I love her, but I only want to have sex with men." These men's behavior may even be overlooked by society if they are meeting the heteronormative masculine responsibilities of being overworked and stressed out. When I first discovered the reality of my sexual attraction to other men, I thought I was doing everything that a heterosexual man was supposed to do.

Although society evolves, sexism persists, and it plays a significant role in men's conflicts about sexual orientation. Successfully competing with other men often defines masculinity more than a relationship with a woman does. Rigid cultural conventions concerning men prescribe that men have a wife and family, aggressively pursue their careers, participate in contests of strength, and demonstrate prowess with women even to the point of objectifying them. Several conservative religious groups demand a dominant role for men over women.

Cultural beliefs about masculinity can affect children from a young age. When I was ten years old, one of my neighbors bought me a gas-powered lawn mower that in the 1950s only a few people had. We agreed that I would mow their lawn and mine, and I could use the lawn mower to mow other people's yards to earn some money for my family. The lawn mower frustrated me considerably. I had a great deal of difficulty with any machine, and I always had difficulty getting that John Deere lawn mower started. One day it would not start. In frustration, I called my widowed mother at work, crying "Mom, I can't get the lawn mower started!"

Helpless, she said to me, "Of course you can! You're a man, aren't you?" I felt as if one of my testicles had just been torn away. Men start machines. I couldn't start mine, so I must not be a man. I was feeling like I could have fixed it if only my dad hadn't died. I desperately wanted someone to teach me to be a man. I needed a counterweight to my mother. Masculinity, I thought, is never nuanced. This feeling of being incompetent at accomplishing manly tasks embedded itself in my brain and penetrated every aspect of my life.

I hadn't considered that I might be gay; my masculinity was unformed like a child's stick figure drawing of a man. Call me anything, but do not call me a sissy. I do not remember any reference to homosexuality as a child other than "Don't wear yellow on Tuesday because it means you're queer." We called each other fairy, but we were thinking Tinker Bell, not faggot. Although we derided others with these terms, they had little to do with sexuality—we only knew it was not good to be called one.

The Complexity of Sexuality

Mature men know what arouses them sexually, but why those things arouse them remains foggy. A growing consensus of scientists believe that genetics determines sexual attraction. Research may help to inform the debate about whether or not sexual orientation is innate, environmental, or both, but those who oppose homosexuality use the same research to make same-sex attraction appear pathological. The exact causes of same-sex attraction may be unknowable, but our society's tendency to describe things in terms of black and white, all or nothing, disallows thoughtful consideration and dialogue.

Nine of the former leaders in the conversion therapy movement have now come out against it with these comments: "We once believed that sexual orientation or gender identity were somehow chosen or could be changed. We know better now. We once thought it was impossible to embrace our sexual orientation or sexual identity as an intrinsic, healthy part of who we are and who we were created to be. We know better now."[8]

One young Chinese student wrote me on my *MagneticFire* blog, and he asked, "What am I? For whom and what do I live in this world?" His questions are similar to many I have received. Many men want to know if they are gay or not, how it will impact their lives, and why they prefer one type of man over another. Most men who are attracted to sex with other men are not concerned about an explanation for the attraction they have. If pressed, they almost inevitably say, "I was born this way." They have a sense of being different from other men, but many of them do not consider themselves to be gay. They profile themselves as masculine and straight-acting, code words for passing in a heterosexual world. They emphasize "No kissing and no anal" when they seek male partners. They believe these self-imposed limits set them apart from being gay. Even though they may desire kissing and anal sex, these are boundaries beyond which they cannot go, or they risk slipping inescapably into the pit of homosexuality.

These barriers allow them to avoid an emotional connection to their sexual partner and maintain their imperfect grasp on being straight. As an indication of their wish to avoid any emotional investment, they often refer to their male partners as fuck buddies or friends with benefits. If they have begun to explore anal sex, by limiting their sexual behavior only to being the inserting partner in the sexual relationship, they can then look at their receptive partner as the feminine one, the weak one, the real queer. They feel they have left their masculinity intact. In *Secret Historian: The Life and Times of Samuel Steward, Professor, Tattoo Artist, and Sexual Renegade*, Justin Spring quotes Samuel Steward's description of one of his regular sex partners: "[I imagine him] standing there, cock uplifted, his hands clasped behind his head (fearful that if he should touch me while I kneel before him, that some of my queerness will rub off on him)."[9]

Straight-identified MSM are from diverse backgrounds—some are raised in the traditions of conservative religions, some are from minority or immigrant cultures and lower socioeconomic groups.

They fear the potential consequences of exposing their behavior. They have made strong commitments to traditional values that they believe belong exclusively to the heterosexual community. They often say they do not want to be a part of the scene. By the scene they are referring to the gay subculture that they perceive to be dominated by the gay stereotype of young men who dance and drink excessively, go to the gym relentlessly, are narcissistically preoccupied with their bodies and physical appearance, and hedonistically spend all of their money on clothes, travel, and restaurants.

As one of the men I interviewed said, "Masculine men are attracted to other masculine men for a reason that is stronger than just sex, a big cock, or a beautiful body." But these men may marry women—not because of some reductionistic idea that they are using women to cover up their sexuality but because they honestly believe this will resolve all their ambiguities of love and sexual expression. They believe in love, romance, and long-term commitment.

Many straight-identified men have difficulty labeling themselves as gay, although they are not homophobic. Some have experienced crushes on other men in their youth and accept that their emotional desire is for a romantic relationship with another man. Other men may have romantic attachments only to women but primarily have sexual attraction to men. They may have examined coming out, but they do not feel that "the gay life" is a true fit with who they are. Some simply reject society's restriction on whom they can choose to have as a sexual partner.

John Howard, discussing MSM in *Men Like That: A Southern Queer History*, wrote:

> [Straight-identified MSM] should not be read as essentialized gay men unable to accept it...Male-male sexualities happened within complicated worlds of myriad desires. To experience or act on homoerotic appetites did not necessarily define the person as gay. Male-male desire functioned beside and along with many other forms of desire—all at some times, in some places, privileged,

oppressed, ignored, overlooked, spoken, silenced, written, thought, frustrated, and acted upon.[10]

For those who have internalized the cultural constructs of masculinity (strong, heterosexual) and femininity (weak, sissy), life is complex and difficult. They secretly and silently feel different from the masculine ideal. Shame and secrecy, lying, self-blame, and self-hatred inform their sexual activities with other men. Some MSM experience a sense of dissonance because who they think they are isn't the same as who they think they should be, and the greater the disparity, the greater the self-hatred.

Sexuality is far more complex than body parts. It includes sexual fantasy, sexual behavior, sexual preference, sexual orientation, and sexual identity; it also includes emotionality and romance. At times, these forces contradict each other even within the same individual. One eighty-five-year-old man who responded to my survey told me that he is quite sexually active and considers himself exclusively gay: "My married life for fifty-four years was the most wonderful imaginable. I never had any gay leanings that I was aware of. I can discern incidents in my earlier life that I now see as [red] flags.

Some MSM experience a sense of dissonance because who they think they are isn't the same as who they think they should be, and the greater the disparity, the greater the self-hatred.

However, I was so happy in my married life that I never gave them a thought. I never even thought about the gay life until age eighty-two." Initially, his story surprised me, but now I have heard many similar stories.

In the rural Nebraska community where I was born in 1943, everyone seemed to have the same values, the same values that some conservatives idealize and to which they think we should return. Conversations about human sexuality rarely occurred, and when they did, they were met with discomfort, embarrassment, and disapproval. Discussions of homosexuality, if they occurred at all, focused on its being unnatural and an invitation to deviancy. We were not only innocent about sex but innocent about almost everything. We did as we were told, and independent thought was discouraged. The roles for men and women were rigidly defined.

Some of the men from my generation that I interviewed described being the best in their class at playing jacks, jumping rope, and twirling a baton, but their pride in their achievements at the time was diminished by a sense of shame at being the best at something a boy should not want to do at all. That's how I felt. At age fourteen, had I known there was such a thing as being gay, I might have understood my life better.

Many of the young boys in rural Nebraska explored their budding sexuality with each other; I know because I explored it with them. As an old, sexually experienced man, I find it hard to think of those experiences as sex. Although we didn't really talk about what we were doing, I don't believe any of us thought of it as homosexual sex, and it certainly wasn't gay sex because *gay* didn't come into common usage until much later. It all seemed perfectly normal to me, and I presume it seemed normal to my partners as well. As I look back on it now, the only difference I see between me and my friends is that perhaps I didn't want it to end when it did. As I grew older, I noticed that the interests of boys my age were changing. I questioned the tardiness of my own attraction to girls, but as for boys' attraction to girls' tits—the only word we ever used for women's breasts—I just didn't get it.

The "Good Me" and the "Bad Me"

Psychologists and psychiatrists use the term *cognitive dissonance* to describe the anxiety resulting from a person's beliefs being inconsistent with his or her actions. One man wrote to me on my *MagneticFire* blog, "I had always been taught that homosexuality was bad, but as I began to accept that I am gay, I could not make myself believe that I had become a bad person." Life no longer fit with what he thought he knew, and his actions were no longer consistent with his previously held opinions. Dissonance creates anxiety that varies in intensity depending on the importance of the issue and the degree of the disparity. Becoming aware of the potential consequences of behavior that departs from traditional expectations only adds to the discomfort. This intense anxiety often drives people to seek a sense of wholeness by changing either their behavior or their beliefs.

Dissonance, when it occurs in those who experience same-sex attraction, is usually attributed in gay literature to *internalized homophobia*—that is, an adoption of the majority culture's fear of or prejudice against LGBTQ people. Self-hatred derives from believing and internalizing those factually unsupported preconceptions about homosexuality. I am not a fan of the term *homophobia*. It seems a bit ironic to detest the word *homosexual* but to cling so tightly to the word *homophobia*. For one thing, it appears double-dealing to be angry about the struggle to replace the term *psychopathic deviants* with *gay* when referring to homosexuals while at the same time labeling the straight community perversely and pathologically homophobic. For another, the term *homophobia* collapses all opposition to homosexuality into one overly simplistic explanation. People are discriminated against because of their language, their religion, their skin color, or anything else that confers on them the status of an outsider. Prejudice is not a uniquely gay experience—all outsiders bleed the same blood when they are wounded by prejudice.

The gay community appropriately promotes coming out as an act that is essential for personal authenticity and social justice. Arguing against that point is hard. In my experience, relationships between straight and openly gay people help remove prejudices. My mother had

Anxiety from believing one thing and doing another increases according to these factors:

- The length of time the beliefs are held
- The importance of the issue
- The degree of inconsistency between beliefs and actions
- The degree of difficulty in reversing a decision
- The higher the anticipation of future problems as a result of the belief

never knowingly met anyone gay until I came out to her. My stepfather was a stern but loving Swede who inhabited his deep, unexamined religious faith and who would never knowingly hurt anyone, but he would say some of the most outrageously insensitive things about others. My parents were not homophobic, but they were homonaïve.

As a young teenager I read muscle magazines that I stole from the Rexall drugstore. I wanted to be like the men pictured in those magazines. Once I ordered a small, white spandex bathing suit from an ad in the back of a muscle magazine. I wore it to the swimming pool to teach swimming lessons, thinking the suit itself would create muscle definition, thereby making me appear more masculine. The senior lifeguard, a very handsome young man who had a body like the one I wanted, called me aside and told me the suit was not appropriate to wear to the pool. He sent me home humiliated. I didn't realize that the suit was semitransparent and meant for posing rather than swimming. I couldn't seem to get anything right about being a man.

Prejudice is not a uniquely gay experience—all outsiders bleed the same blood when they are wounded by prejudice.

Until I was able to afford corrective plastic surgery, I was always ashamed of having gynecomastia, or "man boobs." It was as if the man boobs betrayed a secret about me. Once, my high school football coach shouted at me in front of all my teammates, "Olson, with tits like that, you should wear a bra!" He had just ripped away my other testicle.

Binary reasoning—the idea that only two alternatives exist— dominates contemporary American society, particularly in religion, politics, and advertising. The polar definitions of masculinity and femininity have been ingrained deeply in our psyches. The Marlboro man has become iconic of the tough, muscular man, always ready to get the girl. For the older man, the Viagra man, a little blue pill promises to rescue him from impotence and failure. The pill promises him an adolescent-like erection that with any luck will last just under four hours, right before he needs to call a doctor. A man's movement away from the entrenched image of masculinity can begin a chain reaction of events that culminates in membership in his being labeled a sissy. Beliefs about masculinity are among the longest and most deeply held. Consequently, they yield to change slowly and only with great difficulty. Men may not know why they feel different, but they do know they cannot talk about it. Saying "I think I might be gay" is like unbridling a mustang. Anyone who says "I think I might be gay" is assumed to be gay; otherwise those thoughts would never enter his mind. It is a remark that does not allow a retraction the following morning.

The schoolboys I grew up with were not the first to call men fairies. In the early 1900s the term *fairy* was applied to effeminate men, and the men who had impersonal sex with these fairies were referred to as trade, the same word prostitutes used to describe their customers. Rough trade referred to trade working or criminal class who were often chosen as sexual partners of middle- and upper-class men. The word *gay* referred to pleasure, not an identity.

In the early twentieth century, MSM were not considered abnormal so long as they abided by gender-conforming characteristics, according to George Chauncey, author of *Gay New York: Gender, Urban Culture, and the Making of the Gay Male World 1890–1940*.[11] Interest in same-sex encounters did not preclude interest in heterosexual ones. Achieving orgasm was a more powerful motivator than the gender of one's partner. What Chauncey seems to be suggesting is that during the period he discussed, the idea of a sexual identity didn't exist. Sex was only about pleasure.

Prior to the middle of the twentieth century, coming out of the closet did not exist, because the closet did not exist. In the early twentieth century, the world was not divided into gay and straight; men had to be a lot of things, but being heterosexual was not one of them. Having sex with someone of the same gender didn't come with a value judgment.

In *Just Queer Folks: Gender and Sexuality in Rural America (Sexuality Studies)*, Colin Johnson writes that at the beginning of the twentieth century, the field of eugenics took root in rural America largely through land-grant universities like Iowa State University. The core idea was that if you could breed a leaner pig or a prettier tomato, why not apply the same principles to breeding a better species of man? The idea that sex was for pleasure began to be replaced with the idea that sex was first and foremost about procreation. Pleasure was secondary, and masturbation and homosexuality were considered immoral pleasures. The ideal family was a heteronormative one where boys didn't touch penises—their own or anyone else's—until they were married, and these ideas were promoted through university extension services and the YMCA.[12]

Chauncey traces the increasingly successful challenges to this thinking back to the Stonewall uprising and the beginnings of gay liberation. Chauncey writes:

> Whether homosexuality is good or bad, chosen or determined, natural or unnatural, healthy or sick is debated, for such opinions are in the realm of ideology and thus subject to contestation, and we are living in a time when a previously dominant ideological position, that homosexuality is immoral or pathological, faces a powerful and increasingly successful challenge from an alternative ideology, that regards homosexuality as neutral, healthy, or even good.[13]

Once again we are experiencing a cultural shift as young men and women today find the labels of gay, straight, and bisexual far too restrictive. The study of human sexuality has been expanded since the 1990s through the study of queer theory. Whereas gay and lesbian studies explored natural and unnatural behavior with respect to homosexuality, this newer field of study expands the focus of sexuality to encompass any kind of sexual activity or identity that falls into normative and deviant categories.

The Stonewall Revolution

Although some resistance to the oppression of homosexuality existed earlier, many believe that the Stonewall riots defined the beginning of the gay liberation movement. Police raided the Stonewall Inn, a popular gay bar in New York City, on June 27, 1969. The street filled with violent protesters, and people at the bar fought back.

Following Stonewall, homosexual men and women adopted the word *gay* as a form of self-affirmation. They replaced their shame with pride and staked out a place for themselves in the midst of a hostile society. Gay men rejected the effeminate caricature of their sexuality associated with the term *fairies*—at least in public. *Homosexual* is now considered an offensive term because of its earlier clinical history, which suggested that gay people are somehow diseased or psychologically disordered, and its insistent use by those committed to the idea that homosexuality is a choice and can be cured.

Many during the Stonewall era adopted a masculine uniform of flannel shirts, Levi's, and work boots as a means of expressing a new sense of self. They advanced values and identities different from those prescribed by the dominant culture. The Village People became the archetypes of the new gay masculinity. "It's Raining Men" became the anthem of the gay community. Following the Stonewall riots in New York City in 1969, more men and women publicly disclosed their sexual orientation, and the word *gay* was adopted by the gay community as a term of self-affirmation. They developed a solidarity, visibility, and mutual support that they did not have before.

Not everyone welcomed the higher visibility of the gay community, and for some people, the radicalized counterculture was too much. As one man said during an online interview—one who chose not to label his sexual orientation although he only has sex with men—"I think the gay community is like a club with exclusive membership. If you don't wear the uniform, you cannot belong. I really don't understand the advantage of belonging, except [gay people] do help each other out."

Baby boomers, those men and women born during the decade following World War II, spent their childhoods in a pre-Stonewall society. Having been so deeply closeted prior to Stonewall, many were hesitant to begin to explore their adult lives in a more tolerant post-Stonewall culture.

The "Not Me"

All of us humans have a fundamental need to repress inner contradictions to bring the "good me," the "bad me," and the "not me" into alignment. Powerful psychological defense mechanisms that operate outside the conscious mind prevent unacceptable and intolerable feelings or behaviors from coming into awareness. Not uncommonly, men explain their same-sex indiscretions by saying, for example, "Oh, God, was I drunk! You'll never believe what I did!" or "All I really wanted was a blow job, and I knew my wife would never give me one." These rationalizations are used to justify behavior that might otherwise be unacceptable.

The psychological defense mechanism called denial prevents information, ideas, fantasies, or impulses from reaching the conscious mind; repression banishes them in the event they momentarily reach consciousness. Rationalization seeks to justify them in an acceptable way while hoping to make them appear reasonable. Defense mechanisms can be adaptive and allow us to function normally, and they can help control anxiety when our desires are doing battle with our own values. They also can be unhealthy when they are overused in order to avoid dealing with problems.

During my final year of medical school, I took a trip to St. Louis with my brother. We were exploring a gentrifying neighborhood of the city, and I went into an antiques store. My brother remained outside because he was in a wheelchair and the store was not accessible to him. I stood in the musty-smelling store examining a piece of Red Wing stoneware that I would have collected if I'd had any money. The young, attractive man who owned the store approached me. He was obviously intelligent and well-educated, and I enjoyed visiting with him. He asked me a few questions, and I told him I was in medical school in Nebraska and just visiting. As we talked, he had his thumbs hooked inside the pockets of his Levi's with his fingers extending below. Suddenly, he flared out his fingers and touched my crotch. I thought, "How clumsy of him!" As we continued to speak, he touched me once again, this time a little more assertively.

Psychological defense mechanisms prevent unacceptable thoughts from entering our conscious mind:

- *Denial*—Believing that unacceptable attractions do not really exist
- *Repression*—Pushing back unacceptable thoughts after stealing a look at them
- *Rationalization*—Justifying unacceptable thoughts in an acceptable way

I fled the store and ruminated all day about this encounter. Was it possible to feel violated while at the same time welcoming this man's behavior? Believing I had invited this violation, even in some small way, was completely unacceptable to me on a conscious level. In order to continue affirming my heterosexuality, I had to alter any evidence to the contrary and ignore everything that suggested I might have been accountable for what had happened. Much later, I began to accept that I had unconsciously contributed to what had happened. As long as I could be angry with the proprietor of the antiques shop, I did not have to accept my responsibility. Blaming others for our problems does not transform us. As long as I portrayed myself as the victim and felt anger toward the perpetrator, I was able to continue to use denial, repression, and rationalization to maintain a façade of heterosexuality. As one interviewee said, "We as individuals are responsible for the course of our lives, in bed and out."

Reexamining the "Bad Me"

In 1948, Alfred C. Kinsey published *Sexual Behavior in the Human Male*, which described sexual orientation on a seven-point continuum, from exclusively heterosexual to exclusively homosexual. He suggested that male sexual behavior was far more diverse than held by tradition. As Justin Spring said in *Secret Historian*, "Through statistics, Kinsey had presented these individuals with a whole new way of understanding the sexual self. Among those with a homosexual orientation, feelings of guilt, shame, anxiety, and depression could be particularly intense, and so Kinsey's findings were profoundly enlightening—and, by extension, healing—to these people."[14]

Viewpoints about Kinsey's research are as diverse as his description of sexuality. Opinions range from elevating him as a pioneering researcher in an age of moral hypocrisy to chastising his work as a pseudointellectual exercise intended on shredding the moral fabric of the nation by wrecking the family. Kinsey's work had an unintended consequence, according to Spring: "Only as society became more conscious of the nature and statistical prevalence of homosexuality within the general population did it become more violently repressive of it."[15]

In 1973, the American Psychiatric Association (APA) reversed its position and took the scientific stance that homosexuality is not a mental disorder. Ultimately, most other professional organizations came to the same decision. The APA joined other professional mental health associations in opposition to reparative therapies, issuing a position statement called Therapies Focused on Attempts to Change Sexual Orientation (Reparative or Conversion Therapies). Approved by the APA Assembly and Board of Trustees, it became the official policy of the APA in May 2000. The statement says, in part:

> In the past, defining homosexuality as an illness buttressed society's moral opprobrium of same-sex relationships. In the current social climate, claiming homosexuality is a mental disorder stems from efforts to discredit the growing social acceptance of homosexuality as a normal variant of human sexuality. Consequently, the issue of changing sexual orientation has become highly politicized. The integration of gays and lesbians into the mainstream of American society is opposed by those who fear that such an integration is morally wrong and harmful to the social fabric. The political and moral debates surrounding this issue have obscured the scientific data by calling into question the motives and even the character of

individuals on both sides of the issue. This document attempts to shed some light on this heated issue.[16]

Conversion therapy, sometimes known as reparative or sexual reorientation therapy, is a psychotherapeutic practice that purports to change a person's sexual orientation, literally converting a person from gay to straight. Those who practice conversion therapy cling to the pre-Stonewall word *homosexual* and avoid using *gay* because by doing so, they attempt to create an image that homosexuality is not an identity that is immutable but rather a behavior that can and should be changed. They base their practices upon psychological theories of the early twentieth century where Freudian thought dominated, when homosexuality was seen as developmental arrest, severe psychopathology, or some combination of both. These practices—which have included nudity and intimate touching—have been discredited by virtually all major American medical, psychiatric, psychological, and professional counseling organizations. The validity, efficacy, and ethics of clinical attempts to change an individual's sexual orientation are now being challenged in court.

In 2012, California passed a law, the first of its kind, prohibiting this form of talk therapy for anyone under the age of eighteen, supporting the position that such efforts have never been proven to work and that the therapy can harm young patients. The law was signed into effect by California governor Jerry Brown, but it went through a series of legal challenges over whether or not it was unjustified infringement on free speech or a valid effort to prevent therapeutic malpractice. In 2013, the United States Supreme Court declined to take up the case, supporting California's ban on gay conversion therapy. Other states are now considering similar laws.[17]

To Be or Not to Be Gay

Some MSM feel quite comfortable with Kinsey's nonbinary description of sexuality because they do not see themselves as exclusively homosexual or heterosexual. However, they often express that they feel more normal and comfortable in their sexual relationships with men than they do in sexual relationships with women. One man in my online correspondence with him commented, "It isn't a matter of who penetrates who. Making love [to a man] is way different than hookup sex or a blow job, although some people think it's the same. It is about passion, something that just happens. No rules or agendas. There must be some kind of mutual feeling."

I have often been asked, "How could you not know you were gay until you were forty?" I have been called a liar and a cheat by heterosexuals, and a gay man once said to me, "You have no balls. You're a liar and a hypocrite. There is no way you could not have known you were gay." However, in a society where binary logic dominates, one can be only good (straight) or evil (gay). Ambiguity, nuance, and moderation on ethical issues do not exist; at least, they did not exist for me. It was not until midlife that I could finally accept that being both gay and good is possible.

I met my first gay lover at the gym at Iowa State University when I was forty. One day, when dressing after my shower, I noticed Roberto, an attractive younger man, staring at me and smiling. I looked away nervously, but when I looked back at him he was still looking at me and smiling. Finally, he nodded toward the hallway door as he left the locker room and walked down the hall. As if his smile were pulling me by a magnetic force, I was unable to resist following him. I was astonished when I later learned that it was a married man that had seduced me. Despite our marriage vows, we met each other regularly over the course of about two years.

In some ways it was more acceptable to me that he was married because we shared this duplicitous life and it placed boundaries on the extent of our relationship. Although Roberto and I had had oral sex, we followed the rules: no kissing, no anal. When he finally kissed me, I loved the kiss for what it represented about our relationship, but I hated it for the ways it might change my life. At that moment, "I just went gay all of a sudden." With a rush of insight, I knew that what was true had always been true, and a great deal of my life that I had not understood until then suddenly made a great deal of sense.

My relationship with the thirty-two-year-old Roberto was romantic, passionate, and volatile, as many forbidden relationships are. I experienced a range and intensity of loving and erotic feelings I had never before experienced. Although my adolescent friends' captivation with women's breasts had escaped me, the excitement of an erect penis did not.

Once my relationship with Roberto ended, so did the dissonance I felt about my sexual orientation. I began to accept that, for me, loving another man was as normal as loving a woman is for other men. This was no longer about sex but about loving, and the sex was just an expression of that love. As long as I perceived a sexual partner as nothing more than a body part with which I might achieve an impersonal orgasm, it was hard to see myself as anything more than an instrument for sex. But when I discovered that the body part was attached to a person I loved and whom I wanted to love me, everything changed.

At the moment I knew I was gay, truths exploded inside my mind. It immediately became obvious to me that I had found the answers to questions I'd been asking for forty years. I began to reinterpret my past in the context of my new reality. I no longer felt that being a man was contingent upon accepting the cultural definition of masculinity. It was within my power to define it for myself. I could now go to a party with gay men and talk about football, china patterns, or someone's cute butt. I still found my man boobs unattractive, but I no longer felt that they revealed sexual ambiguity. There were other men who couldn't fix machines. My testicles had been restored.

> *As long as I perceived a sexual partner as nothing more than a body part with which I might achieve an impersonal orgasm, it was hard to see myself as anything more than an instrument for sex.*

2

It's Just Common Sense

Out beyond ideas of wrongdoing
and rightdoing there is a field.
I'll meet you there.

—RUMI

Am I gay? Bisexual? A latent homosexual? Or a heterosexual with issues? While hiding as they search for answers to these questions, mature men who are sexually attracted to other men find themselves caught in the crossfire between those who consider them an abomination and those who think of them as hypocritical, self-hating, closeted gay men. Those searching for answers, however, might not be asking the right questions. Rather than searching for a label that fits them, these men could be asking, How can I understand, accept, and experience the complexities of my sexuality and align my sexuality with my values? But choosing a label and letting the label define you is much easier to do. While I prefer to think of myself as gay, a significant portion of those responding to my survey preferred either another label or no label.

One steamy hot day in August when I was three years old, my dad was making hay. He had hitched a young, high-spirited horse with limited training to the steady and responsive older horse from another team, a common practice in breaking a new horse to drive. My father was working alone. Suddenly, something spooked the horses. They bolted, running about a mile at full speed back to their barn, dragging the hay wagon—and my father who was tangled in the harnesses beneath the horses. My father died several days later, never having regained consciousness.

To reconstruct some image of my father, I created a montage from other people's memories of him. When I was young, I would ask my mother about him, but she had canonized him, and her description was more divine than mortal. I knew that I could never be just like him. Once, when I was in a high school play, I needed to wear an outdated suit. My mother found a suit of my father's in an old trunk. I tried the suit on for size, but it was too small for me. I was too big for the suit, but I was too small to fill my father's shoes. Long before I questioned being gay, I believed that it was my father's death—and the lack of a role model—that informed my feelings of being an unfinished man.

In the Chariot Allegory, Plato described the mind as a chariot pulled by two horses. The charioteer represents rationality, and he holds the reins and uses the whip to assert his authority. One horse in the team is well bred and well behaved. The other is obstinate and difficult to control, barely yielding to the whip.[1] As a man experiencing sexual attraction to other men, that desire was like the obstinate and difficult-to-control horse. Once a man discovers that meeting another man eye to eye—and holding that contact for just a moment too long—betrays his interest, he cannot unsee it, unlearn it, or stop doing it. He forever becomes a participant in this silent communication between men, and therefore is always at risk of losing control over the obstinate and high-spirited horse.

My father had a well-trained team of horses but wanted to break in this new, partially trained horse he'd recently purchased. He hitched the inexperienced horse with the steadiest and best one in his mature team, trying to train the new addition, a common practice in those days when most farming was done with teams of horses. Even a good horseman, like my father was, cannot always control untamed horses.

Former pope Benedict XVI apparently didn't put much stock in Plato's allegory. He wrote that the essence of being human resides in one's reason, and our conscience must guide our physical passions. According to an article on CNN, Benedict published a document in 1986, while still Cardinal Ratzinger, that warned of the "deceitful propaganda" of prohomosexual groups and referred to homosexuality as an "intrinsic moral evil." Citing his failing health but in the midst of several church scandals, Pope Benedict XVI resigned in February 2013, an action not taken in over six hundred years.[2]

In March 2013, a papal conclave convened and elected Jorge Mario Bergoglio, SJ, then bishop of Buenos Aires, who took the pontifical name of Francis. Pope Francis has taken a distinctly more compassionate tone toward homosexuality. As Rachel Donadio noted in a *New York Times* article, Pope Francis said, "If someone is gay and he searches for the Lord and has good will, who am I to judge?"[3] Pope Francis said that he would not judge priests for their sexual orientation. Some interpreted his use of the word *gay*, a word avoided by his predecessors, as an indication of increasing acceptance and an unmistakable departure from the position of Pope Benedict. Never veering far from church doctrine opposing homosexuality, however, Pope Francis remains steadfastly opposed to same-sex marriage.[4]

Pope Francis's statement aligned with many gay men's belief that being gay is innate, existing from birth, and was consistent with Charles Darwin's thought that sexuality is biologically determined. In *The Descent of Man*, Darwin wrote: "At the moment of action, man will no doubt be apt to follow the stronger impulse; and though this may occasionally prompt him to the noblest deeds, it will far more commonly lead him to gratify his own desires at the expense of other men."[5] The subtext of Darwin's message is evident: we frequently do not operate using only rational thought even when our decisions have painful consequences to others. Men and women who are attracted to members of their own sex often enter into this contentious and rigid environment when seeking answers to questions about their sexuality.

When we speak of the self, we are talking about the core of our being, the uniting principle that underlies all of our subjective experiences. The self incorporates our genetic programming with the lessons our parents and culture have taught us. We cannot change our genetic makeup, at least not yet, but as humans we can use our gifts for self-examination and analytical thinking to examine our values and what we have been taught. Buddha got it right when he wrote in the *Dhammapada*, sometimes known as the *Buddhist Book of Proverbs*, "Your worst enemy cannot harm you as much as your own mind, unguarded. But once mastered, no one can help you as much, not even your father or mother."

Many resist Darwin's idea that humans aren't always capable of operating with rational thought. They believe that God gave man a special gift—the gift of reason—that elevates us above other animals. With it, they believe, we always have the capacity to deliberate and decide, to analyze the alternatives, and to weigh the pros and cons. But decisions aren't made using a series of computer chips, and too much thinking can also lead us astray or paralyze us into stagnation. While we may wish to ignore our feelings, we respond as flesh and blood engaged in a palpable world. We have the capacity to deconstruct our inherited value system, analyze it, and reconstruct a value system of our own making; in fact, doing so is essential.

If you believe in the existence of absolutes of right and wrong, someone else has done your thinking for you. A book like the one I'm writing won't be of help to those people, because they will interpret their experiences in the world, including what they read, to conform to rigid, preordained beliefs. For me, successfully understanding, accepting, and deciding how to live within my sexuality required questioning, analyzing, and reassessing some fossilized values that I had never questioned before.

Gay Men Are Born, Not Made

In the mid-1800s, Gregor Mendel chose a small set of traits in pea plants to develop what would become the foundation of modern genetics. Mendel studied discrete characteristics that fit into only one of two different classes with no overlap or blending—green peas versus yellow ones, tall stalks versus dwarf varieties, and so on.

I have what my family calls the Koester nose. At family reunions cousins, aunts, and uncles in the clan all stand in line for pictures, profiles exposed. Cameras click and cousins joke about the dubious heritage of those who don't have "the nose." In looking at those photos, it certainly does not require an understanding of Mendel's peas to have a basic grasp of the power of genetics.

Our fate is not determined exclusively by genes. Although noses may be similar, they cannot be separated into only two characteristic types. Sir Francis Galton, a contemporary of Mendel and a close relative of Darwin, studied the inheritance of characteristics that could be quantified along a continuum—for

If you believe in the existence of absolutes of right and wrong, someone else has done your thinking for you.

example, height and intelligence. Galton's work was the beginning of understanding *multifactorial inheritance*. He discovered that development of any trait requires a combination of genetic predisposition and environmental features such as nutrition. When I was a teenager, boys hoped to reach the magical height of six feet; now that height is common for boys. Girls at that time never reached six feet tall; now they often do. Genetics didn't change—our environment has. But no matter how favorable the environment, if the genetics aren't present for height, some men will never be tall enough to play basketball for the NBA.

Many diseases and most physical and personality traits likely have several genes that trigger their development, but the context in which they develop also significantly influences the way those traits unfold. Being gay may be a consequence of the presence or absence of multiple genes, each with a limited effect but collectively influenced by the environment. In a 1995 article for *Nature Genetics*, Stella Hu and her colleagues reported that being gay is a complex behavioral trait involving multiple genetic factors of DNA on the X chromosome.[6] Even before the ink had dried, the theological press—harking back to the theories of eugenics—began to consider testing fetuses for the "gay gene" and speculated that abortion could cleanse society of the "homosexual curse."

Most gay men accept a genetic explanation for being gay because they believe they were born, not made, into their sexual orientation, and a growing consensus of human sexuality researchers and mental health professionals concede that we do not choose our sexual orientation. Sexual orientation is increasingly acknowledged to be a human trait, like being left-handed. Genes, however, can vary in their expression. In identical twins, if one twin is gay, a much greater likelihood exists that the other twin is gay than in the case of fraternal twins. In a 1991 study of identical and fraternal twins, Michael Bailey and Richard Pillard found that if one identical twin is gay, the chance of the other being gay is 52 percent. In fraternal twins, however, the chance is only 22 percent.[7] And, as studies of twins separated at birth show, strong evidence exists that genetics determines a significant part of our personality—including sexuality.

In identical twins, if one twin is gay, a much greater likelihood exists that the other twin is gay than in the case of fraternal twins.

Biology is a necessary but not sufficient explanation for being gay. In fact, a few studies suggest correlations exist between being gay and being left-handed, being the younger sibling of older brothers, or having hair that forms a whorl in a counterclockwise direction. But correlations only show relationships, and several steps must be taken before causation can be established. After researchers combine correlations with biologic plausibility they look for models in the animal kingdom. In their book, *Zoobiquity: The Astonishing Connection Between Human and Animal Health*, Barbara Natterson-Horowitz and Kathryn Bowers write that animals demonstrate not only homosexuality and heterosexuality but also have monogamy, polygamy, promiscuity, foreplay, seduction, and rape.[8] A person's sexual attractions are a combination of genetic factors decided at the moment of conception and triggered by the environment. Interestingly, with some degree of reliability, child psychiatrists in many cases can determine by the age of five which children will grow up to be gay, and mothers always seem to know.

While sexual *behavior* may be chosen, the preponderance of evidence suggests that sexual *attraction* is dictated by biology, with little or no demonstrated contribution from social factors. Religious conservatives and reparative or transformational therapists who are committed to changing sexual orientation vehemently protest such proclamations. Conservative Christians do not want to see homosexuality as intrinsically human, just intrinsically evil. Either homosexuality is abnormal, chosen, changeable, and hated by God more than all other sins, or being gay is innate and created by a God who doesn't make mistakes. If being gay is innate, it cannot be changed; if homosexuality is a behavior, one can choose to abstain, however difficult reining in the untamed animal might be.

Genes contain DNA, which forms a blueprint for making proteins that impact behavior. The differences in DNA between humans is 0.1 percent—we are 99.9 percent all the same—but that 0.1 percent of gene pairs accounts for millions of potential variations. All of us are much more alike than different, but those differences are many and important. The challenge is to determine how to read the blueprint and understand how all of these many and complex parts work together to make us the people we are. Only about 1.2 percent of our DNA separates us from chimpanzees, and the only real difference between animals and humans is that humans have a need for finding meaning in our lives.[9]

As illustrated in figure 1, the nucleus of our self-identity is first formed from our DNA, which determines a considerable part of our personality. Personality is then shaped by our families, and families are often influenced to a large degree by their religious beliefs, if any. All of this transpires within the larger framework of our culture.

Kinsey's work in the 1950s supported the idea that sexual variations were entirely consistent with genetic theories, according to Justin Spring in *Secret Historian*. Spring writes: "[Kinsey's] findings suggested that variations in sexual behavior were not based on acts of will and individual choice, as religious teachings had always insisted. Rather they were based on widespread biological variations existing within the human population: in other words, on genetic variation."[10]

Those who oppose the idea that homosexuality is genetic use the logic that gay men presumably don't spread their DNA very far because they aren't traditionally reproducing. These critics question how gay

Figure 1: Nucleus of our self-identity

genes could be passed on when only those humans with the traits strongest for survival and reproduction spread their advantageous genes throughout the populations. Evolutionary theory is sometimes applied to argue that homosexuality cannot be genetic because it is nonprocreative, and therefore should have been extinguished, but this interpretation has been countered by the study of other species in the animal kingdom that exhibit nonprocreative behavior. In evolutionary biology, an organism is said to behave altruistically when its behavior benefits other organisms, but the organism does so at its own expense.

By behaving altruistically, the unselfish worker bee produces no offspring, but at the same time, the bee enhances the health of the entire bee community. Its behavior boosts the reproductive capabilities of the queen bee and increases the chances of survival of the entire bee colony. Felix Warneken and Michael Tomasello reported in the *British Journal of Psychology* on March 3, 2006, that they had found an "altruism gene." They suggest that a group in which reproductive and nonreproductive group members cooperate may be much stronger because groups composed of only selfish members would look exclusively after their own interests. The survival of an entire population has advantages over the survival of an individual. Individuals are expendable.[11]

Until recent years when gay people have become parents through artificial insemination and surrogacy, and except for those of us who became parents before uncovering our sexual orientation, homosexuality led into an evolutionary blind alley. Some scientists believe that gay people, like worker bees, serve an altruistic purpose in the larger population. Gay men and women may contribute to the survival of their genetic base by assisting in the care and survival of their family members who share their DNA. In this way, families that contain a homosexual gene—if one exists—might have better survival rates than families who don't, even though some gay people might be an evolutionary dead end.

Ignorance and Common Sense

People who intentionally avoid or disagree with facts—no matter how well-founded—simply because those facts oppose or contradict their personal beliefs exhibit *willful ignorance.* Some conservative religious and political groups are suspicious of all science, including the big bang theory, evolution, and global warming. They consider science to be driven by a conspiracy of liberal academics, the media, and Hollywood. Several years ago, they threw a fit when headlines exclaimed, "Gay Gene Found."

Skeptics are unlikely to accept any genetic explanation for being gay based on a study such as counterclockwise hair whorls. They often attempt to dismiss these studies with sarcasm rather than facts. They are correct, however, when they argue that even when a correlation exists, the correlation does not establish causality. The gay community, eager to establish an innate basis for sexual orientation, too frequently lifts up these studies as proof, drawing conclusions beyond those that can be supported by the data in the study. Both sides of the argument remain in an ideological gridlock.

At the turn of this century, the number of Americans who believed that LGBTQ people can change their sexual orientation equaled the number who believed they cannot, and according to a Pew Research Center study in 2013, four in ten Americans said that being gay or lesbian is "just the way some choose to live," while a similar number said

45

that "people are born gay or lesbian."[12] These statistics are a sobering reminder of just how far this country has to go in terms of LGBTQ acceptance.

As a psychiatrist, I understand the exploitation of facts on both sides of the genetic debate as both proponents and skeptics manipulate well-founded arguments in order to maintain the stability of their beliefs. Discrediting one deeply held belief threatens the security of all other beliefs. Accepting a fact or argument that contradicts one's personal beliefs cracks the barrier that separates good from evil. So, for example, if one accepts that our world was created through evolution rather than being created by God as described in Genesis, everything that follows Genesis in the Bible comes into question. Thinking only in black and white simplifies our understanding of the world.

Moral issues ostensibly are decided on the basis of solid logic, but that is rarely the case. Morality is strongly related to our feelings and outlook on the world, and feelings come before reason. In moral arguments, we first decide that something is wrong; then we search for reasons to justify the wrongness we instinctively feel. Arguments are invented. Like a snowball fight, as one argument is hurled at the opposition, the projectile is deflected, only to be followed repeatedly by another. Jonathan Haidt, Silvia Koller, and Maria Dias, in a still-quoted, classic paper referred to as "Is it wrong to eat your dog?" use the term *moral dumbfounding* to describe how, when people run out of reasons and have exhausted their list of moral justifications, they start arguing without substance, making comments like "Because it's just wrong and disgusting. That's why." Their research dissects moral psychology into two parts: emotion and cognition. They discovered that in moral arguments, we first decide that something is wrong; then we search for reasons to justify the wrongness we instinctively feel.[13] Their findings have major implications for the theological arguments on the morality of same-sex orientation. When we feel same-sex erotic attraction is wrong, we seek arguments to defend our belief, and almost nothing will convince us to change those emotionally charged beliefs.

Psychiatrists have learned through their study of the psychological development of children that values originate in the intimate lives of families, in whose presence children initially feel defenseless. Families socialize us into our communities; friends and loved ones teach us how to participate in our small corner of the world. A system of rewards and punishments directs how we should live. Young children absorb these "truths," knowing almost as if by instinct what is expected of them. Children do not wish to disappoint their parents upon whom they depend for love, approval, and security. Children feel tremendous pressure to conform to their family's values, ideals, and goals, even when these guidelines have not been explicitly stated. For all of us, this pressure forms the basis for our self-esteem, and we internalize it as our conscience, the standard against which we measure all of our behavior. Freud named it the superego. Parents call it common sense, the knowledge that they believe most people consider practical and sensible. Albert Einstein is reported to have said, "Common sense is the collection of prejudices acquired by age eighteen."

We first decide that something is wrong; then we search for reasons to justify the wrongness we instinctively feel.

Theories evolve over time. The classic psychodynamic theory for the development of male homosexuality—one that I read over and over in medical school and in my psychiatric training—was that a distant father and a close-binding mother could cause a child to become gay. Reparative therapists continue to blame fathers primarily for creating their gay sons. They believe that the absence of a happy, warm, and intimate relationship with a father causes homosexuality. According to this theory, the son detaches from his distant father in order to protect himself from the pain of disappointed expectations, and he seeks a sexual relationship with another man to replace what some psychologists have called the encircling arms of the father.

My father wasn't distant. He was dead. How can the complexities of sexuality be reduced to such a simplistic interpretation? If it were that simple, wouldn't a warm and loving relationship with his mother draw a young man toward a similar relationship with a woman? Although many of the men whom I have interviewed had difficult relationships with their fathers, the pseudoscience of the reparative therapy movement has confused correlation with causation. Their theory ignores entirely those gay men who have perfectly warm relationships with their fathers. Could it be that some fathers pull away from their sons simply because they don't know how to be a father to a gay son? As a gay man who is also a father, I'm the first to admit that I felt relieved to have had daughters.

Although far from universal, some themes about the relationship of gay sons to their mothers and fathers come up repeatedly in the stories of the lives of men I have talked with:

- Some mothers sense that their sons are different from other boys and may have valid concerns that their children need protection from bullies.

- Some sons may share interest in more traditionally female activities.

- Sometimes fathers have difficulty finding common ground with their gay sons, preferring other sons whose interests are more compatible with their own.

However, even if a correlation exists between mother-son or father-son relationships and being gay, it does not prove that being gay is a disorder that must be treated rather than a variance that must be understood. The task is not to redefine an individual man, molding him into the heterosexual masculine stereotype, but to redefine the boundaries of what it means to be a man. Being gay is not a disorder that must be cured; it is a variance that must be understood within expanded boundaries of what it means to be a man.

Throughout my adolescence, I consciously searched for men I could model myself after. I felt I had only a fragmented sense of the person I should be. I sought a way to be initiated into the fraternity of men, and my ideas of what it meant to be a man were very superficial and idealistic. I feared that if I didn't know how to be a man, I couldn't hope to hang on to anyone I loved. Being called a sissy or a faggot only hurts if one already believes it to be true. As a young man, I didn't know that the struggle for my identity was the same struggle most other young men were having, albeit with different explanations and outcomes.

While speaking to a group of older gay men, I met a seventy-two-year-old man from Georgia who self-identified as gay although still married to but living apart from a woman. He recalled how he began to hide his interest in art and classical music after being called a sissy. He played tennis in high school and college, hardly the equivalent of playing football in the South. His youthful rationalization for feeling different from other young men was that he had had a more genteel, Southern upbringing, one that led him to be more cultured than his friends. After revealing to me that his first crush was on Roy Rogers, he said, "I know I was born this way and I expect someday a gene will be discovered to explain it."

Being called a sissy or a faggot only hurts if one already believes it to be true.

After more than forty years of thinking about it, I can now confidently reject the empty claims made by the psychiatrists who trained me. Perhaps gay sons reject their fathers so that the fathers don't discover their secret wish to play with their sister's Barbie dolls. Even a boy who can throw a football like a bullet may find it hard to be around his father if the boy finds himself attracted to his father's best friend. Neither my father's death nor having a strong but loving mother made me gay. I am gay, and I always have been gay. My life was transformed as I discovered this truth about myself, and in the process, my discovery forced a change upon the lives of others who love me.

3

God Hates Fags. In Bondage to Dogma

Everyone has a holy place, a refuge, where their heart is purer,
their mind clearer, where they feel closer to God
or love or truth or whatever it is they happen to worship.

J. R. MOEHRINGER, *THE TENDER BAR*

"If you don't believe that Jonah could reach out and touch the walls of that fish's stomach, you are not a Christian." Those were the words I heard from the preacher when I attended services in one of those new big box churches in Ohio a few years ago. Earlier in his sermon about Jonah and the whale, he had established—at least to his own satisfaction—that Jonah had been swallowed by a fish, not a whale. His message was quite clear: believe as I believe or you will go to hell. No ambiguity, no nuance, no discussion. No thought or introspection was required, only obedience. During the sermon he made several jokes about "hom-o-SEX-u-als." Obviously he hated my sin, but I couldn't feel any love for the sinner either. By the time I heard him speak these words, I had grown confident enough in my own sexuality and my faith that I couldn't be shaken by his remarks. But I felt tremendous anger toward him and empathy for his congregants who were being told that to think for themselves would send them straight to hell.

With that experience on my mind, when I became a member of Plymouth Church in Des Moines, I asked the senior minister, "How can you have a conversation with a fundamentalist Christian without getting crosswise with them?" He thought for a while, and then he responded, "I have not found it difficult to have these conversations as long as we focus on the meaning of the Scripture instead of the details of it." Perhaps this is the model that can be used in resolving the conflict in our consciences between the good and evil of homosexuality, the meaning rather than the explanation of it. Although for some MSM, a same-sex relationship may be simply one more way to achieve sexual satisfaction, for many more, the meaning is about a deep and committed love for another person.

Although the message about homosexuals from the preacher in Ohio was subtle, the "God hates fags" message of the Westboro Baptist Church of Topeka, Kansas, is anything but subtle. The congregation of the Westboro Baptist Church published this on its website:

> Since 1955, WBC has taken forth the precious from the vile, and so is as the mouth of God (Jer. 15:19). In 1991, WBC began conducting peaceful demonstrations opposing the fag lifestyle of soul-damning, nation-destroying filth . . . america [sic] crossed the line on June 26, 2003, when SCOTUS [Supreme Court of the United States] ruled in Lawrence v. Texas that we must respect sodomy. SCOTUS sealed your doom on June 26, 2015, with fag marriage. WBC's gospel message is your last hope.[1]

I grew up in Nebraska in a town of just over one thousand people, a number that had remained nearly the same for more than one hundred years until an influx of Mexicans over the last couple of decades swelled the population by about 30 percent, changing the complexion of the community both literally and figuratively. When I was growing up, no one locked the doors of their homes, although some likely do now—needlessly. I once asked my mother why she left the keys in her car, and she responded, "You never know who might need to borrow your car." In my hometown, there were several churches, all Protestant, with more churches in the rural countryside. The church was the center of most social activities, and no one ever questioned singing Christmas carols at school Christmas programs.

During my seventh- and eighth-grade years, every Saturday I attended confirmation classes at my Lutheran church. At the conclusion of our confirmation classes, we had a public examination in front of the congregation. All of the confirmands sat in the choir loft at the front of the church as the pastor drilled us on *Luther's Catechism*. We were expected to testify to our beliefs and our commitment to the faith.

Marcus J. Borg, in *Meeting Jesus Again for the First Time: The Historical Jesus and the Heart of Contemporary Faith*, wrote that "the internalized voice of culture" forms a core value system that impacts all of our later life experiences. It provides a set of rules that serve the interest of all society and forms guidelines by which the majority live. When any subsequent event in one's life occurs, that experience is filtered through this belief system. Ultimately it affects the way we feel and the way we respond to everything.[2]

As shown in figure 2 each event or situation in our lives is a stimulus that gets filtered through an internalized belief system. Our self-talk and automatic thinking, or intervening variables, affect our feelings and behavior as we respond to that stimulus.

This was the world in which MSM like me were born. Since I was raised a Lutheran, I assumed I would always be a Lutheran. I believed that if my life didn't conform to the dogma, it was my life that needed to be changed, not the dogma. For many years, these beliefs remained unexamined and unchallenged. My failure to challenge these inherited beliefs contributed significantly to my coming out late in life.

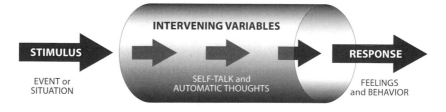

Figure 2: Intervening variables

The Bondage of Dogma

When it comes to religion, the media often presents to us only the two extremes of religion: either homosexuality is an abomination or homophobia created through religious belief is the real evil. Conflict leads to tension, tension lends drama, and drama creates interest. Intermediate positions between the extremes are usually overlooked. Most Americans, even those who find homosexuality morally unacceptable, see the actions taken by the Westboro Baptist Church as extreme and unacceptable. Those who take a more neutral position on the morality of being gay may feel that same-sex erotic desire is acceptable, but only if a person remains celibate or if same-sex behavior occurs only in the context of a committed relationship.

The position of most fundamentalist religions is that everyone is essentially heterosexual and that homosexual *orientation* does not exist. Homosexuality is seen as a lifestyle, as if it were a choice between living in the city or at the beach. Homosexual feelings and homosexual behavior are seen as equally sinful. Homosexuality is considered a product of original sin, a perversion that traps people in a lifestyle of lust. They believe that because gay people are driven by lust that we are incapable of a loving, nonexploitative relationship. When debating the morality of homosexuality, religious conservatives isolate and lift up biblical verses as proof texts showing that homosexuality is an abomination. Many in the gay community think of these as "the clobber passages."

The most conservative religions preach that all of God's truths already have been revealed, are recorded in the words of his prophets, and

Clobber passages are biblical texts often cited as God's condemnation of homosexuality:

- Genesis 19:1–5
- Leviticus 18:22 and 20:13
- Deuteronomy 23:17
- Romans 1:21–31

- 1 Corinthians 6:9–10
- 1 Timothy 1:9–10
- Jude 1:6–7

are governed by objective criteria for right and wrong. Fundamentalist Christians define homosexuality in terms of what gay people do, not who they are. They believe that men who have sex with men should experience emotional discomfort because they are living lives contrary to God's laws. Religious conservatives consider the capacity to reason as the essence of being human and that reason and conscience should be a guide to dealing with the power of physical passions. For the first forty years of my life, I believed that, too.

Many Christians who have been unable to reconcile their sexuality and their religious beliefs have abandoned religion altogether. But one cannot presuppose that all those who assume a gay identity shed their spiritual identity. I receive a lot of correspondence similar to this personal communication from a young man in Indonesia (edited slightly for easier reading): "I am a Muslim but I don't do so well as a Muslim, just enough for me as is common for men of my age. I am having an attraction to men but I am not a gay. I keep it safe from my friends and family. I'm not lying to myself, but I want to marry a woman to do what my religion teaches."

Homosexuality is outlawed and a negative stance against homosexuality is deeply ingrained in much of the Muslim world, with only a handful of exceptions. As Karen Leigh and Asa Fitch noted in the *Wall Street Journal*, most Muslim countries have laws under which gay sex is illegal. It can lead to arrest and torture, and in at least ten of these countries can be punished by death—gay men in these countries have been hung, stoned, and thrown off buildings.[3]

Punishments vary among the major schools of Islamic thought and the most severe punishments are rarely imposed. Many Muslims who live with same-sex attraction and with whom I have communicated have expressed fears that if their attraction is exposed, they might be killed. Most who believe they are gay marry a woman as part of their cover.

The more progressive view of being gay is that sexual orientation is not a moral issue. Morality is seen as having nothing to do with what we do sexually but by how we care for and about others. Sexual behavior, whether homosexual or heterosexual, must be judged as moral or immoral only in the context in which sexuality is expressed. Sexual expression is moral if it is consensual, noncoercive, and safe. Some believe that if these criteria are met, a loving and committed relationship is not essential for sexual behavior to be considered moral.

Can More Than One Road Lead to Heaven?

For about twenty years I struggled with attempting to reconcile being gay with my religious faith. After I accepted that I am gay and always will be gay, I found it increasingly difficult to practice my faith in the manner in which it was handed down to me. Like so many other gay men, I began to feel that the only way for me to feel good about myself was to remove myself from the persistent condemnation I felt. Yet being without a spiritual base also left me feeling unsettled, and I made repeated but unsuccessful attempts to return to the church I had known. Since I knew my attraction to men wouldn't go away, and my success in suppressing it had been only moderately successful for the first forty years of my life, I left the Lutheran Church.

Marcus J. Borg wrote, "[Life in this world] is a life of bondage to the dominant culture." Religious institutions, like religious people, are struggling with the morality of being gay, and the struggle has resulted in divisions within these institutions just as it has resulted in estrangement within families. Between the two extreme positions on the morality of homosexuality, churches have come to different conclusions. Some believe that homosexuality is a behavior that can be changed, and therefore must be changed, and individuals who feel they cannot change must remain celibate. Other churches have taken the position that while being gay is not acceptable, when weighed against promiscuity, same-sex behavior is less sinful if it occurs in the context of a loving and committed relationship. Still other churches, like the United Church of Christ and the Unitarian Universalist churches, have taken the stance that homosexuality is morally neutral and that loving and committed heterosexual and gay relationships are equivalent.

Values and religious traditions are so deeply ingrained in us that they seem almost as hardwired as hair and eye color, making them extremely difficult to change. But when you are gay and your church and family say it is wrong, that is where the change must begin. With increasing maturity, we can begin to see the imperfections in our parents; our heroes fall from grace and the framework of our religious dogma weakens. We learn that prejudices and prohibitions are often based on incorrect assumptions. We begin to realize that social values and traditions are not fixed but rather evolve over time. Rigid and restrictive religion is responsible for much of the shame that gay men feel about their sexual orientation, and many of them have left all religious tradition behind because of this shame.

Religious institutions hold power over their congregants, and the effects of religious dogma can be devastating. This has created a significant backlash against religion in the gay community. For some, however, spiritual identity is more highly valued than sexual orientation. In my interviews some men expressed the view that it can be easier to come out as gay in their communities of faith than to come out as religiously oriented in the gay community. Douglas C. Haldeman suggests that asking people to abandon their religion in favor of their sexual orientation is just as ethically irresponsible as it is for conversion therapists to suggest that people can give up their sexual orientation because of their religious convictions.[4] To suggest that people must choose between their sexual orientation or their religious beliefs can only prolong their internal dissonance.

Uncommon Sense

What people think of as common sense is the set of beliefs that they feel should be shared by everyone. Jesus and Muhammad didn't have "common" sense; they both challenged the conventional wisdom of their time. Reza Aslan, who wrote *No god but God: The Origins, Evolution, and Future of Islam*, and Marcus Borg make the case that the greatness of Jesus and Muhammad resulted from their challenging the conventional wisdom of their time, and they did so not by producing a new set of laws, but by offering insights that challenged people to develop greater understanding.[5]

In recent years, religious conservatives promoted abstinence pledges for teens as a way of discouraging premarital sex, but teenagers who pledged to remain virgins until marriage were just as likely to have premarital sex as those who did not promise abstinence. I knew that no matter what kind of promises I made not to respond to my sexual attraction to other men, I would fail. When reason and passion battle, passion often wins. The one driving the chariot often loses control.

I understood that I didn't have to act on all of my sexual inclinations, but I wanted to act on some of them. I came to believe that moral standards are imperfect and change as societies evolve. I found that progressive churches exist where being gay is seen as morally neutral and natural for a minority of people. I learned that the only resolution to my conflict in values was to unhitch the horses from the wagon. I needed to balance the forces of unrestrained appetites with the force of reason.

The bigger the secret, the greater its impact once the secret is finally revealed. Reverend Ted Haggard was president of the National Evangelical Association, representing thirty million evangelical Christians, when he was disgraced for having a sexual relationship with a male prostitute.[6] Although he preached sermons with antigay messages, he was preaching one thing and doing another. Haggard has been widely criticized by the gay community because, as Jon Stewart said on *The Daily Show*, "People like you [Haggard] make it really hard for, quite frankly, people like you."

The conflict for men and women who come out in midlife is no more or less difficult than coming out is for young people, but in some ways, because they have been passing as heterosexual in a heterosexual world, coming out is more complicated by having avoided reconciliation of contradictory values. Adding children into the dynamic makes it extraordinarily more complex. The conflict for the mature man usually isn't about whether or not to change—most know they cannot. The conflict is about losing a wife and kids, a job, family and friends, and in some cases, religious faith. Although many of the risks of a vaguely perceived future are more imagined than real, when people come out in midlife they may experience an almost total loss of the family and religious community support previously enjoyed.

The power of Haggard's story should not come from watching a dogmatic hypocrite fall. His story has been celebrated as a victory in the ideological gridlock between religious conservatives and liberal supporters of gay rights. Such contradictions are echoed over and over in the lives of millions of men who struggle to beat back their natural same-sex urges. If they relinquish that struggle they may lose their families and friends only to find themselves rejected by the gay community, the very community that should welcome and embrace them.

All gay men have lied about their sexuality at some point. In the mid-1980s, I sat on a committee to define benefits that would be covered by an HMO. One of the managers said that the committee was developing a health questionnaire that was designed to identify gay men so the HMO could deny them insurance because of the potential high costs of HIV treatment. Speaking in a stage whisper, one physician asked, "What do you ask them? Do you like to take it up the ass?" I sat there in stunned disbelief. I had just left my wife and children, was not out professionally, nor was I sure I could be, and I needed a job to pay alimony and child support. I was paralyzed.

My guilt is the painful, personal awareness that I had not lived up to my own moral standards by speaking up, and it has never left me, but my failure to respond was the result of a conflict between my fears of what I might lose and my emerging sexuality. Coming out is not an event, nor is it a linear process. Coming out is like Odysseus's ship, sailing from point to point, but driven off course time and again. As Reverend Candace Chellew-Hodge wrote, "Work out your own demons, and the perceived demons in others suddenly disappear."[7] If one wishes freedom and peace about same-sex attractions, the homophobic bondage inside one's head is the first thing that must be addressed.

Are Morals Relative or Fixed?

Attitudes in the United States are changing. If one rejects the inherent sinfulness of homosexuality, justice demands that the morality of gay relationships be judged by the same standards of morality as heterosexual ones: the degree of commitment, a lack of coercion, safety, permanence, and fidelity. Changes in attitudes among young people account for much of the increased acceptance in the United States, and in contrast to when I was a child, almost everyone has had some exposure to people who are gay. Fewer and fewer people are attributing being gay to upbringing or environment. If one does not accept an inherent sinfulness of homosexuality, justice demands that both gay relationships and heterosexual ones be judged by the same standards of morality.

Introspection and analytical thinking can help individuals resolve inner conflicts. Some may choose to remain homosexually celibate, but that will often require guarding every aspect of one's life to avoid being dragged by a team of horses like my father was. Spiritual beliefs can be a source of comfort but can also prove an irresolvable conflict. Unless people can begin to understand their being gay in the context of a reconstructed value system, the only option may be to pray for a miracle.

Sadly, religion has been used to justify hate, but hating people you know is much more difficult. The more that gay men and women publicly acknowledge their sexual orientation, the more accepting our society will become. However, on an individual basis the decision to come out is a painful struggle no matter how old you are. For those struggling with issues of faith, the struggle can be made less painful by getting to know those people who believe that being gay and being religious are not mutually exclusive. The LGBTQ community walks a delicate line between justifiable and appropriate anger and intolerance and vengeful rage. Both sides of this divisive argument must begin to find common ground. Freedom from the bondage of this internalized ideological conflict comes when one begins to realize on a very personal level that it is possible to be both gay and good.

4

Out from the Shadows:
You're Not the Man You Thought You Were

We stand before a hundred doors, choose one,
where we're faced with a hundred more
and then we choose again.

—RICHARD RUSSO, *BRIDGE OF SIGHS*

I didn't know my mother's father had shot himself until twenty years after it happened, despite the fact that we lived under the same roof with him when he took his life. I only found out as my brother and I passed the home of an old woman who had difficulty with depression and had resisted treatment. I asked him how she was doing.

"She hung herself," my brother said.

"Oh, no," I responded. "I just don't see how anyone could ever do that."

"Well," he said, "I guess it was sort of like Grandpa Koester."

"What do you mean?" I half questioned, half shouted.

"You know, like when Grandpa shot himself."

"What! Why didn't anyone ever tell me?" I demanded.

"I guess we thought you knew," he said.

Years later my sister told me that early one morning our mother had heard a gunshot. When my mother went to the basement, she found

Grandpa. She rushed us off to school so we wouldn't be there when the police and ambulance arrived. News travels fast in a small town, and my older sister learned what had happened from her friends when she arrived at school that morning. My younger sister didn't hear about his suicide until several years later; one of her friends told her. I only now have a hazy memory of being told Grandpa had wanted to go to sleep and not wake up, probably enough of an explanation for a five-year-old. I remember wondering how someone could have known he was going to die, but I had no reference for understanding suicide. I remember riding in the family car following the hearse. As we drove past the school playground I stared out the window at my friends' tiny figures, which seemed to be moving in slow motion. My mother never talked about Grandpa's suicide, at least not to me.

Societies stigmatize both the victims of suicide and their families through isolation and shunning. Although I was too young to recall the impact on our family, the burden of the stigma certainly fell upon my mother. When I was a child, suicide victims were not allowed to be buried in Roman Catholic cemeteries because suicide was considered a mortal sin, and the Church justified its position by saying that it was an attempt to discourage suicide. In recent years the Church has taken the more lenient view that judgment of those who die by suicide should be left to God.

People become depressed when they experience significant losses or if their expectations aren't realized. Although affected to some degree by our family environment, we each have an individual, highly heritable degree of vulnerability or resistance to depression. Research has increasingly proven that some of us are genetically more prone to depression. Some people simply find it easier than others to be happy. In a 2008 article for the *BMJ*, James Fowler and Nicholas Christakis found that people's happiness depends on the happiness of others with whom they are connected. Happiness, like health, is a collective phenomenon. Happy people have more friends, happier marriages and fewer divorces, more successful careers, and longer lives. They learn more easily and recover more quickly from adversity.[1]

For those who are particularly susceptible to depression, anti-depressant medications sometimes can raise their depressive setpoint. Happiness is not a birthright, but neither are we doomed to the level of happiness we have inherited. Changing our thinking is easier than changing the world. In my work, I often hear patients say, "I just want to be happy," and my response is, "What are you willing to do to make that happen, and how will you measure it so you know when you have gotten there?" By taking control over our lives, increasing and nurturing our connections to others, taking care of our health, and developing lives that are meaningful, we can create an environment that helps us resist depression or recover from it more quickly when it occurs. When all of those are not enough, sometimes we must turn to antidepressant medications.

Depression is a common experience for gay men and women as they confront their same-sex attractions. Young LGBTQ men and women experience bullying, physical and verbal abuse, losses of support from family and friends, and disappointed expectations of their anticipated adulthood. For a mature gay man who has passed as heterosexual for many years, the effects may seem subtler, the most common theme being isolation and loneliness. Once I was at a holiday cocktail party and someone turned the television to a college basketball game. Most of the men immediately gravitated to the television set, but two of us who had little interest in the game—but little else in common—remained staring at each other over the punch bowl.

In that moment, as a mature gay man with same-sex attraction, despite being socially active and well liked in my heterosexual community, I barricaded myself emotionally. Many gay men experience similar instances, fearful that too much intimacy might expose their so-called abhorrent desires. In the novel *Blue Boy*, Rakesh Satyal writes, "Nothing is more terrifying than knowing that one glance out of place could destroy my whole existence."[2] For a closeted gay man whose life has been primarily interwoven in a heterosexual world, thinking of leaving the security of that known world can be paralyzing. Isolation and loneliness appear preferable to the unknown but anticipated rejection from the community.

Am I Depressed or Just Sad?

Feelings of loss can accompany loss of a loved one, a pet, a body function, a job, a home, or a community. A sense of loss also occurs when what we expect doesn't materialize. For a few months after my mother's death, I experienced waves of grief. At first the waves would nearly drown me or smash me against the rocks of loneliness and loss. Then they would subside but be followed by another wave, another crash, and then another period of calm. Over time, the waves lost amplitude and frequency, but any unexpected reminder of my mother would trigger an occasional staggering wave of grief.

Depression spans a spectrum of disorders ranging from mild interference with daily function to a sense of hopelessness and a wish to die. Depressed people say that the pain of depression is far worse than the pain of cancer, kidney stones, and childbirth, but those who've never experienced depression can't imagine what being depressed is like. Depression is different from uncomplicated bereavement. Depression can occur unrelated to loss; sometimes it doesn't even include feelings of sadness. Emptiness or agitation is common. What psychiatrists call *neurovegetative symptoms* always accompany depression: difficulty sleeping, apathy, exaggerated guilt, low energy, difficulty concentrating, and changes in appetite. One man told me he couldn't decide which way to walk around his truck. Another woman said she couldn't decide which button on her blouse to button first. We do these things automatically without ever realizing that we're making decisions, but for depressed people, thinking becomes like swimming in molasses, and indecision overwhelms them. When severe, these symptoms significantly compromise functioning.

All depressed people seem to think in a similar way. Predictable distortions in their thinking occur. The thinking of depressed people more closely resembles the thinking of other depressed people than it does their own thoughts from before they became depressed. The word *should* begins to dominate their thinking. They focus on the way they feel to the exclusion of the feelings of others. They see their situation as irreversible and all-encompassing. Depressive frameworks dominate their thinking and create overly harsh judgments about themselves.

Depressed people have a certain kind of distorted logic that makes a great deal of sense to them but to almost no one else. I often tell patients that it's like having Vaseline on your glasses; no matter how much you strain your eyes, nothing comes into focus. Suicide begins to look like the only rational way to relieve the excruciating pain. I imagine that my grandfather's thoughts prior to his suicide went something like this: "I am in more pain than I could have ever imagined. I can see no escape. Suicide is the only thing that will make the pain end. My death will be difficult for my family, but my life is toxic to them. My living will hurt them more than my dying." Depression twists logic; it minimizes the consequences of a stigmatized death and denies any hope of possible recovery.

Secret Identities

I once had an abscessed tooth, and in the absence of a dentist, I seriously considered trying to pull it myself to end the horrible pain. Each of us seeks to maintain a sense of internal integrity while still making a positive impression on others. We are driven by a fear of being discredited. Sometimes that means keeping secrets, especially when the concealed information is sensitive—a history of abortion, a positive HIV status, or sexual attractions.

Secrets are like abscesses waiting to be lanced so the pain will disappear. They are painful; they hurt when we touch them, but we can't stop touching them. A secret that is at the center of our integrity

Depression creates predictable distortions in thinking:

- Experiences are perceived as all good or all bad.
- Everything revolves around the depressed person.
- Conclusions that go beyond the evidence are drawn.
- Details are taken out of context.
- Positives are rejected; negatives are exaggerated.

creates excruciating pain. Secrets produce symptoms of worry, anxiety, and anger that pressure us to disclose those secrets for relief. We long for the momentary intense pain that comes with rupturing the secret like an abscess to release the pressure. We know that once it ruptures, most of the pain will disappear.

Concealment of sexual orientation may occur consciously or unconsciously. Monitoring the secret against societal norms requires considerable effort, constant vigilance, and behavioral self-editing. Although we may wish to disclose the secret, our need to make a favorable impression on others often overpowers our need to disclose. When we consider revealing that we are gay, we sense it will create a vacuum in our self-esteem, and we fear that this vacuum will be filled by all of the shameful, stereotypical characteristics we have internalized of what it means to be gay.

Secrets are like abscesses waiting to be lanced so the pain will disappear.

Coming out is an intimate disclosure that has the power to strengthen or destroy relationships. It defines oneself in a way that acknowledges and integrates feelings and desires that previously were unacceptable, thought to be immoral, and never revealed to anyone. For me, it was a process that began with a life of guilt, fear, and hiding, followed by a period of intense self-examination, and ended with the development of a positive gay self-identity. Although some would say a person cannot be self-actualized until he assumes a complete and open gay identity, many men who have sex exclusively with men say that goes too far. They believe that while disclosure is important, one can still feel actualized without disclosing his sexual identity in every aspect of his life.

In my interviews I commonly found that even though it may have taken decades for a man to come to his own acceptance of his sexuality, he often mistakenly expected his family to embrace it immediately. Families initially may be overwhelmed and unsupportive, but in my experience many learn to modify their own internal value system to incorporate acceptance of their family member's sexuality. Sadly, some gay men and women have found their families completely unwilling to accept them. Their only alternative is to walk away and replace them with a family of choice composed of loving and supportive friends.

Depression in the LGBTQ Community

Due to the adverse social conditions that LGBTQ youth experience as a result of the stigma society attaches to their identities, suicide is one of the three leading causes of death for adolescents and a major public health crisis. Gay adolescents are four times more likely to commit suicide than their heterosexual peers.[3] But in 2013 the CDC reported a surprising surge in suicide rates among middle-aged Americans while there was a relatively small increase in suicide rates among younger people and a small decline in older people during a similar period.[4] Prevention programs tend to focus on suicide among teenagers; until recently middle age had been overlooked. From 1999 to 2010, the suicide rate among Americans ages thirty-five to sixty-four rose by nearly 30 percent with the most pronounced increases among men in their fifties, a group in which suicide rates jumped by nearly 50 percent.[5] The rates of suicide are alarming but even so are likely underreported.

Evidence exists of increased rates of diagnosable psychiatric disorders and substance abuse in the LGBTQ community, but population-based studies of suicide in the middle-aged and older LGBTQ community are virtually nonexistent. The gay community resists discussing the subject of gay suicide because it fears that talking about suicide will reinvigorate the idea that being gay is a form of pathology. The possibility that sexual confusion and conflict about sexual identity might be a contributing factor to suicide in middle-aged LGBTQ people is rarely, if ever, considered.

One of the leading risk factors for suicide is feeling alone. One man in his fifties wrote to me that he was "torn up inside" because of his hidden feelings, but when a man came on to him sexually, "I beat the crap out of him." He began to question what was wrong with him, but he spoke with no one about it. He then turned to alcohol for the next few years. He wrote, "I am sure there are other men out there who are in

Risk factors for suicide may be higher in gay men:

- Depression and anxiety
- Feeling alone
- Loss of relationships, status, income and/or health
- Failure to meet expectations
- Alcohol and other substance abuse
- Unwillingness to access treatment

the same boat as me. Maybe together we could come up with a solution and help one another!"

We all prefer to be a part of a community that accepts and supports us, but for some, isolation makes that very difficult. In their 2000 study of gay and bisexual men and women past the age of sixty, Arnold Grossman, Anthony D'Augelli, and Scott Hershberger found that when people are part of a stigmatized minority, being in the presence of others like them had a positive effect on self-esteem.[6] Many in the gay community who commit suicide do so while contemplating the public disclosure of sexual orientation and gender identity issues. Coming out in midlife is frightening enough, but it would be terrifying if there were no community in which to find support. Having someone to turn to is key, particularly for those struggling with same-sex attraction in middle age, but fewer resources are available for the middle-aged gay community.

Psychiatrists cannot predict who will commit suicide, but established criteria are used to assess risks. Risks include being male, being depressed and lonely, and abusing drugs and alcohol. Unresolved sexual identity issues heighten anxiety, loneliness, and isolation. All of this creates a fear that life is not going to turn out as planned. Because middle-aged gay men fear exposing their secret, they frequently resist seeking help.

Even when they live alone, elderly gay men often continue to have emotionally intimate relationships with others. Those who are isolated may have as much as 65 percent more depressive symptoms. Becoming a part of a community where you don't have to always censor your speech or edit your behavior is remarkably liberating. It creates a feeling of finally coming home again. Grossman, D'Augelli, and Hershberger reported that within research subjects' networks of friends and family of choice, the sexual orientation of their companions was less important than the freedom to be open about sexual orientation. But a supportive community will not seek out a mature man who finally chooses to come out. Finding that community will be up to him.

The Stages of Coming Out

Several different theoretical models for the stages of coming out have been described. One of the most widely referenced is "Homosexual Identity Formation: a Theoretical Model," put forth by Vivienne Cass in 1979 (see table 2). Cass wrote that because gay men and women are raised as nonhomosexual children in an antihomosexual society, their development creates a sense of internal incongruence between how these individuals perceive themselves and how they are perceived by others. According to Cass's model, a need for internal integrity propels people forward through the various stages, and choosing to live with a difference between personal and public identities prematurely halts developmental progression.[7]

Many coming out models, including Cass's, suggest that openly identifying as gay is a linear developmental process. It begins with an

Table 2: Stages of homosexual identity formation as described by Cass

Stage 1. Identity Confusion	"Why am I different?"
Stage 2. Identity Comparison . . .	"I may be gay, but I feel so alone."
Stage 3. Identity Tolerance	"Where are other gay people?"
Stage 4. Identity Acceptance	"I may be gay, but I am still okay."
Stage 5. Identity Pride	"If the world must be divided into homosexuals and heterosexuals, I am gay and I don't want to pass for straight."
Stage 6. Identity Synthesis	"I am okay, and I just happen to be gay."

awareness of same-sex attraction emerging in early childhood, followed by typical timing and sequencing of certain milestones, and eventually reaching the final endpoint of completely coming out. These models have similar, distinct themes: tell yourself, tell your mother (who probably has already figured it out), and then tell the world. Another common theme is that coming out occurs only in a climate of alienation and shame, surrounded by forces that seek to suppress the truth. Often little support exists.

Earlier models imply that one size fits all, and that self-actualization only occurs when one moves through the stages in a regular and progressive way until reaching the point of living an openly gay life. In these linear models sexual development typically ends in the twenties, but always by age forty. An orderly series of ideal or typical stages are posited as the exclusive paths to recognizing, making sense of, and giving a name to emerging gay identity.

These models are useful as a heuristic device that simplifies a complicated process, but they tend to collapse individual stories into common feelings, common thoughts, and common events. They are problematic because they do not provide alternatives—something that I struggled with as a man who came out in midlife. Since my life did not comply with these theoretical models, I began to question whether or not I was gay rather than question the universality of the models.

Many MSM that I interviewed particularly objected to Cass's fifth stage, "I am gay and I don't want to pass for straight." Whether they are primarily gay- or straight-identified, many disclose their sexuality to varying degrees depending upon the situation. They may be completely out with gay friends, out to a few close friends and family, but not at all out to other family members or at work. Those who have an early initial awareness and acceptance of being gay progress through development before having much same-sex experience; these men self-identified early on as gay, and they completed their sexual development as young men. For a wide variety of historical, economic, and social circumstances, other men come to accept their being gay later, sometimes much later, in their lives; many of them have had considerable clandestine sexual experience with other men. Men who choose to come out when they are more mature develop their gay identity later. When gay men have not resolved their internal fears of being gay, they experience low self-esteem, greater social isolation, and greater health risks.

The New Coming Out Model: A Trajectory

Because earlier models for coming out underemphasize sociocultural factors, this stage-sequential framework for gay identity development is being replaced with a hypothesis that multiple trajectories exist for gay self-definition. A trajectory describes how a projectile moves through space—a rocket in flight, for example. Objects moving through space have both individual characteristics and properties in common, but they must obey the laws of physics; they require energy to move them, and their environment influences the progression of their flight. Each object is unlike any other, and therefore it must follow its own unique trajectory.

Rockets are launched only after their propellant is fired; until then, they are governed by the law of inertia. People maintain the status quo unless compelled to alter it. They can't imagine a better future. Future options and outcomes are fuzzy and ill defined. Some choose not to come out because they expect that they might lose much more than they would gain from a future that they can only vaguely visualize.

Some men believe they have always known they were gay. Because the world is a different place now, some young people appear to blast right past all of the milestones, such as admitting their same-sex attractions to themselves and others, and some are completely out in early adolescence or even before. Others who have an early knowledge of their sexual orientation withhold disclosure, delay same-sex experiences, and remain closeted until they are older and have detached from their families. Some younger men may find it easier to come out when they are further along in their education and career. Financial independence provides greater access to a wider range of social options. These men may reach coming out milestones in a more sequential way. Others postpone dealing with their same-sex attractions until midlife or beyond because they have been unable to resolve the dilemma of who might be hurt if they reveal their secret as opposed to how they might be hurt if they continue to conceal it.

Each stage of the earlier models of coming out such as the one described by Cass has a benchmark. Some gay activists insist that those of us who move through the stages grudgingly or stall before the endpoint are defective. When I was in my thirties, I read about the stages of coming out and I discovered that the suggested age for completing all stages was in the mid-twenties. Again, I thought, "I can't be gay. I'm over thirty-five and I'm only in stage two." Although I "just went gay all of a sudden," I didn't exactly throw open the closet door, jump out, and shout, "I'm gay!" My progress toward a public and personal gay identity was halting and tortuous. I didn't come out, I inched out—backward—often waiting to be asked if I was gay rather than confronting the issue head-on.

The trajectory for coming out, as well as the associated milestones, is highly variable. And as I learned firsthand, it doesn't occur sequentially. Some milestones may never be reached, some may happen more than once, and no endpoint can be identified where all of the work of coming out is finished. Most people, including my patients, for example, presume that I am heterosexual. The more men I spoke with who came out in midlife, the more my own story was repeated back to me. Deciding when and to whom to come out is a process that never ends. The following factors can affect the timing of coming out:

- Parents and closeness of family structure

- Age, gender, and level of maturity

- Socioeconomic group, profession, and education

- Race, religion, geography, and culture

- Evolution of societal values

- Idiosyncratic life experiences

In 2010, at a Las Vegas regional meeting of Prime Timers Worldwide, a group of mostly mature gay and bisexual men, one of the men stated he had never been to a "gay" event before. He announced to everyone he met in the hotel and casino that he was attending "a convention for bisexuals." He was in his mid-to-late seventies, had been married for about forty years, and lived in a small rural town in a rural, Western state. In the past, when he had traveled out of town he would be drawn by powerful urges to have sex with a man, and for many years, he lived a "down low" life.

People maintain the status quo unless compelled to alter it. They can't imagine a better future.

He only began to come out following his wife's death. He believed that everyone is bisexual. He had parked his car in the bisexual parking lot, because accepting he was gay would have been driving too far and too fast in the gay lane. I briefly considered labeling myself as a bisexual, accepting that I had some attraction to men while still desperately clinging to my marriage and heteronormativity.

For many men, geography figures significantly in coming out, especially for middle-aged men who have already established communities for themselves, albeit in their heterosexual roles. In 2013 in an article in the *New York Times* Seth Stephens-Davidowitz wrote that on Facebook, about 1 percent of men in Mississippi who list a gender preference say that they are interested in men; in California, more than 3 percent do.[8] Are there really so many fewer gay men living in less tolerant states? For some gay men in rural and suburban areas, their same-sex activity has been primarily a weekend, leisure activity, rather than a full-time identity. Gay men living outside of urban areas more frequently pass as heterosexual, are more fearful of exposure, anticipate more intolerance and discrimination, and have fewer same-sex friendships and sexual encounters.

My own process of coming out certainly did not fit the molds I'd found while exploring my own inner conflicts. I was living out the dictates of my culture as the protector and provider. I fell rather easily into my professional identity. I cannot pinpoint when my marriage to my wife, Lynn, began to fail, but long before I began to question my sexual orientation, I had doubts about my skills at being a good husband and father.

As Lynn and I agonized about the possibility of divorce and breaking the most important commitment either of us had ever made, we searched to reconcile the asymmetries of our potential losses. Neither of us came from a family where anyone had ever been divorced. Every person in our small Nebraska hometowns—about twenty-five miles apart—could have disapprovingly named every couple in town who had been divorced. As a child, I had a younger friend whose parents were divorced and whose father was detached. I could not understand how that could happen. My mother was a single parent because my father had died, but I wondered how anyone could ever lose his father because of a stupid decision his parents had made.

Each Christmas the studio where my daughters studied dance put on performances of *The Nutcracker*. They always needed men for the first scene where the Stahlbaums host a lavish party around a tall Christmas tree. Shortly after meeting Roberto, and long before considering my divorce, I decided to audition and was given the role. At a postrehearsal party for the adults in the cast, I stalled until the other guests had left. I wanted to talk with the rather effeminate younger man who had hosted the party. As we sat with a glass of wine, I told him I wanted to talk to him because I thought I might be gay. He seemed surprised and responded, "I don't know why you would want to talk with me about that. I'm not gay!" I had barely dipped my toe into the coming out pool only to find it filled with hot lava.

Prior to meeting Roberto, I had encouraged Lynn to see a counselor with me to see if we could rediscover some meaning in our relationship. What we had was not enough for me, and it didn't seem to be working very well for her either. After I fell in love with Roberto, I discovered the possibility that I could have something more. Then one evening Lynn brought me some pages she'd printed off my computer. She had discovered some of my writing that journaled details of my relationship with Roberto. She said nothing, just handed the papers to me. A very big abscess was about to be drained.

I felt relieved that my secret was out, but confused about what to do. I knew that I wanted to leave the marriage. How would I tell my mother, who loved Lynn as much as she loved her own daughters? How could I tell the kids that I'd failed at being a father, and I was leaving them when I knew how painful it had been for me not to have a father? Was I putting everyone through all of this pain just for sex? What I had discovered was that I would never be like those other men I was pretending to be. Somehow a barrier had been erected between those other men and me, they were one kind of man and I was another. But now it no longer mattered. I began to mourn everything that had given my life definition up to that point.

I loved my wife as much as I was capable of, yet through no fault of hers it wasn't enough. I wondered if she knew it, too. I had always promised to give my children the father I didn't have, and I had participated in every aspect of their lives, from dirty diapers to Suzuki violin and piano practicing and lessons. I suffered through every dance recital. I love my children more than I ever thought it possible to love another person, and my children were the center of my life. How could I set that aside? I knew that being a good father and being a good noncustodial parent are not equivalent. I was considering giving up being an on-site father because I knew I had discovered that I was capable of experiencing loving a man in a whole different dimension than I had loved their mother.

I didn't tell my mother I was gay; she asked me. Shortly after I had separated from Lynn and moved to Des Moines, she visited me, and before her visit Roberto and I made a plan to test her out by having him drop by my condo. After she went home, she wrote me a brief note: "After our visit, I got to wondering if you might be gay. Love, Mom." I confessed much more than my family needed to know in an eight-page letter that I copied and sent to my brother and sisters.

I was frightened and uncertain about coming out, but with each step I began to feel more relieved, exhilarated, and validated. I anticipated that some friends, family, and colleagues would be shocked, confused, and even hostile. I was certain some would accuse me of exploiting my wife and destroying my family. Those were accusations I was prepared for—I had already made them. My trajectory had progressed through telling myself I was gay, confessing it to a few others, and finally telling my family. It hadn't gone as badly as I'd expected it to. But I was only beginning to make a new way for myself professionally, and I thoroughly believed that being out professionally would undermine my position of leadership in my new job as medical director of psychiatry at one of Iowa's leading hospitals. I led a quiet life as a newly out gay man.

All of life's important decisions are made without enough information, and coming out is no exception. We make our decisions based upon predictions about how our lives will be affected by the possible outcomes. A decision to change must carry with it a substantial chance of achieving something considerably greater than what might be lost, an economic principle called loss aversion. Those of us who have waited to come out until later in life typically have done so because we fear losing something very important in our lives, but the things we value—the things we most fear losing—are uniquely our own.

"Those Fucking Queers"

One of the men I interviewed was a man I'll call Jason McGee, a twenty-seven-year-old man who lives in rural Alabama. He described himself as a black American rather than an African American. He said, "The South expects certain things of you as a man, and being gay ain't one of them. Down here, people like me ain't gay or homosexual; we are queers and fags. For a Southern black man, being called sissy, fag, queer, or homo is one of the biggest disgraces ever." According to McGee, being labeled gay brings shame to your family and you are isolated because of it. He believes that being black and queer would almost certainly make him the victim of a hate crime. He said, "I'm masculine, so no one knows who I don't want to know."

McGee came from a loving and intact family. He considered his father to be his friend as well as his dad, and he was not treated differently within the family. His parents seemed to accept his excuse that he doesn't date because he's busy with school and a job. His brothers were in long-term relationships with women and had given his parents grandchildren. He regretted that he would not be able to. McGee had several gay cousins, although only one of them was out and he lived far away. Starting at age eleven McGee began participating in sexual play with one of his

All of life's important decisions are made without enough information.

cousins. They started by wrestling with each other, and one day McGee ejaculated but didn't understand what had happened. They continued to explore sexual play, but it always began with wrestling. Sometimes they were naked. Later they began to masturbate each other.

McGee was a Baptist who said he loves God and loves his church; he belonged to a congregation composed mostly of white people. Although he saw himself as gay, he was out to no one except his brothers, and only because they confronted him when they discovered some gay porn on his computer. They asked him if he could change, and when he said that he couldn't, they accepted him. He had no intention of coming out to the rest of his family. He believed coming out would mean letting go of so many people he loves, in both his family and his church. He decided not to come out because, he said, "I don't want to bring pain to my family and friends—myself, too."

At times McGee struggled in his church because "it hurts to hear [homosexuality] preached so hard against." He said some members of his church can't see past what their eyes show them, but he did not believe himself to be perfect and did not expect them to be perfect either. He said that he reconciled the issue for himself, quoting Romans 3:23: "For all are sinners and fall short of the glory of God." Then he said, "*All* are sinners. All. Everyone, not just gays. *All*. In God's eyes, no one's sin is worse than another man's sin. People are born in sin, so you can be born gay, as I believe I was."

He described his sexuality as complicated, especially because he was primarily attracted to white men over the age of forty-five, an attraction he discovered through erotic feelings toward his male teachers. He had

had a limited number of sexual partners as an adult. He was not looking for a relationship, but neither was he avoiding it. He said, "I don't act out my sexuality, except maybe online, and even then, I am not feminine by any means." He said that his sexuality doesn't define him or what he does because he doesn't let sex rule his life.

Although McGee had come to peace with his sexual orientation, he was uncertain of what it meant for his future. He wanted a relationship and children. He said, "I look around and I see the type of man I like everywhere, and yet I can't have any one of them. I see my friends with wives and girlfriends and I just go back home to my closet." He remained uncertain how to handle the issue of coming out. He said he had talked with other black men who felt that they have more freedom and more options after having come out, but for McGee coming out was not a priority. He said, "I'm still in the closet because I can't see what good coming out will do in this area. I hear about the free feeling you feel once you're out, but hell, I don't want to be alienated or hated either. There ain't no big gay community for support here. It's every man for himself. I get along fine, but it is still a challenge when you realize you're alone."

A few years ago I met another African American man at the gym. We often worked out at the same time and frequently ran into each other in the dressing room or sauna. Over several months we talked about a lot of things and we were in agreement about most political and social issues. Since only about 3 percent of the population of Iowa is African American, I had not had many opportunities to develop a friendship with a black man. Then one day he said to me, "We've got to do something about the fucking queers in this place." Although we'd never talked about it, I had assumed he knew that I was gay. I was devastated, and I went over to talk with one of my gay friends who was there. I told him what had happened and also about my experience in the Lutheran Church. He said, "You know, it isn't like that everywhere," and he invited me to his church, where all are welcome.

Although society is changing, coming out still means running the risk of losing heterosexual gender role advantages, friendships developed in the heterosexual world, and social status. Men who haven't come out have hidden a fundamental part of themselves because they fear losing love and respect and being abandoned and alone. Some simply fear exposing an imperfect masculinity. Although such negative outcomes can be quite painful, we overestimate the intensity of our feelings of loss and how long those feelings will last. We fail to learn from prior experience that the repercussions from revealing our secrets are almost always less than we anticipate. We underestimate our power to transform negative experiences into positive ones.

Ultimately the strength of a person's support system is the most significant influence in how coming out unfolds. Although the net impact of revealing secrets is typically more positive than negative, and usually more positive than anticipated, the benefits of revealing sexual identity certainly are not guaranteed. Personal revelations are significantly influenced by the response we receive from others. In considering whether or not to come out or how and when to disclose sexual orientation, it is important to develop strategies that are likely to result in positive responses from a network of supportive friends.

Fix It, Put Up with It, or Get Out

As I got older, I felt an increasing sense of urgency to deal with my hidden same-sex orientation. The same was true of the men I interviewed who came out in middle age; time passes quickly, and life begins to seem too short to start over again. As a psychiatrist, I have learned to tell my patients who are dealing with significant life conflicts to simplify the decision-making process. We have only three options: change it, put up with it, or get out. In most cases one of those three options can be eliminated immediately. Since attraction to someone of the same-sex is not going to change, a married man is left only with suffering through it or getting out. Acceptance generally evolves in a positive direction, even when the initial responses to coming out are unfavorable. Change does occur, albeit slowly. Relationships that were once thought to be lost can improve over time as family and friends begin to reconcile their homonegativism with their positive feelings for the gay man.

However, let me be clear; sometimes things really are as bad as they seem. Some of my closest friends from my heterosexual past disappeared from my life completely. For them, change felt impossible, and they reacted by getting out. While criticizing them for being homophobic and judgmental is easy, the truth is that I had never really let them know me completely.

In the process of interviewing for this book, I discovered that many, if not most, mature gay men experienced same-sex attraction as adolescents. But for some, the significance of those early same-sex feelings was not recognized until later; sometimes only after coming out did they really understand those attractions. I have also discovered, however, that many heterosexual men have had very similar sexual attractions as adolescents, although they were reticent to acknowledge them or interpreted them differently. Both gay and heterosexual men spin those past experiences, attaching significance as suits their current sexual identity.

In *Bridge of Sighs* Richard Russo writes, "But at some point, all of that changes. In our weariness we begin to sense the truth, that more doors have closed behind us than remain ahead."[9] When I reached midlife, I didn't find just one closet door out of which to come out. I was confronted by a series of complicated and interlocking doors. There were doors for my spouse, my parents, my kids, my siblings, my coworkers, my friends, and my religious community. I would knock on one door, only to find a solid wall. Other doors I could only peek in, and then realize I must not go inside. Some doors I knocked on over and over again with no one answering. When we come out we don't just open one door and walk through; we move through each of those doors through a process of negotiation.

Coming out professionally remains a significant issue for many gay men. Federal laws do not safeguard against employment discrimination on the basis of sexual orientation, and in 2016 over half of the LGBTQ population live in states that prohibit employment discrimination based on sexual orientation or gender identity.[10]

A study by the Human Rights Campaign Foundation released in May 2014 indicates that most LGBTQ employees (53 percent) nationwide are closeted on the job. Despite significant strides among the Fortune 500 and other major businesses implementing inclusive employment policies and practices, consistent legal protections are not afforded to LGBTQ people state to state. Many LGBTQ people feel unable to talk freely to their coworkers about their partners, and even more don't feel comfortable bringing their partners to corporate social functions.[11]

When I relocated to Des Moines after my divorce, I moved only thirty miles away, but it was an entire world apart from where I'd been while I was married. I knew no one and for a while couldn't even remember my own phone number or the names of any streets, save the one I lived on. I was starting a job as medical director of psychiatry at one of Iowa's largest hospitals. My grasp on my role as medical director felt very tenuous. Coming out as gay to the other psychiatrists seemed as if it would release my grip all together. I threw myself into the job, working seventy hours a week. It also proved to be a great escape from my feelings of failure as a husband and father, and left me little time to think about my loneliness and how much I missed my kids. As Justin Spring wrote in *Secret Historian*, "Normal men do not often have to choose between love and a career. . . . But the homosexual, it seems to me, often finds himself in a place where the choice between a career and love seems inevitable."[12]

I definitely overestimated the consequences of being out professionally, and I am fortunate to have experienced very little in the way of outward discrimination. Only once did my sexual identity seem to be an issue professionally. I had interviewed for a medical director position at a major health system in Indiana. We had completed negotiating the contract, and I was all set to sign. Out of the blue the recruiter called and said the hospital had decided to stop all negotiations and discussions about hiring me. No explanation was given, and in my opinion, none was necessary.

The primary task of coming out is to redefine one's identity so that what was once seen as an aberration is no longer seen as disgraceful.

Heterosexuals don't have to declare their sexual orientation. Men who are "undetectably gay" often encounter the presumption that they are heterosexual. I am frequently asked, for example, "How's your wife?" Until recently most of my patients didn't know much about my personal life, and for a long time that made it easy to pass as heterosexual, something I welcomed. At what point, I have asked myself, and to what degree, should I make a commitment to publicly declare my sexuality? As I became more comfortable as a gay man, I began to ask myself, "Does social justice require that I correct everyone when they make that mistake?"

Being gay does not really tell us much about who we are because there is no single gay identity and no final step in a developmental process. For many, developing a gay identity is a nonissue, and as one matures, sex drive diminishes as the central organizing force of one's life. As men become older, I found in my interviews, they begin to distance themselves from an all-encompassing gay identity and say, "I'm just me." Gay identity is integrated with all other aspects of life, including relationships with family and employers; involvement with church, community, and political organizations; and committed romantic relationships.

Mature gay men refuse to be molded into a universal gay identity, just as they once struggled to be free of the stamp of heterosexual identity. Unlike a rocket, each of us has the capacity to choose our own destination and the trajectory that gets us there. No matter when we confront our sexual identity, as a teenager or in our last decades, we all evolve throughout our lifetimes. Harold Kooden, in *Golden Men: The Power of Gay Midlife*, wrote that each man must direct his own advancement through the sexual development process. By taking more responsibility for his own history, a gay man has a deepening sense of active participation in his life that reduces his feeling of being overwhelmed and out of control. Kooden states that older gay men who are self-accepting and psychologically well-adjusted adapt well to the aging process.[13]

Being gay is not something anyone seeks or plans. In most cases we would have wanted something we once thought of as better, that is, until we accept that what we have is pretty damn good. We are individuals.

Each man who has sex with men must direct his own self-development. We are launched into this world with a presumed heterosexual flight path, but the course our lives take is influenced as much by our own composition as that of the world around us. Eight of the respondents to my survey of mature MSM were over eighty years old. Four of them either came out or were outed in their eighth decade of life. Their life stories defy the universality of stage-sequenced coming out. Our lives evolve as the deniable becomes undeniable. There is no single identity, no single trajectory. No one else can live our lives.

5

Are You Shooting at the Wrong Target?
Detox and Rehab for Addiction to Approval

Therefore the sage is guided by what he feels.
And not by what he sees. He lets go of that and chooses this.

—LAOZI, *DAODEJING*

"Ken's dead." Bruce's call jolted me from my recovering-from-Saturday-night's sleep on Valentine's Day 1988. I had met both Ken and Bruce at a gay fathers' support group that had been formed to help gay fathers deal with the unique personal issues related to coming out as a married man with children. "What!" I screamed into the phone.

"He was murdered last night. The cops were here early this morning and questioned me," Bruce said, with a mixture of anger, fear, and sadness. On Saturday night, we had all spent time together at the Brass Garden, Des Moines's only gay disco.

"What happened?" I had an eerie feeling that perhaps I wasn't really awake. "Who? ... What? ... Where?" I couldn't even formulate the questions.

"Nobody knows anything yet. Turn on your television. That's about as much as I know. It happened at his apartment. I guess someone stabbed him. Jennifer was home, too, but she's okay."

"She was there the whole time? Oh my god!"

As I watched the Sunday morning news, the reality of Ken's murder gradually wedged its way into my brain. It was an odd feeling to see a place where I'd been to dinner parties surrounded by yellow crime-scene tape, but I also realized that given different circumstances, I might have been the one who was being autopsied. It was also the beginning of the AIDS crisis, and I began to wonder what kind of a world I had just joined. Perhaps all of the losses I'd feared were going to materialize, and in an even bigger way than I'd imagined.

The gay fathers' group provided a lifeline for several of us who'd been in heterosexual relationships, some of us still married, and all of us with children. Confused, questioning, and working our way through the questions about our sexuality, we were mentored by others who were further along in the process.

Ken, Bruce, and this group of formerly self-described heterosexual gay men comprised my entire circle of friends, gay or straight, and the only people other than my wife whom I had told about my increasingly unmanageable sexual attraction to men. Medicine had taught me to be thoughtful, rational, and deliberate. I never formed impulsive conclusions. Now my reason and emotion were like two wrestlers locked in a combative embrace, each trying to pin the other.

Ken had been out longer than either Bruce or I had, and when I met him he had a "longtime companion," the euphemistic code words used for gay lovers in all the AIDS obituaries at that time. Ken's relationship with his partner was one I admired and longed for in my own life. When their partnership ended, it underscored my concerns that gay men were only capable of riding one bus until the next one came along. Many straight people, but also quite a few gay people, believe that stereotype. One of my interviewees, who has sex exclusively with men, refuses to refer to himself as gay because he believes transitory relationships based exclusively on sexual attraction are the hallmark of being gay. Ken and Bruce both valued long-term relationships, but both struggled to find them. What I admired most about both of them was their total commitment to being a father to their children.

Ken was a devoted father, and his older daughter, Jennifer, lived with him, first with his partner and him, and then when his relationship ended, with just Ken. Jennifer was a teenager, a good student, and a hard worker. She appeared unblemished by her father's being gay and all of his gay friends. I had hoped she would help my daughters successfully get through the transition of my coming out. Jennifer had been asleep in their apartment during the murder. I couldn't help wondering if I could be putting my own daughters' safety at risk.

After establishing such a close bond with these men, I was shattered to hear that one of them had been murdered. Slowly, a few facts about Ken's death began to trickle in. After going to the theater on Saturday night with a friend, Ken had gone to the Brass Garden. After last call he dropped his friend at home, and then went to the "gay loop," a cruising area where the search for Mr. Right evolves into the search for Mr. Right Now. Ken met two young men there and took them back to his apartment. No one except James Michael "Billy" Green and Gary Titus knows exactly what happened after that, and a search for the facts revealed contradictory stories.

Titus testified that he hated gay people and admitted that both he and Green had a pattern of assaulting gay men for no reason other than their being gay. He now professes to have become a born-again Christian. He said he found Christ after accompanying another prisoner, ironically another one of his former bashing victims, to a prison revival. He has since become a jailhouse preacher. While in prison he received a letter from his brother saying, "Gary, I want you to know I'm gay . . . What if you ran into me at the Gay Loop?" His brother later died of AIDS.[1]

Titus said that preying upon gay men brought power to his otherwise powerless existence, as if he were the real victim of this heinous event. Tragically, this kind of affirmation of power is short lived, and the gay bashing must be repeated over and over to recapture that feeling of strength. Rejecting any responsibility for this despicable act, Titus blamed the murder on Green. Perhaps I'm being cynical or possibly just still angry about Ken's death, but I wonder how many murderers have become born-again Christians when they consider confronting the parole board that will make the decision about their being released from prison.

The Chemicals of Pain and Pleasure

Serotonin is the chemical messenger in the brain that is critical in regulating emotions. Too much serotonin will inhibit sexual behavior, and low levels of it correlate with depression, angry and aggressive behavior, irritability, and impulsivity. Many of the newer antidepressant agents, used for both depression and anxiety, are called selective serotonin reuptake inhibitors (SSRIs). Their net effect is to increase serotonin at the junctions between neurons in the parts of the brain associated with regulating emotion.

Dopamine is the pleasure molecule and too much dopamine can make you crazy. Dopamine neurons take in data we don't consciously comprehend, and they unload dopamine into the brain in massive doses just before a person receives a payoff for some anticipated, pleasurable experience. Dopamine also is associated with controlling movement, emotional responses, and pain. Dopamine rewards can come naturally through eating chocolate and other comfort foods, sexual activity, and approval from others. The dividends of dopamine also come through use of caffeine, alcohol, cocaine and methamphetamine, nicotine, marijuana, gambling, and other risk-taking behaviors like anonymous sex in airport bathrooms.

Grandfathers may not know much about dopamine, but we do seem to know instinctively that you can't tickle your grandchildren unless you raise their anticipation of the tickle attack by playing the I'm-gonna-getcha game. Timing and unpredictability are critical. The heightened apprehension must be managed carefully or it will pass by quickly. Dopamine is dumped in the child's brain during the anticipatory phase of the attack, not during the tickle assault itself. Adults also instinctively play the sexual I'm-gonna-

Dopamine is the pleasure molecule and too much dopamine can make you crazy.

getcha game, although with much different stakes in mind. My friend Ken played that game with unfortunate consequences when he put a gay porn video in the VCR for Titus and Green.

When I was in the navy, I proudly wore the wings of a flight surgeon. As the drug czar for the squadron, I was responsible for the men's drug education. The early 1970s were a difficult time in our country's history. Young men and women protested the Vietnam War and challenged the establishment. The battle cry was "Sex, drugs, and rock and roll." I did not look forward to my assignment to do the sexually transmitted diseases and drug lectures before we left Maine on deployment to Sicily.

I stood before a crowd of young sailors with their arms folded across their chests, staring at the floor. The senior men—there were no women in the squadrons in those days—both officers and enlisted, were adamantly opposed to drug use. Most of the younger men had been drafted into the military and resented the disruption in their lives. Drug use proved to be the perfect way to rebel. However, among the senior officers and enlisted men, alcohol abuse was almost requisite for career advancement. The young men finally sat up and smiled when I denounced alcohol abuse as just another form of drug abuse.

Several of the corpsmen, the navy's medical support personnel, spoke in guarded but rather transparent ways about their use of marijuana. The more they talked about it, the more it intrigued me, and I decided I wanted to try it. I asked one of the corpsmen I trusted if he would help me. One evening, when my wife was visiting her family in Nebraska, I invited the corpsman to come to our house in Maine and to bring some marijuana with him.

Since I planned this to be a one-time event, I was determined to make the most of it. The sailor and I sat in our living room and he instructed me in how to roll a joint. As I began smoking mine, I inhaled cautiously, holding the smoke briefly in my lungs. I could see that he was getting mellow, but I felt nothing. I wasn't sure what to expect, but I didn't seem to be experiencing the same thing he was. I decided I wasn't inhaling deeply enough. I began to take deep drags on the joint, doing as he'd instructed and holding my breath as long as I could. Still I felt nothing, and so I smoked the entire joint before I stopped.

All at once, I was high, very high. I got up and began to pace around the room, trying to ground myself in some reality I couldn't find. I was hit with a very powerful urge to try to have sex with the young sailor. That's when I started to panic. Rumors had circulated around the navy clinic that he was gay, but he had never discussed it with me. Although I was still innocent of man-on-man sex, the effects of the marijuana threatened to unbridle my unconscious desire. Now I can see that I may have wanted him more than the marijuana.

Then the paranoia struck. I began to believe that the Naval Intelligence Service was spying on us through the closed draperies. They would charge me with fraternization with an enlisted man, lascivious acts, and the use of illegal drugs. I would be dishonorably discharged from the navy and lose my license to practice medicine. Once this was exposed, I would also lose my wife and family. Every ambition I had about my future was about to go up in a cloud of cannabis smoke. I was desperate for my rational mind to return and rescue me from the dopamine haze, the NIS, and my psychotic same-sex desires.

Feelings are the summation of information we can't or don't want to comprehend consciously. Very little of our brain is involved in rational thought, while the vast majority of our brain is constantly processing information in its unconscious circuitry. Rational thought is a lion tamer in a cage filled with hungry wild animals. The brain abhors the contest between feelings and rational thought and consumes immeasurable energy binding up information we really don't want to access.

Feelings are the summation of information we can't or don't want to comprehend consciously.

Anticipating rewards is pleasurable, and the anticipation enhances the dopamine effects. But if it goes on too long, the dopamine effect grows stressful. Once, I took my kids to a carnival and we rode the Turbo Force, a one-hundred-foot-tall tower with caged seats that flip over as the tower spins. The ride went on far too long, and I was desperate to get out of that cage. Our screams were amplified to the crowd by loud speakers and only encouraged the sadistic carny to prolong the ride. Our pleadings raised the collective dopamine level of the crowd long after ours were depleted. Maturity is knowing that not every dopamine rush must be gratified.

The Insurgency of Feelings

Successful decision making relies on a balance between deliberate thought and instinctive assumptions. We have two kinds of thinking: intuition, or unconscious thought, and reasoning. Intuition makes up the large majority of all thought processes; it is fast, easy, and indefatigable. Intuition is connected to the brain's centers involved in motivation and reward, while reasoning is not. Reasoning is slow, arduous, and demanding.

Most of the work of the brain does not occur at a logical level. When buying a new car, I read all about the cars recommended in *Consumer Reports*, but in the end, I buy the one that I fall in love with. Often we believe we are making a rational decision when we are really making an emotional decision, and then we begin to search for justifications to make our decision appear rational. As our brains collect bits of experiences, our rational minds quickly create rational explanations for things that can't be explained or are simply untrue. As Benjamin Franklin said, "So convenient a thing it is to be a reasonable creature, since it enables one to find or make a reason for everything one has a mind to do."

Our minds are engaged in a continuous conflict that operates outside of our awareness. The most important thing we can do is to listen to what every part of our brain is telling us. We must consciously search for the facts we need, but then allow our brains to incubate those facts together with our feelings before making a decision.

According to the Prospect Theory of economists Daniel Kahneman and Amos Tversky, "In human decision making, losses loom larger than gains." Because we undervalue the future, they argue, our decisions are impacted more by a fear of losses in our present life than the prospect of potential gains.[2] Therefore, we opt for the status quo, often making uninformed decisions based on fear. This principle seems to govern many men's decisions to remain in the closet and, as was my case, in their heterosexual relationships long after they've begun to have sexual relationships with other men.

Our brains carry a negativity bias, meaning that criticism has more impact than compliments do. Bad is stronger than good. As political campaigns demonstrate, nastiness in the form of mudslinging can be extremely effective. Researchers have demonstrated that in personal relationships a very definite ratio exists between the positive interactions that are necessary to compensate for the negative ones. John Gottman, author of *The Seven Principles for Making Marriage Work*, wrote that five positive interactions must occur for each negative interaction to establish a satisfying balance in marriage, to diminish conflict, and to make marriages more successful.[3]

Various parts of our brains have been identified as serving different functions. The bottom of the frontal lobes integrates visceral emotion into decision making, connecting feelings to higher, more rational thought. But the engine of this part of the brain can become flooded with too many facts, causing a person to no longer be able to make sense of a situation. Other parts of the brain generate negative emotions like fear, anxiety, and acrimony, which impact decision making. Small wonder that often mature men make the decision to come out only after they have been confronted by a situation that forces them to do so.

A part of the temporal lobe of our brains helps us theorize what others are feeling and allows us to empathize with them. Individuals vary in their capacity for empathy, from far too much to almost none. The world is full of impulsive people who, like Titus and Green, appear to have a major functional deficiency in their capacity for empathy. Empathy helps us with moral decision making. We treat others fairly because we know how it feels to be treated unfairly and can conceive of what we would feel like in another person's situation. The dopamine reward system of the brain responds to being treated fairly in the same way it responds to hitting a jackpot or eating a hot fudge sundae. Those with lower levels of serotonin are more sensitive to unfair treatment.

Some people seem to have a particularly heightened capacity for empathy, often caring more about others' feelings at the expense of their own. One gay man I visited with following a speaking engagement told me that the primary pleasure in his relationships with men comes from pleasing his partners. When I asked him how he received his own sexual pleasure, he said, "I can always take care of that myself." He went on to say that his attractions were bittersweet since he was only attracted to older men, and he had lost five different partners through death. Then he added, "At sixty, the only place left for me to cruise is in a nursing home."

In-Groups and Out-Groups

We care about our behavior and the ways in which we interact socially with others. For me, that translated into caring about the brain. I was drawn to psychiatry because of its complexity; psychiatry is a profession where nuance and ambiguity coexist with the gelatinous facts of brain science. When I told my mother I wanted to be a psychiatrist, she said, "Why do you want to stop being a doctor?" For her, psychiatrists were physician outsiders. In the late 1960s, her only reference was small-town Nebraska, where if someone went to see a psychiatrist, they never returned. It may also have triggered memories of my grandfather's suicide.

Categorization is a useful tool our brains develop to reduce the complexity of the world; it can also be destructive.

Categorization is a useful tool our brains develop to reduce the complexity of the world; it can also be destructive. Labels are often static, arbitrary, and far too restrictive. Although people and societies evolve over time, labels, once assigned, resist change. Sexuality is far too complex to divide into just two categories, gay and straight, with bisexual thrown in as a default category for those who don't fit easily into the other two. Historically, the word *queer* was used to describe men who felt a sense of difference and saw themselves as outsiders, marginalized by society.

In the antebellum South, just "one drop of blood" was enough to brand someone as black. The primary purpose of the "One-Drop Rule" was to expand the slave population. Today an extremely diverse group of people are called Hispanic, even if the only thing they have in common is that their first language is Spanish.

In an 1869 pamphlet arguing for the opposition of Prussian antisodomy laws, Karl-Maria Kertbeny coined the word *homosexual* by combining a Greek and a Latin root. He hoped that by labeling homosexuality a medical problem, homosexual men who were being blackmailed would find compassion.[4] The word *homosexual* stuck, but instead of creating compassion it fixed the idea that homosexuality was a form of pathology.

In 1871, Paragraph 175 was added to the German Reich Penal Code. A precise translation is complicated because the phrase *Unzucht treibt* doesn't have a polite English equivalent. Basically, the original law prohibited sex between two men and between humans and animals, although it was later expanded under the Nazis to include two men kissing, fondling, or masturbating each other. These behaviors were punishable by imprisonment and loss of civil rights for tens of thousands of men accused of these offenses. They were sent to concentration camps where they were forced to wear a pink triangle and treated brutally. Many died before the camps were liberated; some who were liberated still faced imprisonment.[5]

The law of small numbers forms the basis of all stereotypes and prejudices. Simply put, it states that what is true for some must be true for all.

The law of small numbers forms the basis of all stereotypes and prejudices. Simply put, it states that what is true for some must be true for all. If some gay men are sissies, all must be. Applying this principle, societies describe groups of people by isolating one or two easily recognizable characteristics, elevating those traits to the highest level, and then generalizing those characteristics to everyone in the group. Once done, the search for any invalidating evidence stops, and stereotypes become fixed.

Sociologists tell us that all groups of people behave in similar ways, and they define the behavior in terms of in-groups and out-groups. They suggest that these principles hold true whether we examine behavior in religious groups, political parties, school friendships, or gay and straight communities. I joined a college fraternity because I was trying to satisfy a need for connectedness. I believed membership would confer on me some positive feelings of acceptability. Sociologists call this "basking in reflected glory," but as I found, borrowed respect vanishes quickly.

In all groups, individual interests are sacrificed and merged with the interests of the whole, the most extreme example being the military, where an esprit de corps inspires devotion, honor, and obedience. Members of units within the military speak about the intense love each has for the others even though their relationships may be quite brief.

People who identify most strongly with a group see themselves as typical of all group members. They become outspoken and begin to believe they speak for everyone. These guardians protect the group from problematic or contradictory information that interferes with group cohesiveness. This behavior is apparent when we consider conservative talk show hosts like Glenn Beck and Rush Limbaugh, who exalt their norms and thinking as if they are universal truths. But this is also true of some of the most outspoken gay activists. In the documentary movie *Out Rage*, Elizabeth Birch, former executive director of the Human Rights Campaign (HRC), said of Senator Larry Craig, "We don't want him anyway." It created a great laugh line for what appeared to be the largely gay audience. I have a great deal of respect for Ms. Birch and the HRC; however, where do people go for group membership when they're not wanted by the HRC, the nation's largest lesbian and gay political organization? I believe that Ms. Birch's remarks were motivated by her strong loyalty and commitment to the HRC rather than any particular hostility toward Senator Craig.

Powerful leaders like Senator Craig who are hypocritical about their sexuality are in a position to do great damage to a large number of people. Concerning the outing of public figures, former congressman Barney Frank said, "I think there's a right to privacy. But the right to privacy should not be a right to hypocrisy. People who want to demonize other people shouldn't then be able to go home and close the door, and do it themselves."[6] Many of us have lied about our sexual orientation, particularly while we were in a state of confused transition. For some, that state of confusion lasts a very long time, and in the process, we have hurt others. That holds true for Senator Craig just as it holds true for me.

Because I can identify with some of Senator Craig's motivations for concealing his secret life, I felt stung by Ms. Birch's remark. I thought, "I've been a hypocrite. Maybe they wouldn't want me either." But gay men and women are subject to the same principles of sociology as everyone else, and we must guard against the possibility that loyalty to our own community might also create for us a sense of moral superiority.

Sociologists explain that as we become members of a group, we begin to know other members well, eventually seeing ourselves as similar to them. However, we satisfy our need for individuality by recognizing that the group is more diverse than it originally appeared. We are connected emotionally to them, we hurt when they hurt, and we experience joy when they do. We also begin to exaggerate the positive characteristics of our group and may begin to see ourselves as having a higher moral authority than other groups. Marilynn Brewer wrote that many discriminatory behaviors are not motivated primarily by antagonism toward the out-group but rather by a desire to promote and maintain positive relationships in our own group.[7] However, the very factors that make allegiance to our own group important create fertile ground for distrust of those outside. The need to justify the values of the in-group creates a sense of moral superiority. Loyalty to our own group then conspires to create disdain and hostility toward the out-group.

Because we associate primarily with members of our own group, we don't really know other groups, and we see them as more homogeneous and generic than they actually are. Some who have little or no experience with gay people feel confident that they can define us. They believe that gay people are unrestrained and disregard all laws or morality.

We assign negative characteristics to the other group and begin to see them as more evil than they are. Conflict escalates from name calling to discrimination to attacks, hate crimes, and genocide. Propaganda that characterized all Jews, Gypsies, and gays as subhuman and a threat to the Aryan race allowed the Nazis to exterminate those they felt threatened by. The Germans hated the Jews for a reason, but the reason was fear based and founded on a distortion of facts. American history is replete with crimes of hatred and prejudice, including lynchings, cross burnings, vandalism of churches and synagogues, and hate crimes like the murders of gay and transgender men and women.

The term *hate crime* did not become a part of the nation's vocabulary until the 1980s during a wave of bias-related crimes including Ken's murder. Perhaps Titus's and Green's brain chemistry or their family environments led them to kill Ken, but judging by their own statements the more likely explanation is that they felt threatened by gay men. Their hatred caused them to make preemptive attacks on gay men, making themselves self-appointed warriors for all homophobes out there—the law of small numbers in its most brutal form.

The dominant heterosexual community has at times blamed gay men and women for having brought hatred upon themselves. When those in the out-group feel morally excluded, threatened, and vulnerable, they begin to exalt themselves, claiming higher moral authority, and they degrade, hate, and attack the opposition.

Following Stonewall, gay people became a more powerful group. No longer hidden, they became bolder and more unified, even making their own preemptive attacks on the powerful, through groups like ACT UP, as described by Jason DeParle in the *New York Times*: "To the businesses, bishops and bureaucrats that they accuse of slowing the fight against AIDS, [members of ACT UP] often seem rude, rash and paranoid, and virtually impossible to please. And they are. . . . Members of ACT UP, the AIDS Coalition to Unleash Power, refer to themselves as a despised minority, literally fighting for their lives. And that they are as well. Another word helps describe ACT UP: effective."[8]

Contact between a dominant majority group and a racial, ethnic, religious, or other minority group reduces prejudice. Psychologists call this the *contact hypothesis*. Research has demonstrated that heterosexuals' attitudes about being gay are changed most significantly when a homonegative person has an open discussion about same-sex attraction with two or more close friends or family members who are gay. When

When a homonegative person discusses being gay with two or more people who are gay, prejudices against gay people are diminished.

a homonegative person discusses being gay with two or more people who are gay, prejudices against gay people are diminished. From a global perspective, it is easy to suggest that social justice demands that those of us who are gay must share our sexual orientation with others, but when it comes down to how these decisions impact the people we love, coming out becomes far more difficult.

Early in my years of coming out, the extent to which I took up the task of implementing the contact hypothesis by coming out was limited. In 1992 I participated in the March on Washington for Lesbian, Gay, and Bi Equal Rights and Liberation with my friend Bruce and my partner, Doug. Organizers estimated that one million people attended the march, but the National Park Service estimated attendance at three hundred thousand. Either way, my presence didn't make a substantial difference, but experiencing the great diversity of men and women there made a tremendous impact on me. The march was organized to bring attention to the government's lack of response to the AIDS epidemic.

Being in the presence of so many gay men and women revealed to me how large and diverse our out-group was. It also confronted me with the stark reality of how many of our group had died from AIDS. During the march, a final display of the AIDS Memorial Quilt covered the entire National Mall. Bruce, Doug, and I located the panel of our friend Jim, who had died of AIDS. I was filled with grief for the tens of thousands of people who were victims of this devastating disease. Had I come out earlier, I believe that one of the three-by-six-foot quilt panels might have had my name on it.

I experienced great empathy for those men my age who searched for quilt panel after quilt panel of the many people they had loved and watched die. I felt no peace just because my name wasn't there on a quilt. I only felt a sense of connectedness to those who had died and the enormous guilt so often felt by those who escape the consequences of terrible tragedies.

Being Gay and Feeling Good

Believing that we are competent, attractive, well-liked, and morally good are the touchstones of self-esteem. I often worry too much about whether I am liked by others, and I expect rejection to the point that I look for evidence even when it doesn't exist. During the first year of my relationship with Doug, he was unable to decide whether or not to remain in Iowa to be with me. Because of my exaggerated fears of loss, I kept pressuring him to make a commitment. Doug was frustrated by my anxiety and reminded me to live in the moment of our relationship.

In describing their motivations, Titus and Green, who murdered my friend Ken, perceived that acting on their hatred for gay people would compensate for their feelings of powerlessness and finally give them some self-respect. They, like me—albeit in a completely different, violent, and ineffective way—were seeking self-esteem.

Our ideal self, the person we wish to be, is the sum of all traits, values, and issues we consider to be important. This is the main organizing principle of self-esteem, the nucleus formed early in life. It enlarges and becomes more complex with maturity. For example, having perfection as an ideal creates a chronic gap between what is expected and what is achieved; when perfection and failure are the only two options, a sense of failure is inevitable because perfection is not achievable. We filter each new experience through these negative constructs, resulting in a broad range of negative generalizations about ourselves and a growing tendency to personalize everything. Self-criticism and self-blame begin to dominate our thinking. Events are polarized into good and bad, and because we seem to have a bias for it, we selectively focus on things that are negative. This negative thinking is generalized to our assessment of the world, leading to isolation and loss of motivation and resulting in the physical signs and symptoms of depression.

Andrew Tobias, in *The Best Little Boy in the World*, describes how many gay men try to compensate for what they feel are their deficiencies by going to extremes to please others.[9] As a young man, I had believed that since gay was bad, I couldn't be bad. So I was going to be good, and I'd be the best at being good that I could be. This was a very common theme in the interviews that I conducted. But my measure for being good had been to be what others expected me to be. Choosing to be a psychiatrist rather than a family care doctor became the touchstone for my evolving decision-making process; I didn't need my mother's approval of my professional choice. If I wanted to be a psychiatrist, I would be a psychiatrist. If I wanted to be gay, I would be gay, too. I could be gay and still be good, but it would mean giving up an expectation of approval from others.

Several years ago at a meeting in Arizona for medical executives, I heard Dr. Harry Levinson, emeritus professor of psychology in the Department of Psychiatry at Harvard, discuss a model for self-esteem using a formula based on the effects of the reciprocal number. The rules of reciprocal numbers suggest that the larger the number on one side of the equation, the smaller the number on the other side becomes. In Dr. Levinson's formula for self-esteem, illustrated in figure 3, the smaller the difference between our ideal self and our actual self, the smaller the denominator on the right becomes, and the larger the number on the left side of the equation (our self-esteem) becomes. In other words, the closer we believe we are to becoming the person we have always wanted to be, the better we feel about ourselves.[10]

$$\text{Self-esteem} = \frac{1}{(\text{Ideal self} - \text{Actual self})}$$

Figure 3: The formula for self-esteem

I tried using Dr. Levinson's formula on some of my patients, but many of them responded to me with a glassy-eyed, math-anxiety look. I

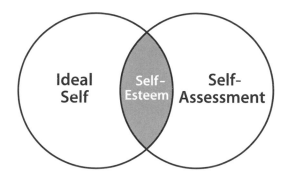

Figure 4: Self-esteem diagram

began to use the diagram in figure 4 to explain this to my patients, and almost immediately they began to understand the issue.

In this diagram, the greater the overlap of the circle representing our ideal self with the circle representing our actual self, the larger our self-esteem becomes. To develop a positive self-esteem, we must work to align the ideal self with the actual self.

Dr. Levinson suggested that we have the power to modify the ideal self, the person we believe we should be, but the word *should* suggests that this ideal self has been set for us by our family, our religion, and our culture. In working with my patients, I have discovered that many of them have never given any thought to their ideal self, what they would like to become. They either have been content to let someone else set that ideal for them or have never received much encouragement to become more than what they are.

As we develop across our life span, we begin to have the maturity, experience, and wisdom to examine those shoulds and determine if they represent our values or someone else's. Often the actual self, the person we think we are, is based less on the facts of who we are than on a negative bias in our brains. In other words, we tend to be overly harsh in our self-criticism. The task, then, is to eliminate the distortions by focusing on the facts of who we really are. What is striking about this formula is that it contains *nothing* about approval from others; lasting self-esteem, Dr. Levinson insists—and I completely agree—can never be achieved by seeking approval from others.

Using this diagram, my patients began to see, as I had, that energies directed at pleasing others would never lead to a predictable and lasting feeling of satisfaction with oneself. Always seeking approval drives us to become what Stanley Hauerwas called "a quivering mass of availability." We make ourselves available to be controlled by what others expect of us. Anna Freud had the same insight when she said, "I was always looking outside myself for strength and confidence, but it comes from within. It is there all the time."

This was a dramatic revelation in my own life. If I wanted to feel good about myself, I had to analyze all the things I had been told I must be and then assess which of those things I wanted to commit myself to being. I felt a new sense of freedom as I took complete control of this ideal. I realized that seeking approval from others is nothing more than a form of addiction. A "hit" of approval creates a rush of good feelings that lasts but a moment. The search for the next hit begins immediately. To achieve a lasting sense of self-esteem, I had to choose for myself a high but achievable standard, work hard to reach it, and be objective in measuring my progress. Getting to know other gay men whom I admired and respected was an important step in deconstructing the old and reconstructing that new ideal.

It was after I came out that I realized I needed to be fair and accurate with my self-appraisals. I recognized that seeking approval for being someone I didn't really want to be undermined my self-esteem. The remarkable thing is that often when we choose outside of what is

---

You can take three steps to improve your self-esteem:

1. Take control of the ideal self and make it your own, not something you inherited.
2. Learn to see yourself as you are; avoid exaggerated self-criticism.
3. Look inside yourself for strength and confidence; approval from others is fleeting.

Typical, inherited societal values tell us that in order to be happy, we must meet the following criteria:

- Not make mistakes
- Be successful
- Be accepted by all people all of the time
- Have a wife/husband and a family

expected, others approve of us as much as if we had chosen according to expectations.

Cognitive therapists talk about automatic thinking, which creates a cascade of those thoughts like this:

1. I cannot start my lawn mower.

2. Every man should be able to start a lawn mower.

3. In fact, I can never do anything most men should be able to.

4. I am a worthless man.

5. I am a drag on my family and society.

6. I may as well kill myself.

These negative pathways are practiced so frequently and successfully that a depressed person can instantly shift from something as banal as mechanical trouble to extreme existential angst, a response that goes far beyond anything justified by the original circumstances.

The basic principles of cognitive therapy suggest that these thoughts have their origins in early life, incorporated through role models, feedback, and culture. Although these thoughts, especially the earliest ones, are difficult to change, they are subject to modification, meaning that distortions in our thinking can be corrected. Cognitive therapy does not question the existence of unconscious thinking, but it does suggest that looking entirely at the roots of these distortions, as traditional psychodynamic psychotherapy does, is unfruitful.

Automatic thoughts have the following characteristics:

- They are habitual, learned, and practiced.
- They are global and generalized.
- They are specific and discrete.
- They appear to be plausible, intuitive, and factual.
- They lead to negative events being taken out of context and magnified.

Men who struggle with their same-sex attractions can feel as if they are being dragged by a strange new force. Desire and reason are pulling these men in two different directions: they desire other men but reason that they should be attracted to women because that is normal. While this turmoil may initially appear during the emotional upheavals of adolescence, it can persist, as in my case, throughout adulthood. The cultural values of masculinity, femininity, and sexuality are incorporated into our ideal self in often unrealistic and unattainable ways. This gap in expectations and outcomes creates the sense of difference that gay men feel. It creates additional distortions in thinking and causes *should* to dominate thinking: I *should* like women, I *should* be able to fix a lawn mower, and I *should* have known not to have dressed as a girl for Halloween. These are things we believe a boy should know instinctively. Failure to attain the *shoulds* can create a sense of shame that translates into the rage some gay people feel toward a homophobic culture. Although anger toward an unjust society is appropriate, and actions directed at changing that culture are admirable, unfortunately that alone will not help anyone feel better.

The first step in improving the way we feel about ourselves is to take a good look at the ideal self of our childhoods and begin to modify it into something that is more representative of our own values and gifts. One important way to do that is to seek out others whose values are more consistent with our own. The isolation of many MSM perpetuates their stereotypical beliefs about the gay community. Joining the fathers' support group changed all of my preconceived ideas about gay men. I met MSM whom I loved, admired, and respected. I learned to recognize alternatives to the prescribed values I had obtained as a child. The *shoulds* melted away and the *want-to-bes* began to dominate.

"There is nothing either good or bad, but thinking makes it so," Hamlet says to Rosencrantz and Guildenstern in Shakespeare's *Hamlet*. One of my patients continued to be tormented by a long-term same-sex relationship he had with a classmate in high school. He could not set the incident aside, and he was constantly plagued by his memories of it. Although he was married, he lived a lonely life, never speaking to anyone other than me about these thoughts. In our sessions I was reminded of another line from *Hamlet*, where Queen Gertrude says, "The lady doth protest too much, methinks." Even in our sessions, my patient was unable to integrate into his sense of self that he stayed in the relationship because he wanted it as badly as his sexual partner. The thought that he might be attracted to someone of the same gender was far too unimaginable to him. For years he had been plagued by guilt, telling himself, "I shouldn't have wanted that!"

Moral integrity, in psychiatric terms, is the formal relation each of us has to ourselves. Integrity includes knowing our desires, not deceiving ourselves about those desires, and acting upon them. It means resolving the ambivalence and inconsistency in conflicting feelings. Some may have compelling reasons to avoid neatly resolving incompatible desires, but the cost of not resolving them can be great. Searching for this authenticity, this wholeheartedness is never ending—life is complex and multifaceted. But achieving integrity means incorporating all parts of our personalities into a harmonious, uncorrupted, and intact whole.

Ain't Nobody's Business:
Tricks of the Trade

An individual life is the accidental coincidence
of but one life cycle with but one segment of history.

—ERIK ERIKSON, *IDENTITY AND THE LIFE CYCLE*

A headline stretching across the entire front page of the *Idaho Statesman* on November 1, 1955, announced to the citizens of Boise, Idaho, "Boiseans Held on Moral Count." Two days later, the paper ran an editorial headlined, "Crush the Monster" in which the editors called homosexuality everything from a moral perversion to a cancerous growth. Beginning with the arrest of three men in October 1955, an investigation began into allegations that more than one hundred young men and teenage boys had been involved in sexual acts with a ring of adult homosexual men. The newspaper editors demanded that the entire situation be "completely cleared up, and the [city] premises thoroughly disinfected."[1] Anonymous calls flooded the Boise Police Department switchboard as people turned in the name of any man who was suspected of paying too much attention to any young boy. Parents hovered over their children like hens over baby chicks, and the city's gay residents realized that a witch hunt was in full swing.

At least twelve men from Boise were arrested for "infamous crimes against nature." The national news media goaded the public with headlines like "Male Pervert Ring Seduces 1,000 Boys."[2] By the time the investigation wound down in January 1957, some fifteen hundred people had been questioned, sixteen men faced charges, and fifteen of them were sentenced to terms ranging from probation to life in prison.

On November 20, 1955, the *Idaho Statesman* abruptly softened its position, noting that homosexuality existed in every community and had existed "as long as the weaknesses of the human mind have been evident." The *Statesman* declared that homosexuals were not criminals and incarceration was not an appropriate response. It claimed that so long as the focus was on punishing the adult men, the involved boys, now "infected" by the homosexual men, would eventually "travel the same path and carry the identical threat to the next generation of youth." The scandal limited the debate to seeing homosexuality as a mental illness requiring treatment or as a criminal act that should be punished.[3]

Coercive sex with anyone, and in particular with children, is wrong. Although the investigation was framed in terms of protecting children from adult predators, the probe was not confined to investigating charges of men having coercive sex with underage boys. Some of those convicted and sentenced to prison were found guilty only of sexual encounters with other consenting adults, their previously private sexual identity accidentally colliding with a short but tumultuous segment of Idaho's history. I have no doubt in my mind that the events in Boise shaped the developing consciences of young boys who were just becoming aware of their sexual urges. Perhaps former Idaho senator Larry Craig, ten years old and living in Boise at the time of the purgation, absorbed a lesson that sexual indiscretion (or the perception of it) could ruin a man's reputation.

The same "Lavender Scare" wind was blowing over Nebraska, where I grew up. The *Daily Kos* reported that in 1950, when I was seven years old, Nebraska's Republican senator Kenneth Wherry was quoted in the *New York Post*: "You can't hardly separate homosexuals from subversives.... Mind you, I don't say that every homosexual is a subversive, and I don't say every subversive is a homosexual. But [people] of low morality are a menace in the government, whatever [they are], and they are all tied up together." Senator Wherry, quoting "reliable police sources," said that 3,750 homosexuals held federal jobs.[4]

It was the height of the Cold War and people feared that foreign infiltrators abetted by homegrown subversives were preparing attacks against the United States. These fears penetrated our minds as children, and our games morphed from cowboys and Indians into soldiers fighting Stalin and foreign terrorists. Gay men were lumped into the category of subversives, not because they were considered Communists but because they were thought to be susceptible to blackmail and could be coerced into revealing government secrets.

When people fell under suspicion of government agencies, the question they feared the most was "Are you now or have you ever been a member of the Communist Party?" However, a close second was "Information has come to the attention of the Civil Service Commission that you are a homosexual. What comment do you care to make?"

The term *McCarthyism*, named for Republican senator Joseph McCarthy of Wisconsin, was applied to the witch hunts in the late 1940s and early 1950s promoted by McCarthy and his fellow conservatives in their attempts to expunge Communists and homosexuals from American public life. Many conservative Americans were fearful that the country was in a state of moral decline, and gay and lesbian civil servants were demonized as part of the Washington bureaucracy. McCarthyism presumed an overlap of Communists and "the homosexual menace," and the term has since come to signify all political extremism and civic hysteria. Senator Wherry bragged to reporters, "If you want to be against McCarthy, boys, you've got to be either a Communist or a cocksucker."[5] McCarthy's conflation of cowardice, homosexuality, and treason covered anyone left of the Right, especially those who also worked for the State Department, leading to the popular consensus that homosexuals were immoral, emotionally unstable, and untrustworthy, which justified their punishment and stigmatization.

In June 1950, the Senate authorized an official investigation, the first of its type in the history of the United States, popularly referred to as the pervert inquiry. For gay men and lesbians, the period was one of police harassment, witch hunts, suspicions of disloyalty, and dismissals from jobs, especially in the public sector. Throughout the 1950s in the United States and Great Britain, thousands of individuals were arrested and imprisoned on homosexual charges. Concerns were continuously being raised about the danger of homosexuals in government, citing an alleged lack of emotional stability and weakness of moral fiber as defining characteristics of homosexuals.[6]

Presidential candidate Adlai Stevenson was described as feminine, dainty, and weak—not a tough-talking man's man. Rumors were spread that he was gay. J. Edgar Hoover, director of the Federal Bureau of Investigation for nearly fifty years and considered by some to be the most powerful person in the United States, was said to have been a cross-dresser. Hoover hated Stevenson's liberal politics and attempted to brand him as queer. The term *pinko fag* became the era's worst slur, one I remember hearing as a child. Having been born in 1943, during the early years of my life fears about communism were pervasive, particularly in conservative states like Nebraska. Although I had no understanding of either *pinko* or *fag*, I knew that being a pinko fag was about the worst thing one could become.

Presidential candidate Dwight D. Eisenhower and his running mate, Richard Nixon, were portrayed as regular guys in favor of morality. In 1952 the incumbent Democratic administration was alleged to be engaged in immoral behavior, and the Republicans finally won the White House, campaigning under the slogan "Let's Clean House." Issues of morality were debated across the tables in the coffee shop in my hometown in Nebraska, and while they were intentionally shielded from my ears and the ears of my peers, the fears of communism and homosexuality certainly leaked into our developing unconscious minds.

Despite the mainstream fear, early gay activist groups existed. In the early 1950s, one of the earliest American gay movement organizations, the Mattachine Society, began to challenge some of society's ideas about being gay. Given the fearful political climate, Mattachine Society meetings often took place in secret with members using aliases. A poll taken at that time suggested that 95 percent of homosexuals would *not* be willing to take a pill, if one existed, to become heterosexual. Respondents also indicated that they would not wish their own brother or son to be brought into a society that scorned them. The Mattachine Society asserted that one should have no more guilt about being homosexual than one should have about his skin color. The primary goals of the society were to

- Unify homosexuals isolated from their own kind

- Educate homosexuals and heterosexuals toward an ethical homosexual culture paralleling the cultures of the Negro, Mexican, and Jewish peoples

- Lead the more socially conscious homosexual to provide leadership to the whole mass of social variants

- Assist gays who are victimized daily as a result of oppression[7]

Despite the Mattachine Society's efforts, at the time I was in high school in the late 1950s, three thousand men were arrested by the Los Angeles Police Department for lewd acts in public places. The police alleged that men having sex with men was occurring more and more conspicuously in public places and therefore was justifiably punishable by the law. The LAPD said its goal was to reduce immoral sexual behavior.

In March 1967, by the time I was just completing my third year of medical school, I heard the national broadcast of "CBS Reports: The Homosexuals." For most of an hour, Mike Wallace, a familiar figure from *60 Minutes*, provided his audience with some of the most disturbing antihomosexual propaganda ever heard. Wallace's report, which followed the general mentality of the time, reminded viewers:

This much is certain. Male homosexuals in America number in the millions. And their number is growing. They are attracted mostly to the anonymity that a big city gives them.... The average homosexual, if there be such, is promiscuous. He is not interested in or capable of a lasting relationship like that of a heterosexual marriage. His sex life, his love life, consists of a series of chance encounters at the clubs and bars he inhabits, and even on the streets of the city. The one-night stand is a characteristic of the homosexual relationship.[8]

Airing to hundreds of thousands if not millions of viewers, the report spread an inaccurate and exaggerated portrayal of gay men. I don't remember exactly what impact Mike Wallace's report on homosexuality had on me at that time, but in retrospect I am sure that I tried, somewhat unsuccessfully, to believe that it really didn't apply to me except as evidence that I wasn't gay. I was still a part of that large majority of Americans who looked upon same-sex relationships with discomfort, disgust, and fear. Ignorance surrounding homosexuality was the norm in the 1960s; Wallace later admitted his ignorance of homosexuality and regretted his involvement in the report's creation.

Movies, too, added to widespread misconceptions of gay people in the 1960s and '70s. According to Vito Russo in *The Celluloid Closet: Homosexuality in the Movies,* in about four out of five films with gay subtexts, gay characters either committed suicide or fell victim to violent death. The movies suggested that being gay was so dramatic, unpleasant, and frightening that it would drive even an otherwise well-adjusted person to self-destruction. Even those gay characters who survived for the length of the film had little in their cinematic representations to be admired.[9]

The first movie that portrayed coming out in a nonsensationalistic way was *Making Love,* a 1982 movie starring Michael Ontkean as a happily married doctor who falls in love with Bart, played by Harry Hamlin. *Making Love* was the first movie to depict gay men as normal and capable of loving each other in healthy, emotionally rewarding ways.[10] As my wife, Lynn, watched the movie on television, I sat behind her pretending to do paperwork, riveted to what I was seeing but careful not to show Lynn that I had too much interest in it. In the movie, two gay men were shown as normal and capable of an emotionally rewarding relationship—living a life others might aspire to. The movie profoundly touched the lives of many gay baby boomers by portraying gay men as men who did not have to be victims or victimizers with tragic but inevitable outcomes. In 1982, at the beginning of the Reagan era and before the explosion of AIDS, this film lacked some of the edge it would have had if it were made today, but it took many people outside of their comfort zones.

Making Love was the first movie to depict gay men as normal and capable of loving each other in healthy, emotionally rewarding ways.

Senator Craig, Ted Haggard, and others like them believed they were just straight MSM. When asked if they were gay, they said no because they did not see themselves as infected with the immorality, emotional instability, and untrustworthiness of gay people. They were patriots, capable of tough talk with their masculinity intact. In their mind's eye, they were not traitors, feminine, or weak. They were men's men who just wanted a blow job because it was so much easier to find a man who was willing to do that. I know that's what they were thinking, because that's what I thought, too.

Why is it that it took a movie in the 1980s to awaken me? Why is it that some gay men who, like me, grew to adulthood during Stonewall believed the propaganda about homosexuality while others rebelled against it? Were some of us more predisposed to buy into stereotypes as a result of some personality traits? Was it perhaps related to our relationships with our fathers, or the influences of our social community? Were the flames of our fears for loss of job, friends, and family more easily fanned? Or did a high need to please and a low tolerance for conflict make us more susceptible to accepting the values handed to us?

For those of us who were born in the 1940s and '50s, the heteronormative culture was the only one imaginable, and homosex was not seen as *real* sex. No wonder that until middle age someone like me couldn't confront his sexual identity—an identity essentially denied by the dominant culture. However, later in my life, I came to understand that each of us is unique. We live in discrete cultures with different values that are impacted by our particular place and time in history; therefore, no universal explanation for sexual expression exists. I now see that how people choose to deal with conflicts about sexual orientation cannot be generalized, but understanding the social and historical context of the time of our sexual development offers some clarity into my life and the lives of my contemporaries.

The Loneliest Years

When I was in medical school, I made and cancelled three separate appointments to see a counselor at the University of Nebraska Medical Center. I was very lonely and unhappy. I remember thinking how much I would welcome some chronic, minimally painful, yet terminal illness so I could die a heroic death and not have to live the next part of my life. Although I had some very good friends, I always felt outside the social fabric of my class. I wanted someone to share my life with me, but I seemed to have difficulty connecting with women on an intimate level. I dated some very bright, articulate, and beautiful women. I was aware that some of their mothers wanted them to fall in love with me, although I never believed their fathers felt the same way.

I thought the only logical explanation for why I was still single was my own father's absence; I lacked a role model for how to be a husband and father, and I needed someone to mentor me through the relationship process. Once my sister told me that she also had some confusion about just what a father's role is in a family, her confusion validated my own misguided perspective. I hoped my life would come together when I got married and had a regular, acceptable sexual partner, but I was having doubts about finding someone.

The Vietnam War was in full force as I approached the end of medical school—it was a reality I couldn't ignore. Military recruiters assured us graduating med students that unless we were women, veterans, or disabled, we were not likely to escape the draft. In my junior year of medical school, I signed up for the navy, also taking on the extra commitment of flight surgeon training. I had a year between medical school and the navy, and I decided to interview for medical internships in Chicago, New York, St. Louis, and New Orleans. Although unaware of it at the time, I now can see that the unconscious forces of my mind were pushing me toward the anonymity and permissiveness of an urban environment. However, around the same time, I met my future wife. "Rational thought" captured my mind, overpowering whatever unconscious motivations I had. Rather than pursue an urban life, instead I married and moved to Lincoln, Nebraska.

Absent Father, Close Binding Mother

The psychiatric literature I read in medical school did nothing to challenge the cultural values I acquired in my youth. No defense of homosexuality could be found in the earliest edition of the *The Diagnostic and Statistical Manual of Mental Disorders*, which listed homosexuality as a pathologic deviancy.

Two psychiatrists, Dr. Irving Bieber and Dr. Charles Socarides, wrote in the mid-twentieth century that homosexuality develops because a child who is barely able to function as a heterosexual seeks to extract masculinity from his male sex partner. This theory, like the one about conversion therapy, suggested that the homosexual man craved the "encircling arms of his father," and it resonated with me because of my fears that I was not masculine enough to be a real man. In hindsight I am shocked that I could ever have believed either of these theories. It makes no logical sense that two men, supposedly both deficient in masculinity, could expect to extract masculinity from each other. And yet some still continue to believe it.

In 1962, Dr. Irving Bieber headed a nine-year study of 106 gay men, at the time the largest of its kind. Bieber concluded that, "a constructive, supportive, warmly related father precludes the possibility of a homosexual son; he acts as a neutralizing, protective agent should the mother make seductive or close-binding attempts." Male homosexuality, according to Bieber, is an adaption to a disorder in one's relationship to other men. Homosexuality develops, in Bieber's view, because an overly protective mother senses that her son is vulnerable and, fearing that he will be injured, pulls him close to her. She isolates him from his peer group and siblings and develops an overly intimate relationship with him as her favored child. Bieber believed that a child in this position becomes closer to his mother than her own husband does, and the father, resenting that closeness, pulls away even further. According to Bieber, a good father will reassert himself and take control away from the mother. His intervention rescues the child from the undesirable future of homosexuality.[11]

Although discredited by his professional peers, Dr. Bieber remained steadfastly committed to his controversial theories. Even late in his life Dr. Bieber defended his work. Steven Lee Myers wrote Bieber's obituary, in the *New York Times*. Myers wrote that in 1973 Dr. Bieber told an interviewer, "A homosexual is a person whose heterosexual function is crippled, like the legs of a polio victim."[12]

Dr. Charles Socarides, another leading psychiatrist whose work I was exposed to in medical school, was featured in Mike Wallace's report on homosexuality. He, too, argued that homosexuality was a "neurotic adaptation" and that in men, it stemmed from absent fathers and overly doting mothers. Dr. Socarides was one of the cofounders of the National Association for Research & Therapy of Homosexuality (NARTH). To this day, NARTH focuses on promoting reparative therapy for homosexuals, and propagates the conservative perspective that many in the United States seek to redraw American culture by making being gay the equivalent of heterosexuality. NARTH holds Drs. Bieber and Socarides up as two of its leading prophets. NARTH treats their writings as scripture even though they have been discredited by peers in their own profession.

Throughout his life, Dr. Socarides continued to maintain his position that homosexuality is not a normal variation, despite the fact that his son, Richard, is openly gay and has been active nationally as a gay rights advocate. When asked about his relationship with his father for Dr. Socarides's obituary, Richard said that "it was complex" and that they "tried to relate to each other as father and son." Dr. Socarides may well have felt some guilt about absentee fathers, having divorced the first three of his four wives, a fact never mentioned by family-values conservatives.[13]

In the mid-twentieth century, same-sex behavior was not seen as a crime in most of Europe, but England was one of the last countries to change its laws. Some societies were beginning to question whether or not the interests of the public were being served by prison sentences of up to sixty years for consensual man-on-man sex. Were gay men really twice as dangerous to society as second-degree murderers? In England, prison sentences for same-sex behavior were six times as long as for abortionists, more than twice as long as for bank robbers, and more than seven hundred times longer than for public drunks.

Integrating Genetics, Psychology, and Culture

My training in psychiatry—emerging from the homophobic world of the 1950s and developing in the rapidly changing 1960s—followed a rather classical Freudian tradition. Sigmund Freud proposed a structural theory of the brain that said that much of our mental life is unconscious and our feelings are a consequence of underlying conflicts. Freud's theory hinges on the id, the ego, and the superego. The id is the unconscious cauldron of raw drives, particularly sexual and aggressive ones. The ego is both conscious and unconscious, containing the elements of rationality and reasonableness plus the responsibility for maintaining contact with the external world. The superego also contains both conscious and unconscious elements; it develops early and is learned from parents, teachers, and others in positions of authority. The ego mediates in conflicts between the primitive forces of the id and the restraints of conscience or the superego. According to Freud, a person achieves optimum mental health when the id, the ego, and the superego are brought into equilibrium.

By the time I entered my psychiatric training, Ivan Pavlov's classical conditioning theory and B. F. Skinner's operant conditioning theories were beginning to weaken the hold Freud's psychodynamic theories had on psychiatry. The focus of psychology moved from the theoretical unconscious to observable behaviors—although it appears we may now be moving back toward a rediscovery of the forces of the mind that operate outside of consciousness.

In order to understand the complexities of how the mind works both in cases of mental illness and in health, I have found most helpful the biopsychosocial model described by George Engel in *Science*. This model looks at all of the known, broad forces that affect us: biological, psychological, and sociocultural elements. One single factor might weigh heavily or not at all. In my professional experience, I have found that this model can be used to gain insight into how being gay manifests itself within individuals as well as societies. The forces of genetics, childhood development, and an individual's sociocultural context interact to determine psychological health or illness.[14]

Previously I discussed the genetic basis for homosexuality. A growing consensus of scientists believes that a biological predisposition to being gay exists but is not a sufficient explanation for the expression of being gay. Arguments that being gay cannot be genetic because their sex is nonprocreative, and therefore would eventually be extinguished, have been countered by the study of

The forces of genetics, childhood development, and an individual's sociocultural context interact to determine psychological health or illness.

other species in the animal kingdom in which there exist nonprocreative individuals. These individuals may contribute significantly to the overall success of the biological community.

The brain and behavior are inextricably linked, and although the balance in psychiatry has shifted to a more biological orientation, we are once again realizing that all behavior cannot be understood only through an expanding knowledge of synapses, receptors, and the circuitry of the brain. The biopsychosocial approach helps us capture the dynamic complexity of each individual by taking the biological evidence and combining that data with each individual's unique concerns, values, and life context. Whatever the cause of being gay, the coming out process must be approached in a person-centered way, and conflicts related to decision making must be worked out on an individual basis.

All of this discussion of psychological theory matters because all of us must live our own lives. Although a man with same-sex attraction may struggle to discover what is right for him about his sexual identity, he must learn to trust himself to know how his experiences intersect with the lives of others and how his life connects him to the culture around him. The gay man is the only one who can weigh the potential price he will pay for coming out against the possible gains. The benefit of understanding that his sexual identity is uniquely tied to a combination of biology, psychology, and environment should allow him to recognize that he is not limited only to the binary choices of gay and straight, out or closeted. Alternatives related to his specific life and personal makeup do exist.

Not One but Many Closets

Cultural context and differences across discrete social groups and historical events greatly impact perceptions of homosexuality. In the fourth century, Plato said, "Homosexuality is regarded as shameful by barbarians and by those who live under despotic governments, just as philosophy is regarded as shameful by them, because it is apparently not in the interest of such rulers to have great ideas engendered in their subjects, or powerful friendships or passionate love—all of which homosexuality is particularly apt to produce."[15]

Years later another philosopher, Plutarch, whose homeland of Greece had been conquered by the Romans, wrote, "The intelligent lover of beauty will be attracted to beauty in whichever gender he finds it." Romans were largely indifferent to gender and gender orientation, and Roman laws made absolutely no restrictions on the basis of gender. Latin lacks words that mean *homosexual*; the primary linguistic distinctions in ancient Rome were based on the dichotomy of masculine or feminine qualities, like dominance or submissiveness.[16]

Some American Indian tribes were also rather indifferent to gender. In those tribes, gay people were described as having two spirits, were considered to have special gifts, served as shamans, and in some cases had a same-sex spouse. Joe Medicine Crow is quoted by Walter Williams in *The Spirit and the Flesh: Sexual Diversity in American Indian Culture*: "We don't waste people the way white society does. Every person has their gift."[17] Of course, acceptance of homosexuality was not universal in all tribes, and now because of the influence of the dominant culture, gay American Indians are discriminated against in some of their communities.

In some cultures, same-sex behaviors are part of a coming-of-age ceremonial rite, and help men cultivate spirituality and personal bearing in relationship to other men. Shirley Oliver-Miller of the Kinsey Institute wrote about anthropological reports of the Sambians of Papua New Guinea. These reports described a culture of "ritualized masculinization," where young men fellated their elders in order to receive the "masculinizing force" of semen. When the boys grew up, they married and then became the recipients of fellation by younger boys. All males participated in their adolescence, but as adults, they were expected to marry. At the same time, some Sambian males were described as homosexual in the Western, sexual-erotic sense of that term, and they existed in the same proportions as estimates of homosexuality in Western cultures.[18]

These examples—Greek, Roman, American Indian, and Sambian cultures—illustrate that alternatives to contemporary Western interpretations of homosexuality exist. The idea that being gay is unnatural, something at odds with dominant norms, only persists because a portion of our society has judged it disgraceful, creating a culture of secret sexual expression. That culture, in my experience, can only be harmful to individuals.

The rich are said to be able to afford their indiscretions because they have the power and money to conceal them. Gay professional athletes, actors, wealthy businessmen, and politicians are notable examples, but in the end, money wasn't enough to help Lord Browne of Madingley, the chief executive of British Petroleum (BP) who was forced to resign in 2007. As Ginny Dougary reported in the Times, Lord Browne perjured himself about the nature of his relationship with Jeff Chevalier, a gay escort he had met on a site called Suited and Booted.[19] Lord Browne allegedly had misused BP resources by making substantial payments to Chevalier, establishing him in luxury accommodations, taking

The rich are said to be able to afford their indiscretions because they have the power and money to conceal them.

him on holidays, purchasing clothes for him, and setting him up in a business. The House of Lords rejected Lord Browne's attempt to keep his relationship with Chevalier secret and exposed Lord Browne as a liar, humiliating him in the process.

Lord Browne, reportedly unaware of a gay subculture when he was young, began frequenting gay bars for the first time in New York City after Stonewall. He relied on the discretion of others to keep his secret. For several years, even though his being gay was something of an open secret, Lord Browne had steadfastly denied his gay identity, a victim of the culture of secrecy. He told Dougary, "It was obvious to me that it was simply unacceptable to be gay in business, and most definitely the oil business." He is now in a relationship with a man, and said, "I'm happier than I've ever been. I feel amazingly fortunate. Amazingly."[20]

The closet Lord Browne inhabited is quite different from that of a twenty-one-year-old man from the South who posted this personals ad early in 2010: "Are there any other bi/closeted/gay rednecks like me around?" He went on to describe wanting someone who would hunt, fish, and chew tobacco, but he also required that if his friends came around, "no one would be able to tell. I ain't out and I don't wanna be!"

The size of a closet and the thickness of its walls vary from one person to the next. Sometimes it resembles a bomb shelter. Living a hidden life is far more complex for those in rural America, for many immigrant populations, and for those practicing fundamentalist religions, where the key institutions are home, church, and school. For many of them, being gay is seen by the community as an otherworldly decadence, and homosexuality is seen as an act, something one does—not an identity, something one is.

Non-Western and Immigrant Perceptions of Being Gay

In some of the most extremely fundamentalist societies, heterosexuality is compulsory. In September 2007, while speaking before an audience at Columbia University in New York City, Iranian president Mahmoud Ahmadinejad was asked about the alleged execution of two hundred homosexuals in Iran earlier that year. He responded by saying, "In Iran, we don't have homosexuals like in your country. In Iran, we do not have this phenomenon. I don't know who has told you that we have it."[21] In fundamentalist societies homosexuality is considered evidence of the degradation of American society.

Homosexuality was made illegal in thirty-eight African countries after antisodomy laws were introduced during African colonialism.[22] Because the culture in Uganda defines all sex as heterosex, no recognition of a separate gay identity exists. Those who do identify as homosexual are ostracized, seen as a subclass, and are disempowered or discriminated against. As encouraged by Christian fundamentalists from the United States, a law threatening the death sentence for serial homosexual offenders or active homosexuals living with HIV also was introduced in 2009 and debated by the Ugandan Parliament in early 2010. This proposed death penalty law drew international outrage, and the law was briefly shelved when Britain and other European nations threatened to withdraw aid to Uganda. Family and friends who failed to report homosexuals, and landlords who rented to them, would face up to seven years in jail. People working in public health agencies counseling homosexual men on HIV prevention would also face the possibility of imprisonment.

After replacing the death penalty provision with a proposal of life in prison for acts in which one person is infected with HIV, serial offenders, and sex with minors, Ugandan parliament passed the law in 2014.[23] In spite of this law, the Uganda AIDS Commission revealed that the proportion of Ugandans infected with the HIV virus is trending upward with a steady rise in new infections.[24]

Most countries in Africa have compulsory, legally enforced heterosexuality. Anyone wishing to engage in same-sex practices must live two lives. Homosexual activity is largely concentrated in networks, mostly urban and interconnected. In 2015, prior to his visit to Kenya, President Barack Obama was warned to leave "the gay agenda" at home, but despite the protests, Obama met with gay leaders, addressed the Kenyan people, and candidly addressed Uganda's discrimination against sexual minorities. Kenya's officials have rejected homosexuality as un-African and identified deviations from heteronormativity as the legacy of white, Western imperialists. President Museveni dismissed President Obama's criticism of the law as social imperialism and held that homosexual behavior is unnatural, a matter of choice, and disgusting. He went on to say Ugandan scientists had proven that same-sex behavior is not innate.[25]

David Kuria, a former chairman of the Gay and Lesbian Coalition of Kenya and the first openly gay candidate for public office in Kenya, explained the situation for LGBTQ people in Kenya by saying, "For now there is no political leader who has shown enough courage even to be equivocal or appear 'undecided' on the issue of LGBTQ rights....Poor or weak LGBTQ people will most probably experience violence or be denied services but they will not be connected to a social network that can help them access legal redress. It is interesting that in Kenya today, married gay men face the highest levels of blackmail and it's fairly routine."[26] Gay men feel imprisoned in their marriages, although Kuria also said that many married gay men love their spouses and most cannot see themselves living in societies where anything other than a heterosexual family relationship is the norm. In rural areas of Africa there is a particularly high demand for the appearance of heteronormativity.

On my *MagneticFire* blog, a man in India sent me a letter that said "I am a thirty year old Indian, married and have one son. I am sexually attracted to older men, but I love my wife and do have sex with her. How can I make this stop?" Although homosexuality appears in old scriptures and paintings, today homosexuality is a taboo and highly stigmatized subject; same-sex behavior is hidden and can lead to harassment by police. The criminalization of homosexuality in India dates back to 1860, when the country was still under British rule, but in 2009, the New Delhi High Court repealed Section 377 of the Indian Penal Code, decriminalizing consensual sex between LGBTQ adults. The Supreme Court threw out that ruling in 2013, effectively once again recriminalizing "carnal intercourse against the order of nature." On February 5, 2016, activists were given new hope when India's Supreme Court agreed to reconsider the 2013 ruling.[27]

In Japan many people live by the rule "If it smells, put a lid on it." According to one interviewee who had spent considerable time in Japan, same-sex activity is compartmentalized, and the Japanese are more comfortable than Americans in living with contradictions, as long as order is maintained. Japanese men are expected to maintain a respectable life on the surface. The gay community in Japan is less public than the community in the United States, but finding gay bars and saunas that serve as gathering places for men of all ages is not difficult. Not all of the clientele are gay, and many of them are looking for a quick sexual release. School bullying is notorious in Japan and has been for decades. For LGBTQ youth in particular, the harassment, threats, and even violence in schools can be unbearable.

Gay characters appear on Japanese television, but the rule is that no matter how entertaining, same-sex behavior is still perverse. Gay men are often seen in the same category as prostitutes, bar girls, and the criminal underground. But change is coming. In 2016, the Shibuya and the Setagaya wards in Tokyo became the first municipalities in Japan to pass an ordinance that would acknowledge same-sex unions as equivalent to marriage, while cities outside Tokyo announced possible future arrangements for same-sex partnerships.[28]

Asian immigrants are often noted for having a strong work ethic, humility, and strong family ties, but these traits also may contribute to their difficulty in coming out. I received this correspondence from a thirty-five-year-old man who immigrated to the United States from Vietnam with his family when he was nine years old:

I am out to my friends as bisexual, but as for my family, it's don't ask, don't tell.... Basically I am prioritizing one battle at a time. I did tell my father that I am bisexual and he was somewhat supportive and hoping that I will like girls more than guys. Growing up being discriminated [against] and coming to the USA, it's harder for me to speak out about [being a part of a] sexual minority because of fearing that I, too, will get discriminated against. So I hide in the closet until the time is right. We waste too much time and energy on sexual orientation and shame.

In analyzing cross-cultural notions of heterosexuality, some commonalities arise: In many cultures the homosexual male who is more feminine and acts as the passive sexual partner is typically devalued, just as many women in those cultures are. The transgressions of those who are the active partner are more easily forgiven or overlooked. As in the United States, some men simply opt out when adult expectations force heterosexual dating and marriage after an age where same-sex play may have been ignored or tolerated. Other men engage in "trade," hiring male partners for sex in which the hirer is almost exclusively the penetrative partner, an acceptable masculine behavior. Some men will seek out anonymous sexual partners in public venues. Often they do not discuss it with others, so a culture of secrecy exists worldwide.

Gay immigrants experience a kind of double jeopardy by having difficulty establishing an authentic sexual identity that is different not only from mainstream American culture but also from the family values and ancient cultural traditions of their parents. This exposes them to the possibility of multiple oppressions: racism, sexism, generational clashes, and stigmatization from both outside and within their immigrant communities. Because of this, they may resist being labeled gay and struggle with a decision about whether or not to come out.

Immigrant families are frequently tied together much more tightly than other families in America, and being gay may be seen as deviant and bringing dishonor and shame to the family. For many immigrants, coming out involves setting aside cultural mandates and being forced to choose either a gay identity or an ethnic one. Coming out can mean rejection from their families as well as from their community of friends who have immigrated to the United States. Male children have strong obligations to marry, create families, and sacrifice their own interests for the benefit and tranquility of the family.

For many ethnic minorities, coming out involves often having to decide whether their ethnic identity or their sexual identity will take precedence. If they choose their ethnic group, they will surround themselves with homonegativism; if they choose a gay identity, they may lose the social support of their primary ethnic group and have no buffer against racism.

Closets Can Be Dangerous

Closets are dangerous places when it comes to issues of public health. Criminalization of same-sex activity generally creates an underground of sexual activity. Where acceptance of being gay is low, gay people are likely to have more concurrent heterosexual relationships, increasing the risks for HIV and other sexually transmitted diseases. Andrew Francis and Hugo Mialon report that where acceptance of gays is higher, HIV rates are lower, and where tolerance—although most in the LGBTQ community would prefer they had used the word *acceptance*—is low, the HIV rate of men who have sex with other men in underground cruising areas, such as parks, beaches, and restrooms, is higher. Their findings were thought to have so much potential impact on policy decisions that in 2009, Emory University published the report on its website prior to its publication in a peer-reviewed journal.[29]

The culture of secrecy can lead gay men to engage in illicit sex in clandestine, sometimes sleazy venues. The risk of exposing themselves and their partners to disease is high, not to mention the risk of public humiliation. Living a secret can only reinforce a sense of shame and guilt. But that isn't to say that these encounters are purely anonymous. In those societies where heterosexual expression is mandatory and oppression is extreme, gay men and women create underground communities, invisible gay spaces.

Sometimes we believe that we have made great progress in our understanding and acceptance of being gay over the last decades. After seeing Mike Wallace's 1967 CBS report, I never could have imagined that I would one day live in a place where Doug and I could be legally married. That said, many of the same social forces that caused me to delay coming out until midlife continue to operate, and in some places those forces are more severe than anything I had to encounter. However, as my personal experience attests, life-changing societal evolution does happen. If it didn't, women would still be waiting to vote and we might all still be either slaves or slaveholders. American culture for gay men and women is far from perfect, but things are moving in a positive direction.

Where acceptance of being gay is low, gay people are likely to have more concurrent heterosexual relationships, increasing the risks for HIV and other sexually transmitted diseases.

How to Have Sex in a Tree

I'm supposed to sit around and love him
while he decides what to do with his fucking wife and daughter.

—TIM TURNER, *OUT LATE*

"Hey, Loren, I wanna show ya somethin'." My friend greeted me almost immediately after I jumped out of the car at his parents' farm in Nebraska. I was about ten and he was a couple of years older. We ran off to the barn, where he took off his denim jeans—back then only sissies wore shorts—and in less than a minute, he masturbated to the point of ejaculation, likely not his first time that day. He launched my education in sex as he announced, "I just shot my wad." Farm boys knew more about sex and at an earlier age than town boys like me, but their knowledge wasn't much more nuanced than "It takes a bull and a cow to have a calf." At that time, I still believed that to make a baby, a man must pee on a woman's crotch.

Discovering ejaculation introduces most boys to sex, and their education builds slowly throughout adolescence and young adulthood. Ejaculation is what men do that women can't. It is a man's role in reproduction. For a young boy, ejaculation is the essence of becoming a man; fortunately, it is also immensely pleasurable. But education encompasses both information and disinformation, and education is shaped by cultural attitudes. When a man discovers he is gay, his education must begin all over again.

Discovering our sexuality is much like observing the night sky. One evening, my younger daughter and I were returning from a family reunion in Wyoming. It was August, and at dusk we lay down on the asphalt in a parking lot in the Badlands of South Dakota to watch the stars. The setting sun introduced the earliest and brightest stars. As night unfolded, more and more stars appeared as darkness lay over us like a blanket. The constellations and the Milky Way began to interrupt the darkness that then exploded with so many shooting stars we didn't have enough wishes for all of them. When a boy first discovers ejaculation, it is like the first visible star in the evening sky, but its appearance is only a tiny hint of a world that will unfold.

Young boys are sexual beings, and erections and erotic dreams begin long before boys know their significance and well before they can ejaculate. During this period of sexual discovery in early adolescence, group sexual play is not uncommon. After dark, on our Boy Scout camping trips, we would strip off our clothes and run around naked. Although often accompanied by erections, being naked created a sense of excitement that was far too amorphous to call it sexual. Sexual exploration with other boys was accepted, up to a point, and if my sexual attraction to other boys surpassed that of my friends, I wasn't aware of it.

Young boys are sexual beings, and erections and erotic dreams begin long before boys know their significance and well before they can ejaculate.

During my childhood summers, I spent time on my friends' and cousins' farms, and we couldn't wait to get to the hayloft and shed our clothes. No one discussed masturbation, although the Boy Scout manual mentioned something about "unhealthy behavior." I masturbated a lot, sometimes several times a day, but probably no more than most of my friends. I would promise myself that I would touch myself only briefly and then stop, but I never could. Sometimes I thought, "That was fun. Whatever it is I want to do it again. I think I will do it again now." Tissues were a luxury, so my mother, without comment or censure, washed a lot of handkerchiefs.

The adults who supervised us never seemed particularly concerned about our nakedness and exploration. Looking back, it seems as if their attitude was that boys will be boys. If there had ever been any concern that these activities might have made homosexuals out of us, the adults certainly would have intervened. As we grew older, I felt a growing sense of disconnection from what other boys might have been experiencing, but no one ever talked about it. It was as if a wall were gradually being built, with me on one side and all of the other boys on the other.

Emotional Networks

Our brains are hard-wired for several different emotional systems, each with its own anatomical location: fear, attachment, maternal nurturance, anger, anticipation, play, and sex. These primitive structures in the brain remain constant in all humans from one culture to the next. As our brains mature, these centers progressively interconnect in ways that are unique to each individual. Early on, scientists pinpointed the limbic system as the seat of emotions and motivation.

As the secrets of the brain are revealed, neuroscientists have seized upon a portion of the limbic system called the amygdala as the brain's emotional control center. The amygdala allows us to respond quickly to danger; through the experience of fear, we appraise a situation and choose a protective response. The amygdala assigns emotional significance to events and modifies how experiential memories are recorded in another part of the limbic system called the hippocampus. Although some emotion enhances detail in our memories, when emotions run too high, the amount of detail recorded in the memory of the hippocampus may be reduced. Memories stored in the hippocampus modify our thinking whenever we encounter an emotional situation, and through a series of feedback loops, memories also influence the emotions recorded in the amygdala.

Multiple emotional centers of the brain function through a series of integrated networks, and the networks change dramatically through our learning. Between the ages of nine and seventeen, our brains undergo enormous changes that refine our physical and emotional functions. As young children, not all our neural connections are yet formed. The labile emotions we associate with adolescence are a consequence of incompletely formed neural connections. As a result of our continuing neural development, during adolescence we gradually shift from characteristically childlike emotional reactions to greater self-regulation, social awareness, and emotional control. The onset of hormone production in remote parts of the body during adolescence complicates all of this, as anyone who has been around a teenager knows. As we reach adulthood, the amygdala relinquishes control over our emotions to the prefrontal cortex of the brain.[1]

Multiple emotional centers of the brain function through a series of integrated networks, and the networks change dramatically through our learning.

Although our brains are all similarly hard-wired for several emotions, the way the networks interconnect the parts of our brains where emotions are centered varies considerably from person to person. Our different life experiences create unique, fine structural areas in our brains. These connections evolve and expand throughout our lifetimes as new learning adds complexity. In the novel *Blue Boy*, Rakesh Satyal writes, "Only now am I able to fully understand what being called gay means.... It means that you are wired for a different life entirely. It means that your body, your feelings, your responses toward all other people are different. You do not look at men the same, you do not make love to them the same way."[2]

My first real awareness of being in the presence of something that might have been homosexuality—although I didn't recognize it as such at the time—came when I was about nine years old during a rare family vacation to Chicago. As we visited the shore of Lake Michigan, just east of downtown, I darted barefoot across the hot sand to change into my swimsuit in the men's bathroom. In a concrete-block building that was open to the sky, naked old men crowded driftwood-colored wooden benches lining the perimeter of the changing area. The men were more distressed by the presence of their young, unwelcome guest than by their nakedness.

When I walked into the room, all activity—if there was any—froze. Perhaps my discomfort came just from being in the presence of naked men. With no men in our household, it was the first time I had ever been in the presence of a totally naked man. And here was a room full of them. No one looked at me in a sinister way, no one talked to me, and no one touched me. I didn't see anything overtly sexual (although until I was nearly forty, everything relating to homosexuality went unnoticed). In fact, I have absolutely no evidence that anything sexual was happening. But when I remember the incident, the emotional memory it creates is similar to the feelings I've had as an adult when I've been in a highly sexually charged environment. The circuitry of my brain wasn't wired enough to assess the situation and plan an appropriate response. I changed quickly and ran back to the beach and the security of my mother.

The first girl in our class to have her period was the first person to help me connect some of the centers in my brain. She happily shared the details she remembered from the movie shown to the girls in the fifth grade. We boys never saw it. A new scheme preoccupied me: if I could just have sex with a girl, I would finally feel like a man. In the seventh grade, I pinched a girl's breasts while we were roller skating to see if she might want to have sex with me, but she angrily skated off. I was disappointed—not because she rejected my primitive attempt at seduction but because I felt nothing when I did it.

Emotions change how we think, and thinking alters our behavior. In the 1960s, Stanley Schachter and Jerome Singer developed the two-factor theory. The theory proposed that emotion has two parts: physiological arousal and cognition. Emotion-provoking events induce physiological changes such as an accelerated heart rate and shallower breathing; those sensations make us aware of an emotion. This sends a message to the prefrontal brain, which plans and executes the appropriate response.[3] The two-factor theory suggests that people label their emotions according to their physiological clues and their environment.

In the mid-1980s, while still exploring my own sexuality, I discovered a park near Des Moines where gay men were said to meet for sex. It was an uncommonly beautiful August day, sunny and mild with very little humidity. A little while after I parked my jeep, a pickup pulled in behind me.

My heart began to pound and my breathing became shallow as a young man walked up to the Jeep and said, "How're ya doin'?"

"Fine."

He went on, "I'm from Oklahoma, here for the state fair. Came out here to see if I could meet someone." We spoke in meaningless conversation for a while, and then he said, "I'd really like to suck your dick." His directness shocked me. Not all sexual negotiations between gay men are nonverbal. I told him I wasn't interested.

He walked away, but I knew he hadn't given up.

He returned to my Jeep and said, "I really want to suck your dick." I said no again, but with slightly less resistance.

I continued to refuse, and he walked away again. A short while later, I got out of the Jeep and walked deep into the woods. He followed me into the woods, as I was sure he would. I sat down on the trunk of a fallen tree. He walked up to me, and with his two large hands pulled down my shorts, exposing me. This was more than not-quite-sex. I had not anticipated that having sex in a tree would ever be a part of my gay sexual development.

When the young man walked up to my Jeep, I experienced the physiologic response of shallow breathing and a racing heart. At that point I could not be sure whether he intended to assault me or have sex with me. Although I was in an environment known as a gay cruising area, it was only after our interaction began that I was certain of his intent. The hesitancy in my response was an opportunity for messages to be sent to my prefrontal cortex, where I could process the information and then make a cognitive decision to walk deep into the woods or to speed away in my Jeep.

Alone Am I

Although the basic elements of all our brains are similar, the intricate networks connecting these elements do not all develop in the same way for everyone. Children have been characterized as either inhibited or uninhibited. Inhibited children hover near their mothers, are quiet, and avoid strangers. Most children fall on a continuum between the two.

As adults, some who were more inhibited continue to have difficulty separating from their families and connecting with others in intimate ways. Throughout their lives their primary emotional commitments are to their families of origin. Coming out for them can be especially difficult. The death of their parents represents a huge loss. Although they may long for a meaningful relationship, they continue to isolate themselves, preferring no attachments. Their relationships are more instrumental than emotional. Uninhibited children spend less time with their mothers and embrace new activities. Because they are less sensitive to the judgments of others, coming out for them may be less difficult.

A thirty-seven-year-old gay man from Canada who contacted me online was trapped in a life from which he saw no escape. He was a school administrator in a small town where living as an openly gay man would have been extremely difficult. Being an experienced teacher with a master's degree, he had reached the highest level of the salary scale, reducing the possibility of professional mobility. As an only child he felt a responsibility to care for his parents. His father had developed Alzheimer's disease and required full-time care, and his family had few resources to pay for it. It became financially expedient for his mother to live with him, destroying his last boundary for privacy.

Although faced with these difficult realities, he also seemed to be toward the inhibited end of the spectrum. His only escape was watching gay pornography or chatting in sexually explicit chat rooms, but he could not masturbate without fearing that his mother would discover him. Consequently, he began to stay awake far into the night, compromising his performance in school the next day. He was losing hope that he could ever have someone to share his life with, and he had no one with whom to discuss his frustration and disappointments. Although loneliness was imposed upon him by his role as a caregiver, he was more fearful that the loneliness would become worse once his role as a caregiver to his parents had ended.

Meeting someone involves taking risks, and one of the biggest risks is facing rejection. After speaking to a group of gay men, one man I met said, "Gay partners don't just fall into your lap." Many men are shy about meeting others and waste evenings wanting to talk with someone but being unable to do so. Knowing what to say is only half the battle; knowing how to listen and ask questions is equally important. Urban areas are often home to a variety of gay men's groups that center on hobbies, books, politics, sports activities, potluck suppers, and coming out groups. These can serve as vehicles for developing a network of friendships. Putting a notice on Craigslist about a fathers' support group could be a good method for finding other men who have families. Gay bars, arts events, fundraisers, and LGBTQ resource centers can also expand networks of friends as well as people to date.

We seek intimacy, pleasure, affirmation, and approval from our partners and peers. The brain is the most complex organ, and we want to understand it because we care about how we behave. Our DNA determines how the emotional centers of the brain are established, but each of us builds an intricate and evolving structure in our brains as we interact with our own changing environment. Life cannot be defined by a genetic code. We do not connect with humanity purely on a biological level. Developmental and cultural differences exist, and these experiences make us unique.

Pulling the Pin on a Hand Grenade

If discussing sexuality places a target on your back, a discussion of pedophilia, pederasty, and age of consent is like picking up a hand grenade without a pin. Ignoring the topic does nothing to defuse its explosive potential. Gay men wrongly and frequently have been accused of molesting children and recruiting children to "the homosexual lifestyle." So much distorted information has been produced by those who condemn homosexuality that the topic begs for comment. First of all, let me make it clear that I am not advocating for pedophilia, lowering the age of consent, or sex with animals.

After I read an essay online in the Roman Catholic press in 2010 alleging that homosexuals are responsible for the sex abuse scandals in the Roman Catholic clergy, I posted this response: "I am a sixty-seven-year-old gay psychiatrist, and almost nothing you have written fits with my own personal experience or with the experience of any gay men that I know."

In response to my post I received an e-mail from a well-educated young man who began, "Homosexuality is just wrong." He went on to say that gay rights leaders have acknowledged that "pederasty is at the core of the gay rights movement." I was more than a little shocked, so I wrote back and said that because I had never heard anyone in my psychiatric training or in my personal life use the word *pederasty*, I had to look it up. I wrote him that if pederasty was supposed to be at the core of the movement I'd joined, I ought to find out something about it.

We began a friendly and thoughtful correspondence. We were eager to learn from each other. He loved the Roman Catholic church, was a lay leader in the church, and worried about how the Church had come under attack over a series of scandals exposing widespread abuse of children, many of which dated back several decades. He expressed that as a father he had concerns about protecting his children. I wrote that I knew that some young people felt victimized by men and women who abuse the power of their positions, but I felt like he was conflating pedophilia, pederasty, and homosexuality, which are entirely different.

I told him that I knew some gay men who as teenagers had had sex with an adult and didn't feel forced into it or traumatized by it; some admitted to initiating it. None considered pederasty central to their thoughts about being gay or a part of the gay rights movement. We continued our correspondence in discussions about maturity, age of consent, and abuse of power. He said that he wanted very much to understand, and his curiosity seemed intellectually honest. I corresponded with him because I believe that prejudice is only shattered when our antagonists have a personal relationship with someone who is gay.

In another response to my comment on the essay, I had a much less satisfying exchange with another man whom I will call George.

George: [You do] not think that homosexuality is wrong. Homosexuals fit the description of Nietzsche's Übermensch, the man above other men. He stands above other men because he does not submit to a moral law that he did not himself devise. That is to say, his behavior is not restrained by any law. Pederasty, homosexuality, the corruption of the clergy, the devolution of society into paganism, it all hangs together.

Loren: You don't know me.

George: Oh, but I do know you! You have identified yourself as a homosexual, an immoralist. If a person can define for himself that homosexuality is perfectly good, nothing stands in the way of defining pederasty as perfectly good. Nothing binds his conscience. Morality is a matter of taste. Homosexual-, fornication-, and abortion-embracing churches are literally dying before our eyes.

Loren: You are as unable to see the evil in yourself as you are to see the good in me. You have attributed to me stereotypical characteristics of being gay with no attempt to know me as a Christian or a human being. You don't know me.

Shortly after the essay appeared, CNN World reported on the outrage displayed by gay rights groups over comments made by Tarcisio Bertone, a senior cardinal and the Vatican's secretary of state, linking homosexuality to pedophilia: "Many psychologists, many psychiatrists, have demonstrated that there is no relationship between celibacy and pedophilia, but many others have demonstrated, I was told recently, that there is a relationship between homosexuality and pedophilia."[4] This CNN report went on to state, "A Vatican spokesman said Wednesday that just 10 percent of the abuse cases against priests that were reviewed by the Vatican constituted 'pedophilia in the strict sense,'" because 60 percent of those incidents were between priests and teenage boys. James Cantor, editor-in-chief of *Sexual Abuse: A Journal of Research and Treatment*, rejected suggestions of a link between homosexuality and pedophilia. "Although there have been claims that child molestation is a result of homosexuality (or of celibacy), there is absolutely no basis in science for either conclusion. The scientific evidence instead suggests that pedophilia and hebephilia are caused by atypical brain development occurring near or before birth."[5]

According to the American Psychiatric Association's *The Diagnostic and Statistical Manual of Mental Disorders*, pedophilic disorder is characterized by the "recurrent, intense sexually arousing fantasies, sexual urges, or behaviors involving sexual activity with a prepubescent child or children." Pedophilic attraction is sexual attraction in which it is *obligatory* that the partner is a prepubescent child, usually thirteen years of age or younger with the perpetrator being age sixteen or over and at least five years older than the child. The *DSM-5*, the newest revision of the diagnostic manual, also attempts to distinguish between atypical sexual *interests* and sexual *disorders*. Atypical sexual interests—also known as paraphilias—include things like fetishes, S and M, or cross-dressing. This subtle but crucial difference makes it possible for someone to engage in consensual but atypical sexual behavior without being labeled with a mental disorder. Most people with atypical sexual interests do not have a mental disorder.

Having an atypical sexual interest by itself is not enough to consider it a mental disorder. To be considered a mental disorder it must do one of two things: *either* create personal distress, *or* cause emotional or physical harm to another or involve someone who cannot or will not give consent. Because a child has not yet developed enough social awareness and emotional control to be able to understand the meaning of consent, pedophilia is by these criteria a mental disorder.[6]

Almost everyone agrees that it is wrong to have a sexual relationship with a preadolescent or when coercion is present. Parents and governments have an obligation to protect vulnerable children from adults who disregard their interests and easily manipulate them. People who oppose homosexuality frequently quote a few seriously flawed studies that suggest that pedophilia exists more commonly in homosexuals.[7] I am a gay man, but I am also a father and a grandfather. How could anyone believe that any gay person, but particularly gay fathers, would accede to a gay rights movement that would sacrifice the sexual innocence of their children or grandchildren?

My correspondence with the young man, which began with his claim that "homosexuality is just wrong" screeched to a halt when on May 5, 2010, the *Miami New Times* broke a story along with photographs about George Rekers, one of the leaders of the Christian conservatives, as he returned from Europe accompanied by a twenty-year-old male prostitute he had hired on a website called Rentboy.com. Rekers claimed that he hired the young man from this gay, male escort site to help him carry his baggage.[8] Rekers, a clinical psychologist and a Baptist minister, began his lucrative career by writing a book advising parents on how to raise children so they would not turn out gay. He promised that homosexuality could be cured, and he had been responsible for some of the most vicious assaults on homosexuality. Rekers has since divorced the antigay organizations he helped found, the Family Research Council (FRC) and NARTH, both of which believe homosexuality can and should be cured. In leaving he wrote, "I'm not gay and never have been."[9] His damaging writings and public appearances tell us more about his fractured psyche than they do about homosexuality. Rekers's exposure had been profoundly disappointing to my correspondent.

I want to avoid sweeping generalizations about those who oppose homosexuality; however, history has repeatedly shown that conflict about same-sex attraction often besieges the men who are caught up in rigid ideological judgments against being gay. Occasionally, their passion breaks free and they find release in clandestine man-on-man sex.

A Field of Land Mines

Prior to having received the initial correspondence from that young educated man, I had never before read anything that suggested that pederasty "forms the core of the gay rights movement." In fact, the word *pederasty* rarely crosses the lips of anyone other than those who condemn homosexuality. In that context, *pederasty* is frequently and incorrectly interchanged with the word *pedophilia*.

Several definitions exist for pederasty. The different uses of the word are important. The definition that provides the least reproach to homosexuality describes pederasty as a nonspecific sexual activity where one of the two participants is a minor—that is, between the ages of thirteen and nineteen. A more restrictive definition states that pederasty means anal intercourse between two men where the receptive partner is a minor, a definition that implies coercion. In contemporary American society, depending upon the jurisdiction that defines age of consent, an adult who has engaged in pederasty could be charged with felony sexual assault.

One of the gay leaders whom conservatives connect with pederasty is Harry Hay, who died in 2002 at age ninety. Stuart Timmons chronicled Hay's life in a book, *The Trouble with Harry Hay: Founder of the Modern Gay Rights Movement*. Hay had once been a member of the American Communist Party, and he had a brief marriage to conceal his being gay from the party. Prior to his death, Hay was considered an elder statesman of the gay rights movement. He was one of the founders of the Mattachine Society in the early 1950s. Hay reported that his first same-sex encounter occurred at age nine. At age fourteen, he discovered same-sex lovemaking with a twenty-five-year-old sailor. He described it as "the most beautiful gift that a fourteen-year-old ever got from his first love!" Hay's defense of his experience with the sailor disturbs many, and confounds our contemporary notions of adolescent sexual maturity.[10]

Different cultures celebrate the transition from childhood to adulthood with various traditions. Quinceañera is a traditional Latin American celebration for girls when they turn age fifteen. Historically it signified the young girl's eligibility for marriage. During the ceremony, adults present the honored teen with a pair of high heels as a sign of her ascent into womanhood. She, in turn, gives her younger sister a doll as a symbol of relinquishing childish interests. Bar mitzvah—bat mitzvah for girls—is a solemn ceremony held at age thirteen to admit a Jewish boy or girl into adult membership in the Jewish faith. This ritual communicates that a young Jewish person is entirely responsible for adhering to Jewish law.

But the brain does not mature on one celebratory day and maturity varies from individual to individual, across cultures. Some adolescents are capable of thoughts and actions with unusually high levels of maturity, and some come from societies that demand it. I once had as a patient a twenty-five-year-old African man who was studying in the United States. I hospitalized him for his first episode of acute mania. He sent for his African wife, who was but fifteen years old and had infant twins. I told him I doubted her ability to travel thirty-six hours with two infants and without being able to speak English. He said, "Dr. Olson, you don't understand our culture," and I didn't. It was an important lesson for me to learn: understand people in the context of their lives. My patient's culture demanded of his wife a high degree of emotional maturity, whether or not I believed she was capable of it.

Although we may not be surprised to learn that men and women in undeveloped countries reach maturity at younger ages, the same thing happens in urban environments even in the United States as a man from Baltimore described to me on my blog, *MagneticFire*. He said that urban children grow hyperaware of their environments in order to deal with whatever comes up. He went on to say that most who live outside of the inner city cannot imagine what this experience is like. He grew up in a city with pervasive drug problems where sexual activity and other dangerous situations were commonplace. He wrote that surviving in such an environment demands a high level of maturity at a very young age. In his case, by the age of eleven, he was physically mature and sexually active.

This young man's experience in the Baltimore ghetto and the world of my patient's African wife are vastly different from the world of my youth. Although my life's circumstances dictated a high level of emotional maturity, I maintained a high degree of sexual innocence, perhaps even longer than I should have. Adolescents may reach physical and sexual maturity long before they reach emotional maturity, but emotional maturity may also precede the loss of sexual innocence. These difficult transitions will be experienced differently by a child who is "inhibited" than by one who is uninhibited—whether in the Baltimore ghetto or in rural Nebraska. Some adolescents can function with higher levels of emotional and physical maturity than others. No universal age stands at which an adolescent becomes capable of giving consent for sexual activity, and those who cannot protect themselves must be protected from those who would exploit their innocence.

Strong emotions change how we think. Discussions of the age of consent enrage some people beyond the point at which any sensible discourse can occur. People disagree passionately and vehemently over the age at which a boy has the emotional maturity to give consent for sexual

No universal age stands at which an adolescent becomes capable of giving consent for sexual activity, and those who cannot protect themselves must be protected from those who would exploit their innocence.

activity, but particularly if that sex is with another boy. Although I felt very sexual as an adolescent, the drive I experienced seemed to be diverted from its logical target. With a growing awareness that my friends were becoming more sexually active, I began to feel more and more disconnected from them, but I didn't know why.

Sexual maturity is a very complex issue from a genetic, cultural, and neurological standpoint. Both heterosexual and gay adolescents usually do not have the capacity for the commitment and permanence of adult relationships. The brains of adolescents have not developed sufficiently to be able to understand all the consequences of their behavior. Today, even in our more liberal society, if two adolescent boys were engaged in sexual activity, the older one would be called a sexual predator, even if the younger adolescent initiated the activity. Other than the sex of the partner, these relationships are no different than comparable heterosexual ones, but because the participants are gay, they come under far harsher scrutiny. Let me say once more that I am not endorsing pedophilia, pederasty, or changes in our social definitions of age of consent. Our society has a responsibility to protect the safety of children and adolescents and to assure that sexual behaviors are not the result of coercion and manipulation. What I am suggesting is that our society is blatantly hypocritical in the way it approaches gay adolescent sexual behavior compared to the way it deals with the sexuality of heterosexual adolescents.

Is it not unjust for the age of consent to be different for homosexuals than the age of consent is for heterosexuals? In 2000, the Sexual Offenses Bill became law in the United Kingdom, equalizing the age of consent of all heterosexual and homosexual acts to age sixteen. Prior to the reign of Queen Victoria, gay sex was punishable by death. In 1967 being gay was legalized for those of twenty-one years of age. It was not until 1996 that it was suggested that the different ages of consent for homosexuals and heterosexuals breached human rights. Any change in the law was opposed by the House of Lords under the pretense of protecting children and preventing sixteen-year-old boys from falling prey to older men.[11]

When do the emotional networks in the brain become mature enough for sexual expression? Variations in development mean that the age of consent cannot be defined simply by a number representing age. Developing gay sexuality must be considered in the context of all adolescent sexuality. By the age of fifteen, 18 percent of all boys have had sexual intercourse at least once. By the time adolescents reach the age of nineteen, 69 percent have had sexual intercourse.[12] Gay or straight, sexuality emerges between the ages of fourteen and nineteen. Most adolescents, however, receive little advice on how to understand and explore their developing sexuality, making them more vulnerable to those who would exploit them.

Those with strong feelings against homosexuality would certainly disapprove of an ongoing sexual relationship like the one I had at the age of twelve with Randy, a male friend who was a couple of years older. It would be scrutinized more harshly and considered to be far outside the realm of normal adolescent heterosexual experimentation. When it comes to adolescent same-sex experimentation, many fear the awakening of a sleeping giant, as if all adolescent same-sex activity is transformational. That issue is further complicated when age of consent comes into play—because Randy was older than I, a relationship like ours is by default construed as predatory, even though I was always the initiator.

No matter how carefully I have written this part of the chapter—and I have rewritten it many times—I am aware that some will misinterpret my words to mean that I am advocating for man-boy sex. Some people are so horrified by this thought that their emotions will interfere with understanding. Let me be explicit: Sexual encounters that result from the use of coercive power of one over another are wrong. Period. But they are wrong for all ages and for all sexual orientations. They are not more wrong or less wrong when the two are of the same sex.

Snap Judgments

One of the tasks of adolescence is to learn how to be a sexual person—a task that is no different for heterosexuals than for gay people. I have never spoken with a gay man who felt that he would have been heterosexual but for some adolescent same-sex exploration. Some men remember their adolescent sexual experiences with older males differently—as neither reciprocal nor voluntary but rather based on an imbalance of power. An adolescent who wishes to refuse an adult's advances may be too intimidated by the power of authority to say no to a priest, a coach, a youth leader, or even worse, a parent. A child's inability to say no must never be taken as consent.

Although I have no regrets or guilt about my same-sex experiences in early adolescence, sometimes I become anxious when I remember how I was unable to resist my attraction to Randy. I remember that relationship with Randy as being reciprocal, and I do not feel I was victimized or abused. We were both adolescents, incapable of understanding sexuality from a more mature perspective. Many of the men I interviewed for this book described very similar experiences. Even though I pursued Randy, today he might have been considered a sexual predator, put on a registry for sex offenders, and given a legacy that would have followed him the rest of his life. The sexual activity that I had with Randy did not convert me to being gay. As I look back on that experience, I see it as an unfolding of my sexual orientation that began long before and continued long after my involvement with Randy.

Many boys, both gay and straight, relate a history of sexual activity much like what I had with Randy. If both are young, it may be ignored as boys being boys. But what of adolescent boys—and there are many— who like Hay had a relationship with an adult male? Apparently already aware of his being gay, Hay made it clear he had no intent to say no to the sailor. One of my gay friends has a gay son who late in adolescence had an ongoing sexual relationship with an adult man. My friend insists that the relationship was abusive, but his son, who is now an adult, continues to defend it as being reciprocal. Although some adolescents may be harmed by these relationships with adult men, none are converted into becoming gay through these relationships. More than a few men have told me that as adolescents, they pursued an older man. Because of the differences in age, and presumably power, these are complicated issues. But they should be no more complex for homosexual relationships than for heterosexual ones.

Bishop to Pawn

Kristijan is a mid-forties gay American man of Croatian decent whom I interviewed. Although he is now inactive in the church, he was raised as a Roman Catholic, attended Catholic schools, and served as an altar boy. When he was thirteen, on a Friday night after an eighth-grade dance at his parochial junior high school, he waited for his brother under the lights on the front patio of the school. Although it was late, he was typically the last to be picked up and wasn't too concerned. As he stood there, someone started a car at the adjacent nuns' convent. The car slowly circled Kristijan and stopped near where he stood. The dome light came on and revealed the driver as the bishop.

The bishop waved Kristijan over to the car. Kristijan walked to the passenger side as the bishop lowered the window. He greeted the bishop, who asked why he was alone. Kristijan explained he was waiting for his brother. The bishop, a very handsome, midfifties man with striking blue eyes, said, "I don't want you waiting alone." Kristijan responded that even though it was late, his ride was coming. Kristijan was aware that the bishop intended something more than keeping him safe, but the bishop was so insistent that Kristijan got into the car with him.

The bishop told Kristijan, "Don't worry about your ride. I will take care of you." As he reassured him, he reached over, put his hand on the inside of Kristijan's upper thigh, and snuggled his hand against Kristijan's crotch. Then the bishop said, "It's okay, you're with me now." Kristijan said his body was flooded by feelings of fear mixed with sexual desire and excitement. He looked down at the bishop's hand and then into his face, which he described as warm and kind. The bishop nudged his hand into Kristijan's crotch again as he said, "It's okay. You can come with me." Although he very much wanted to go with the bishop, he thanked him and got out of the car. The bishop then said, "I'm sorry to see you go." Kristijan told me that he has no question that had they driven off together they would have gone to the bishop's house and had sex. Kristijan accepts that pedophilia is wrong, but he does not consider the bishop a pedophile or himself a victim. To this day, Kristijan regrets not leaving with the "incredibly sexy" bishop. His story indicates how complicated these issues are.

A 2003 survey of the number of sexual abuse complaints against Roman Catholic priests and deacons found that over 10,000 people had lodged complaints in every diocese in the United States against nearly 4,400 priests. David G. Clohessy, national director of the Survivors Network of Those Abused by Priests (SNAP) said, "It's at least plausible that as many or more nonordained people are abusers as there are priest abusers."[13] Comments made by Pope Francis during his 2015 visit to the United States disappointed some abuse survivors. He said, "I deeply regret that some bishops failed in their responsibility to protect children. It is very disturbing to know that in some cases bishops even were abusers. I pledge to you that we will follow the path of truth wherever it may lead."[14] But for many victims, Francis's comments were not enough to overcome their sense of disappointment. Upon his trip back to Rome from Armenia in 2016, Pope Francis said that the Roman Catholic church should apologize for the way the Church has treated gay men and women.[15]

How can we explain the disparate experiences of adolescents? Why are some crippled by their experiences while others transcend them? The interpretation of these experiences does not rest on the act of sex alone. Recalling the two-factor theory of Schachter and Singer, the interpretation comes from the physiological response, the context of the experience, and the way our cortex processes the experience.[16] Changes in the brain, physical changes of the body, and psychological maturity all come together in puberty, and the rate of change varies considerably from one teenager to the next. The effects of premature sexual activity are greater for children from chaotic and abusive families that offer little support than for children in less dysfunctional families. Sexual abuse by a family member carries the greatest consequences. These consequences are also greater if the abusive activity was frequent and invasive and occurred early in adolescence.

Thinking holds power over emotion. Some of my experiences have taken on a new interpretation since I accepted being gay; my brain was rewired to incorporate this new knowledge. Perhaps the difference between those of us with negative experience and those of us with more positive experiences is related to the way we have reconstructed the narratives around these experiences.

Children must be protected from sexual practices where there is an imbalance of power; sexual exploration and sexual exploitation are *not* the same thing. While sexual abuse is more common than once thought, in the 1980s the legitimate concern about abuse rapidly developed into mass hysteria. All memories are but reconstructions and are factually inaccurate, but these concerns about sexual abuse produced an epidemic of false, recovered memories. In *Prescriptions for the Mind: A Critical View of Contemporary Psychiatry*, psychiatrist Joel Paris, wrote, "Therapists, beginning with Freud, believed that everything that happens in one's life is recorded in the brain.... But that is not true. We do not remember most of what happens to us, and what we do remember is more a narrative than a recording."[17] In society's attempts to deal with its collective guilt for ignoring sexual abuse of children for so long, in some cases we have created overly harsh penalties for sex between a young boy and an older one. For example, some very young adolescents have been labeled sexual perpetrators and incarcerated in sexual abuse treatment programs, yet limited evidence exists for the effectiveness of these programs. Protecting our children is vital, but doing so in an informed way is critical. And our children must also be protected against overly harsh, ineffective, and in some cases, inappropriate treatments.

Children must be protected from sexual practices where there is an imbalance of power; sexual exploration and sexual exploitation are not *the same thing.*

The emotions of trust and fear recur frequently in stories like Kristijan's. When the Roman Catholic Church ordained pedophile priests, it gave them the mantel of trusted men of God. The Church offered sanctuary to troubled children who may not have been able to trust their families. When trust is destroyed by severe or repeated abuse, fear ignites the amygdala, incinerating the capacity to trust even when no danger is present. Children must be protected from sexual practices that involve an imbalance of power and an abuse of trust. What could induce greater fear than a breach in trust by those who proclaim to be our protectors?

Although same-sex sexual exploration is often disregarded as "boys will be boys," sexual education that would better equip a young boy to deal with his expanding sexuality encounters tremendous resistance, as if the innocence of boyhood would be unleashed, resulting in out of control, sexually driven automatons. In the 1950s, girls were shown a movie about menstruation, but boys got nothing. In Nebraska, farm boys learned about sex in the context of breeding farm animals, and city boys learned about sex from farm boys. Many of those who oppose sex education feel the need to protect the innocence of their children. Opponents believe that sex education undermines the values taught by parents and see sex education as a subversive attempt to remove parental authority. But ignorance and preaching abstinence is no protection of innocence.

Sex education should be so much more than a ten-minute discussion of good touch and bad touch, ideas that are to be shed magically like wedding clothes upon entering the honeymoon bed. Sex education could teach young boys that they have a choice, and that a failure to express their choice is not the same as giving consent. It could teach them about how to deal with an imbalance of power with someone in a position of authority. It could teach them about safe sex. Whenever children do not receive a healthy education about sex, they will seek to educate themselves. That sleeping giant is going to wake up.

8

Hookups and Not Quite Sex

If one does not want to suppress his nature
and yet is afraid of expressing it, what is he to do?

—JUSTIN SPRING, *SECRET HISTORIAN: THE LIFE AND TIMES OF SAMUEL*
STEWARD, PROFESSOR, TATTOO ARTIST, AND SEXUAL RENEGADE

I first explored hookup culture in 1976 in a movie theater around Fifty-Seventh Street and Broadway in New York City. I was in the city with my wife; she had other plans, so I decided to go to a movie. The marquee of the theater revealed enough for me to know that I was entering a theater playing gay porn. As I walked through the doors into the theater, I stopped at the half wall that separated the entrance from the seating area. I stood there in the darkness and watched the screen, where for the first time in my life I saw two men having sex.

As my eyes accommodated to the darkness, I could see that the theater was filled only with men. Unlike most movie theaters, the men moved constantly from one seat to the next. I chose my seat in the same way men choose a urinal: always take the one that gives you the greatest possible separation from another man. None of the other men obeyed that rule—solitary viewing wasn't why they'd bought a ticket.

When I returned home to Maine, I continued to think about what I had seen in the theater. I did not want to want what I was wanting, yet I could not stop myself from wanting it. The men in the theater validated the stereotypes I held of a gay culture where the hallmarks are impersonal and casual sex. The possibilities of losing my family, friends, and job had not yet entered my mind. The harder I tried to ignore these feelings, the more miserable I became. These desires began to boil over inside me and were not going to be content simmering on a back burner. Not long after this experience, I arranged another trip to New York, where I had my first adult sexual experience with a man. I began to lay down some entirely new interconnections in my brain.

Casual and impersonal sexual encounters are said to be the prized trademark of gay men's sexuality. The term *hookup* was borrowed from the drug culture. A hookup is a casual sexual encounter that is based on pleasure without commitment. Hooking up has its own rules and expectations. A person looking for a hookup does not think about even a casual relationship with the other person; he only considers the moment and his own pleasure. I once asked a young Muslim how he reconciled his homosexuality with his religion and he responded, "I am not gay. This is only about pleasure."

One younger man, just beginning to explore his attraction to men, said he had received a hand job and a blow job. He was shocked when I referred to it as having sex with a man: "These were hookups, not quite sex," he said. He expressed concern about meeting a man he really cared about, knowing he might want to have anal sex. He considered anal sex to be the most intimate contact one man can have with another man; if it happened, it would erase any defenses he had built protecting him against being gay.

Pitchers and Catchers

For most of my early adult life I existed in a state of homonaïveté. I could not imagine how two men could have sex with each other, at least beyond the limits of the most obvious ways. I only thought about man-on-man sex in sexual terms, not as an expression of love and commitment. No middle school movies enlighten men about how to have an intimate relationship with another man. In the weeks that followed my visit to the theater, the only man-on-man sex I would allow myself to think about was being the passive partner in oral sex. I had no fantasies about anal anything; that would have been taking the gay fascination way too far.

We categorize gay sexual roles in the same black and white binary way we categorize everything else: tops and bottoms or pitchers and catchers. Before I accepted being gay, I wondered how men negotiated their sexual roles. I thought that perhaps after men established a relationship they begin to communicate about their sexual activity. But in the world of cruising I had observed in the movie theater, men expressed their attraction or availability in mostly nonverbal ways. With virtually no prior experience as a gay man, I had only a heterocentric paradigm. As I later learned when I entered my gay adolescence, finding a same-sex partner is not always that simple.

One gay man I visited with online said, "If the anus was not meant to be a receptacle for the penis, they wouldn't fit so well together," but anal sex is not practiced strictly by gay men. It can be mutually pleasurable for heterosexual partners as well. Some men have a strong or even an exclusive preference for one role or the other. Other men describe themselves as versatile, with no absolute preference for one role or the other; they say that their sexual role preference depends upon the man and the moment. In the bedroom, gay men simply do what they feel comfortable with and mutually agree to do.

A 2003 study published in the *Journal of Sex Research* offered these findings regarding tops, bottoms, and versatiles:

- Self-labels are meaningfully correlated with actual sexual behavior. For example, tops more frequently engage in insertive behaviors.

- Tops are more likely than both bottoms and versatiles to reject a gay self-identity and also have a higher degree of self-loathing related to their same-sex desires.

- Tops are more likely to have had sex with a woman in the past three months.

- Versatiles enjoy better psychological health than tops and bottoms do.[1]

Trevor Hart and his colleagues found that men who live in cultures that are strongly opposed to homosexuality tend to be more highly invested in the role of being a top.[2] Many of these cultures devalue women. In my conversations with Muslim men, very few—at least initially—express any interest in being the receptive partner in anal sex. Being a bottom is looked upon as abdicating masculine power and authority to become more like a "weak and powerless" woman.

Those men who are tops and also engaged in heterosexual behavior may serve as a bridge of transmission of HIV and other sexually transmitted diseases. The greatest risk of HIV transmission appears to come from men who only occasionally serve as a bottom because they perceive themselves to be at a lower risk for contracting HIV. Hart and his colleagues found that the use of condoms does not correlate with men labeling themselves as a top or a bottom, but in general bottoms appeared to have a better understanding of their risk.[3]

The Lowdown on the Down Low

"Everything you think you know about the down low is wrong," according to Keith Boykin, who wrote *Beyond the Down Low: Sex, Lies, and Denial in Black America*. Before it was appropriated by a broader community, *down low* or *DL* was a term used primarily in the African American community to describe an underground society of men who secretly have sex with men while also regularly having sex with women. The word *gay* is considered to be a term used by white people and filled with stereotypes, especially feminine connotations. Men who describe themselves as being on the down low reject any term that might emasculate them and incorporate them into the gay community. They typically prefer to have sex with straight acting, masculine men. The men engaged in DL behaviors, Boykin explains, are often dedicated to wives and children, churches and communities. Like hooking up, the DL attitude does not include a desire for any relationship beyond a physical one; hookups are simply about sexual pleasure.[4]

J. L. King, who wrote *On the Down Low: A Journey into the Lives of "Straight" Black Men Who Sleep with Men*, put a face on DL activities, but his broad and exaggerated generalizations about the African American community provoked a great deal of criticism.[5] His expertise was not as a sociologist or healthcare provider but came primarily from many years of living a sexual double life. One of King's biggest errors was to suggest that the DL phenomenon was exclusively African American. Men and women of all ethnicities and sexual orientations regularly partake in sexual relations outside of committed relationships. I have no doubt, however, that his appearance on *The Oprah Winfrey Show* started a national conversation about men who have secret sex lives with both men and women.

According to Justin Spring in *Secret Historian*, Alfred Kinsey discovered that significant class differences are reflected in sexual expression, particularly in attitudes toward premarital intercourse, prostitution, and homosexuality. Spring says: "Young men with only a grade school education experienced four or five times as many homosexual experiences as did young men who went to college. Moreover, lower-class males tended to be quite promiscuous in the early years of marriage, had a higher tolerance for homosexuality, and were much more direct, even blunt, in their approach to sexual acts of any sort."[6]

The label *bisexual* sparks controversy with opinions ranging from "everyone is more or less bisexual" to "there is no such thing as bisexuality." Some insist that bisexuals are really gay men who haven't completed all of their rewiring. Some challenge the existence of the DL and insist that DL men are just a variation of bisexual. The term has also been adopted by some men who reject being called anything that they believe emasculates them. In the past, sexuality has been thought of as a continuum from homosexuality to heterosexuality with bisexuality as a kind of waystation between the two, as if a competition exists between gay and straight with one eventually winning out. Bisexual people are often stereotyped as promiscuous.

A consideration of bisexuality points out the different ways we speak of sexuality in general. Are we speaking of sexual attraction? Fantasies? Behaviors? Identities? Taken literally, *bisexuality* means that a person has at least *some* sexual attraction to both men and women, and even though these erotic attractions may coexist in an individual, it does not mean that they cannot or will not be constrained. For example, a straight-identified person may have sex with a person of the opposite sex while experiencing lustful feelings toward someone of the same sex. Those who define themselves as bisexual face several stereotypes. They are described as promiscuous, going through a phase, imagining it or trying to camouflage their being gay.

A more contemporary understanding acknowledges that human sexuality is far more complex and fluid than this simplistic explanation. Instead of a continuum, I have come to view sexuality as more of a complex matrix of sexual expression. The sexual orientation grid described by Fritz Klein in his book *Bisexual Option* more closely approximates what I have found clinically. This grid compares several dimensions of sexuality—attraction, behavior, fantasies, emotional preference, social preference, lifestyle preference, and self-identification—and relates them to past, present, and idealized future behavior.[7] But even this model is inadequate because it does not include atypical sexual behaviors or paraphilias. In my experience, men who consider themselves bisexual often feel caught between gay and straight societies. They feel neither group accepts them. Younger people seem to find it somewhat easier to talk about a fluid sexuality, and many say that falling in love with a person's personality and character exceeds the importance of the gender of the person.

In 2005, a group of researchers published a study in *Psychological Science* asserting that, "Most bisexual men appeared homosexual with respect to genital arousal." They also found that bisexuality "appears primarily to represent a style of interpreting or reporting sexual arousal rather than a distinct pattern of genital sexual arousal."[8] Controversy surrounded the publication, and the findings were attacked by both gay and bisexual communities. Several difficulties in studying bisexuality relate to its being a hidden community as well as its dependence upon whether or not it is defined by fantasy, behavior, or self-identification. Although the number of bisexual activists is growing, in my experience people who have bisexual fantasies or participate in bisexual behavior far exceeds the number who view bisexuality as a self-identity.

Gay Spaces

People outside of the LGBTQ community see gay culture as far more unified than it is, with common aspirations, common interests, similar lives, and even a shared agenda. The truth is, few things bind gay men and women together other than the choice of someone of the same gender as a sexual partner. Oppression is another common element, but even that is not the same for everyone. Older gay men are likely to have experienced greater oppression because of their sexual orientation and may have chosen to remain deeply closeted; many have suppressed their sexuality or lived in self-imposed celibacy.

Gay men often gather in gay spaces, including gay bars and restaurants; gay neighborhoods; gay sports leagues and gay rodeos; and gay resorts, campgrounds, and cruise ships. Many gay men migrate to urban areas to find acceptance and understanding. If a stigmatized condition is concealable, being in the presence of others who are similar has a positive effect on self-esteem; those who feel they can't come out may benefit from finding a community that will coach them through the process. These microcommunities become places to see and be seen and to search for potential partners. The larger cultural effect of unified gay spaces is greater public awareness. The political and economic strength of these communities has grown and has brought about a gradual increase in civil-rights protection and fewer repressive restraints.

While in earlier decades the LGBTQ community adopted a kind of uniformity that caused members to resemble one another, today it is far more diverse and dispersed than most imagine. The gay community penetrates far beyond the confines of gay spaces into all areas of society. Gay men who hold more traditionally heteronormative values have settled in suburban areas. In accepting environments, they integrate with the straight community; in others, where gay men must be circumspect about their identity, sexual activities are confined to weekend leisure activity.

Gay spaces typically emphasize a youthful culture, and attractiveness is a prerequisite for attaining and maintaining membership. Some gay friendships, much like their heterosexual counterparts, begin with sexual attraction, a one-night stand or perhaps some dating. Some of these casual relationships lead to strong, long-lasting but platonic friendships. Older gay men may be excluded from these spaces because being old is equated with being unattractive. The stereotypes for old people and gay men are combined to form a dual prejudice against older gay men. Older people are sometimes considered to be politically conservative, senile, fanatically religious, or incapable of sexual interest. Loss of resources, incompetence, and dependency are all a part of the stereotype of aging.

The stereotypes for old people and gay men are combined to form a dual prejudice against older gay men who are seen as sexless and yet preoccupied with sex.

Combining the stereotypes of old people with those of gay people paints a picture of the aging gay man who is poorly adjusted psychologically—sexless and yet preoccupied with sex. This stereotype certainly doesn't relate to my life or the lives of my older gay peers. Although some of my friends live on restricted, fixed incomes, they remain engaged in their lives and are active socially and sexually. While some gay men are childless and have large amounts of disposable income, many gay men are parents of biological children through arrangement, adoptive children by choice, or children from prior heterosexual relationships.

Gay spaces for older men do exist, and entrepreneurs are just beginning to recognize potential markets for gay baby boomers. This coming together in gay spaces has ramifications far beyond those spaces. In 2016, when several states began to pass anti-LGBTQ legislation in the name of religious freedom, the LGBTQ community found allies in surprising places: big corporations. Corporate America's response to laws proposed and passed based on religious freedom has been these laws are "bad for our employees and bad for business." *New Yorker* reported that when several states proposed or passed laws making anti-LGBTQ discrimination legal, some of America's largest companies began to push back with a more progressive agenda. Executives expressed opposition, and businesses moved production and canceled plans for expansion. Several state governors responded immediately by vetoing discriminatory laws based on religious freedom.[9] This has caused some dysfunction in the blended families that coalesced under President Ronald Reagan of probusiness conservatives, national-security hawks, and the Christian right. Many conservative business leaders consider today's social-conservative agenda anachronistic and harmful to the bottom line.

Virtual Cruising and Sex

The Internet has put millions of men in contact with gay culture in ways that were previously reserved for those who live in major urban areas. The Pew Research Center reported that Internet usage among those 65 and older has more than tripled between 2009 and 2013. Social networking sites are increasingly used to keep up with close social ties, and the average user of a social networking site has more close ties and is half as likely to be socially isolated as the average American.[10] People are more likely to be drawn to the Internet if they know others who have used it successfully. New opportunities for meeting partners now often begin without leaving home; about 60 percent of LGBTQ relationships begin online. From January 2011 through January 2014 there was an 80 percent surge in users age 55 and above. As boomers flock to Facebook, teens have begun to stay away in order to protect their privacy.[11]

The Internet can be risky. Websites often warn against sharing too much personal information and suggest that the first face-to-face meeting between online acquaintances should take place in a public place. The Internet creates opportunities for MSM to skim profiles and anonymously meet new sex partners who have similar interests. An older study reported that men who meet partners online are more likely to take sexual risks and be exposed to HIV than are MSM who do not seek partners on the Internet, but subsequent studies have shown no greater risk from meeting online.[12]

Pornography is ubiquitous, and its use exploded with the onset of the HIV/AIDS crisis. Some estimate that 30 percent of Internet traffic is related to porn. The nearly universal use of the Internet means that even young children have been exposed to porn, either by choice or by chance. One Canadian research group wanted to compare people who had been exposed to pornography to those who had not, but they abandoned their study when they could not find a control group that had never seen pornography.[13]

Now you can even have sex with someone without being in the same room. The virtual world of the Internet offers dozens and dozens of sites with interactive webcam chats. Many gay men who meet on gay dating and hookup sites continue their relationships with naked and sexually explicit conversations on Skype. For some in long distance relationships and MSM who are isolated by heterosexual marriages, geography, or culture, the Internet may be their only connection to a same-sex erotic life.

Porn has distorted how we view normal sex; it is no substitute for good sex education. Sex does not always involve endless copulation and oral sex, nor does it always end with a star-spangled, explosive ejaculation.

Wanking to Yang

A young physician related to me his struggle to understand his sexuality. I said to him something about struggling with his yin and yang, and he responded, "Recently, I've been spending a lot more time with my yang." He fantasized about both men and women when he masturbated, but he felt increasingly anxious about his indecision. He said, "I feel so ill at ease talking with women. Nothing seems to come naturally. I could never chat with them on the Internet because I wouldn't know what to say. Talking with men is easier. I'm not gay, but I don't understand the difference." For this young man, he was able to explore his sexual uncertainty through masturbation.

People who masturbate have more sex and more satisfying sex, according to the 2010 report "Sex, Romance, and Relationships: AARP Survey of Midlife and Older Adults."[14] This report stated that of all men in their fifties, 42 percent masturbate to ejaculation at least once a week. Men masturbate for all sorts of reasons. Masturbating helps men learn what sensations arouse their bodies and how to control their orgasms so they may have more satisfying sex lives. Men masturbate as a stress reliever or a pick-me-up. Masturbation satisfies sexual needs in the absence of a partner. Prolonged absence from sexual activity can impede a return to satisfying sex, and 90 percent of men over the age of eighty still fantasize about sex. Fantasizing and masturbating become acceptable substitutes for hidden or forbidden wishes. When you masturbate, you are in complete control of all the variables.

Whether or not the Bible prohibits homosexuality hinges a lot on the interpretation of the Greek word *malakos*, which has been translated as both *homosexuality* and *masturbation*. I am neither a Biblical nor a Greek scholar, but I bet that when the committee met to decide whether masturbation or homosexuality was the real abomination, not many men were going to say that malakos meant masturbation. The gay people on the committee were going to lose either way.

Individuals differ tremendously in how much they masturbate. Some people masturbate two or three times in their lives and others two or three times in a day. Although some people feel that those in monogamous relationships should feel no need to masturbate, most men continue to masturbate even if their partnership is completely satisfying. Unless masturbation in some way compromises the sexual relationship with a partner, masturbation is not problematic.

Sex Addition

Controversy surrounds the concept of sexual addiction, or as it is sometimes called, *hypersexuality disorder*. A large group of committed people believe that addiction to sex is the same as addiction to drugs, while a group of other researchers and therapists argue that hypersexuality is a concept that should not include the language of addiction. The jury is not in. The frequently mentioned criteria for hypersexuality disorder include a loss of control, failed attempts to stop the unwanted sexual behavior, and a pattern of negative consequences such as anxiety, depression, legal troubles, sexually transmitted diseases, and relationship problems. Some say that using this model makes sexual behavior morally wrong and denies the enjoyment of positive sexual experiences with as many people as one likes, any way one wants. Its validity as a diagnosis is challenged by not only psychiatrists and other mental health professionals but members of the general public who believe that sexual addiction is just another excuse for cheating.

Sexual behavior can become a problem and may be considered compulsive when it begins to interfere with normal daily activity. Problematic behavior includes having multiple concurrent sexual partners, objectifying sexual partners, excessively masturbating, exposing oneself in public, and feeling compelled to have sex when stressed, anxious, or depressed. These behaviors become compulsive when a person feels driven by sexuality and out of control. Compulsive sexual behavior is particularly problematic if a person neglects his partner or becomes deceitful in a primary relationship.

Some people refer to the Internet as the crack cocaine of sexual addiction. For some very sexually active people, sex is the only source of pleasure, soothing, and acceptance. Others use it to guard against loneliness, emptiness, and depression. Still others are addicted to a constant flow of validation and approval from complete strangers, or they ignore their needs for love and intimacy by constantly having sex. I once communicated with a man who said that he had masturbated up to thirteen times that day. Living in Pakistan, he said he was unable to explore his same-sex attractions in a more intimate way, and the Internet numbed and alleviated some of the pain of his loneliness and isolation, but I had to wonder how much time he had left for anything else.

Some people refer to the Internet as the crack cocaine of sexual addiction.

The science associated with sexual addiction is thin, although people who compulsively have sex may experience real suffering. Most of the clinical descriptions of and treatment programs for sexual addiction are copied from the treatment programs for alcoholism and drug abuse. Treatments based on talk therapy and twelve-step programming continue to expand across the country; most are not reimbursed by insurance. That wide net catches many wealthy fish.

Dr. Jack Drescher, a New York psychiatrist who has treated many patients for sexual problems, wrote that the research showing a correlation between chemical change and sexual addiction has not been determined. Dr. Drescher believes that no one's ever decided what the proper amount of sex is. He also believes that so-called sex addiction is usually a mask covering deep-seated issues, like alcoholism or drug use, or abuse suffered in childhood.[15] Psychiatrists generally believe that multiple psychiatric disorders can include compulsive sexuality as one of the symptoms.

'Til Death Do Us Part

Many gay people as well as heterosexuals reject the idea of marriage, arguing that marriage is paternalistic and based on a need to control the behavior of another. At the same time, however, gay culture is profoundly reactive to and conditioned by the traditions and values of present-day American heterosexuality. Some MSM find it difficult to let go of the heterosexual marriage paradigm. They resist the next step of forming a bond with another man. They are unwilling to forsake either the pleasures and freedoms of nonmonogamous sex with men or the favored status of heterosexual privilege that accompanies having a family.

Many people believe that where an affair occurs something has been profoundly wrong in a marriage. Across the thirty-nine countries polled by Pew Research Center, a median of 79 percent of people consider infidelity unacceptable, including an overwhelming 84 percent of Americans; this belief is especially widespread in predominantly Muslim nations.[16]

Scott James, writing in the *New York Times*, noted that gay couples often have more relaxed rules about monogamy. Reporting on a new study, he said that monogamy is not a central feature of many gay and lesbian relationships and that some people argue that their relationships are stronger, longer lasting, and more honest because of this openness. This study found that in the San Francisco Bay Area about 50 percent of those surveyed have sex outside their relationships with the knowledge and approval of their partners. Consent appears to be the keystone of these arrangements. For people in open relationships, sex outside of marriage does not carry negative connotations, and some experts say that these boundary-challenging relationships represent an evolution in marriage.[17]

People who have affairs outside their committed relationship tell their friends, "No one has ever loved me like he has," or "No one has ever understood me like she does." In our electronic era the definition of infidelity keeps expanding from sexting, to cam sex, to fuck-buddy relationships. It has never been so easy to cheat or so difficult to keep a secret, and infidelity can shatter the expectations of perfect love. People are sometimes drawn into affairs because they fear their own mortality—they begin to wonder, Will I ever have that feeling again?

> *It has never been so easy to cheat or so difficult to keep a secret, and infidelity can shatter the expectations of perfect love.*

Falling in love is almost always a psychotic experience even under the best of circumstances. If you say to someone engaged in one of these affairs, "Can't you see who he really is?" the typical response is "You don't know him like I do!" But that person is actually falling in love with who he imagines the other person to be. A person engaged in an affair isn't turning *toward* another person; he is turning *away* from the person he's become. He wishes to once again feel important, desirable, and special.

Fidelity has more to do with the head than the genitals.

In theory, marriage is a lifelong commitment. Some fear that marriage will end in spite of the commitment; others fear that the commitment will keep it from ending when it should. More than 50 percent of marriages end in divorce, but in Massachusetts, where same-sex marriage has been legal for several years, divorce rates are the lowest in the country. William Sloane Coffin wrote, "The argument that gays threaten to destroy heterosexual marriage is an assertion only, not an argument. If anyone destroys marriage, it's married people, not gays."[18]

Our sexual drive is a powerful, universal biological drive. We are born into a culture with identifiable norms and values about sexual expression and intimacy that are based almost entirely on a heterosexual paradigm. A stable expression of gay sexual identity depends upon a reassessment of those values and norms. It requires that we deconstruct those values and reconstruct a value system for how we express our sexuality and intimacy.

The default setting for marriage—an exclusive sexual and romantic relationship throughout the marriage—is difficult for most humans, gay or straight, to maintain. What seems to render extramarital sexual relationships damaging is secrecy and lack of honesty. In *Lust in Translation: Infidelity from Tokyo to Tennessee*, after reviewing several polls researching adultery in different cultures around the world, Pamela Druckerman writes that although 80 percent of respondents thought infidelity was wrong, most of those who got caught cheating didn't think of themselves as "the cheating kind." Only other people who committed infidelity were cheaters.[19] In the previously mentioned AARP survey, about half of the respondents said that an affair had no effect on their primary relationship and about one quarter said the affair actually made their primary relationship better. Spouses who discovered and had not consented to their partners' affairs were less inclined to dismiss them.[20]

M. V. Lee Badgett, in *When Gay People Get Married*, wrote: Marriage "has the power to define a relationship that others might not understand. Couples can use marriage to express to others what their relationship means and how it should be treated."[21] Being gay is a social role as well as a sexual behavior. It is far more than genital sex. Homoerotic desire is one thing, but living the life of an openly gay man in a relationship is quite a different matter that often means living a life informed by the values of heterosexual sexuality and intimacy.

The Risk of HIV and the Hope of PrEP

Statistics can be hypnotic, but please, stick with me here. HIV/AIDS has impacted all communities, all races and ethnicities, and all levels of society. The community of MSM includes all men who have sex with other men regardless of how they identify themselves—gay, bisexual, heterosexual, or other. The CDC stated that in 2014, in the United States, gay and bisexual men accounted for 83 percent of the estimated new HIV diagnoses among all males, although MSM make up only about 2 percent of the population, with the percentages declining by 6 percent among white gay and bisexual men and increasing by 13 percent among Hispanic/Latino gay and bisexual men.[22]

A number of studies have shown that MSM who seek sex partners online are at greater risk for HIV and other STDs than are MSM who do not see partners on the Internet. Because of the high percentage of gay and bisexual men living with HIV, MSM have an increased risk because of multiple-partner exposure and less commitment to safe-sex precautions. MSM have more opportunities to have sex with someone who can transmit HIV or another STD. Most MSM acquire HIV through anal sex. Unfortunately, many gay and bisexual men are still unaware they have HIV. Had I come out earlier in my life, I likely would have been among the over three hundred thousand gay and bisexual men who have died from HIV. Francis and Mialon's study found that the incidence of HIV decreased considerably during the 1990s as attitudes toward gays liberalized, but the incidence of new cases has been increasing again.[23]

Sexual risks account for most HIV infections in MSM, particularly the risk of having anal sex with someone other than a primary HIV-negative partner. The highest risks appear to fall on those casual sexual partners who have sex without a condom, a practice known as barebacking. Older men with a large number of sexual partners, young men who use "circuit party" drugs like ecstasy and ketamine, and older men who use amyl nitrite or "poppers" to heighten sexual arousal carry a high risk of exposure to the virus. Older men continue to be a significant source of HIV transmission to young gay men.

One in eight people living with HIV is unaware of his infection. Young African American MSM in the study were especially likely to be unaware of their HIV infection. A lack of knowledge is tragic because many MSM reduce their risky behaviors after they test positive for HIV infection. Knowing they are positive could help protect their sex partners and fellow drug-users from HIV infection. Those who are unaware of their HIV infection cannot take advantage of medicine that could help them live longer.

Many MSM continue their false belief that they are at low risk of becoming infected or infecting their partner. Treatment successes have hidden many of the negative aspects of HIV, leading to false assurances about the risks of death or, for that matter, how difficult living with HIV can be. Young gay and bisexual men, unlike older gay and bisexual men, have not witnessed the ravages of the HIV/AIDS epidemic.

Studies have shown a significant reduction in new HIV infections with use of preexposure prophylaxis (PrEP). The CDC's published "Preexposure Prophylaxis for the Prevention of HIV Infections in the United States" states that in 2012, the Food and Drug Administration (FDA) approved the use of the HIV drug Truvada for PrEP to help prevent infection with the AIDS virus for people at high risk for infection. The FDA panel voted overwhelmingly to approve PrEP for MSM and for uninfected partners of HIV-infected people. This is the first time that the FDA has approved any PrEP drug for the protection of uninfected people against HIV. The drug is not to be used as a sole preventive measure but is to be used in combination with other risk reduction strategies including regular use of condoms, safe-sex practices, counseling, and regular HIV testing.

The risk of acquiring HIV infection substantially increases with any of the following:

- An HIV-positive sexual partner

- A recent bacterial sexually transmitted disease

- A high number of sex partners

- A history of inconsistent or no condom use

- A history of commercial sex work

Truvada is expensive, and only some commercial insurance and employee benefits programs have policies that cover PrEP. Public insurances vary in their coverage. In many cases, a healthcare provider may be required to complete a prior authorization to have the medication covered by insurance. For patients who do not have health insurance, or whose insurance does not cover PrEP medications, or whose personal finances are inadequate to pay out of pocket, the manufacturer of Truvada, Gilead Sciences, has established a rather liberal PrEP medication assistance program. Applications are available for patients at the Truvada website (https://start.truvada.com/).

Hepatitis B (HBV) is an STD of the liver spread like HIV that leads to severe liver disease, including cirrhosis (liver failure) and liver cancer. Although HBV is found mostly in blood with lower concentrations in other body fluids (e.g., semen, vaginal secretions, and wounds), it can be transmitted through unprotected sex. HBV can be prevented by HBV vaccines and safer sex. In the United States, chronic HBV infection results in an estimated two thousand to four thousand deaths per year.[24]

HBV and other STDs, such as syphilis and gonorrhea, increase the risk for getting an HIV infection, indicate participation in high-risk sexual behavior, and can facilitate the transmission of HIV infection to a sex partner. The use of alcohol and illegal drugs also increases the likelihood of risky sexual behavior. Sexual decision making is complex; it requires an optimally functioning brain.

HIV is not necessarily transmitted every time a person has sex, but regular testing is critical. Many places provide testing for HIV infection, including local health departments, HIV clinics, LGBTQ resource centers, offices of private doctors, and hospitals. An HIV test result reveals only the test taker's HIV status; a negative test result does not reveal whether the test taker's partner has HIV. Currently only two home

HIV tests are available that produces results in approximately twenty minutes: the Home Access HIV-1 Test System and the OraQuick In-Home HIV Test. When buying a home test online, make sure it is FDA approved. Positive results from rapid HIV tests must be confirmed with a follow-up test in a testing facility before a final diagnosis can be made.

In parts of the country where acceptance of homosexuality is low, underground cruising areas become the predominant venue for the sexual activity of MSM. Rates of risky sexual behavior are higher in those places. The most certain way for MSM to avoid becoming infected with HIV, or HBV and other STDs is to abstain from sex (including oral, anal, or vaginal sex) until they are in a monogamous relationship. This sounds simple, but when a brain is flooded with dopamine, alcohol, or illicit drugs, sexual drive can easily overpower rational thought.

9

Midlife Crisis: Is It Too Late for Me?

*Midlife crisis is that moment when you realize
your children and your clothes are about the same age.*

—WILLIAM D. TAMMEUS

The universal description of the midlife crisis includes a time of personal turmoil, sudden changes in personal goals and lifestyle, realization of aging and physical decline, and feelings of entrapment in roles that are seen as unwelcome and too restrictive. When I first came out, I was already a decade past "over the hill at thirty" as gay men said at the time. I am sure some people believed that my coming out was just a midlife crisis. One man I corresponded with online wrote, "I will not say my life was better when I was younger, but [it was] definitely totally different. In ten years it will be totally different again."

All people have a moment when mortality finally becomes personal. We realize that less time remains of our lives than has already passed, and we begin to check things off our to-do list without ever having done them. Midlife is a time when we review our life experiences and begin to consider the need to develop a legacy, a suitable ending to our life story. Midlife is a time of disengaging from the world of the young to pursue a greater range of social roles and to engage a more cognitively complex, ambiguous, and uncertain world. Midlife is also a time of higher cognitive complexity, when values and institutions are seen with more ambivalence and uncertainty. As we mature, we become more critical of groups and institutions that once had a great influence in our lives.

The exact ages for midlife seem to be quite elastic, extending from the thirties through the sixties. At the time I was born in 1943, life expectancy for a man was about sixty-eight years, so at seventy-three years old, I have already received a gift of five years beyond what was expected when I was born. I used the Social Security life expectancy calculator to determine that today, my life expectancy is 86.3 years, or another twelve or thirteen years.[1] When I was a child, a seventy-three-year-old man looked pretty damn old. The image of seventy-three that I carried in my head for a long time was of a person who had lived five years beyond the best-if-used-by date. But life expectancy has increased over my lifetime.

Midlife is a time of disengaging from the world of the young to pursue a greater range of social roles and to engage a more cognitively complex, ambiguous, and uncertain world.

Because I'm not dead yet, I'm considered a survivor, but sometimes I wonder, How many of those years will be good years? When will I change from one who has always been a care provider to being one who is dependent upon the care of others? I prefer to think of midlife as the middle of adult life, which would put it at the beginning of my fifth decade. Whatever age one chooses, all people reach a point where they begin to have some awareness that they are aging, that time is passing by, and that they are "halfway home."

Midlife can be a tumultuous time where every aspect of a person's life comes into question. Much of what is revealed is horrifying, including the destructiveness in others and the recognition that we have been responsible for some of the pain experienced by those we care about. What we aspired to be and our current achievements may be significantly different. We are stretched between a strong investment in maintaining the status quo and the urgent desire to modify our life.

The period of midlife transition is characterized by disillusionment as we recognize that long-held assumptions and beliefs about ourselves and the world are not true. This can be experienced as both a loss and liberation. When gay men come out in midlife, they may be daunted by deconstructing the straight-and-narrow, nice-kid-next-door pose they had assumed for decades. In maturity people begin to act in ways that are more in concert with their reconstructed internal values rather than revert to their old patterns of pleasing others. Priorities change, and the external world is no longer the reference point for what is correct.

One interviewee described his late coming out in this way: "A mature person has a highly personal value system that they have constructed from the best parts of different systems to which they have been exposed. Prior to maturity they adopted the value system of their parents and peers, or they rejected those values completely and reactively developed opposing values. In either case, values are still dominated by the values of their parents. Midlife allows us to integrate those values with our own later experiences."

As men undergo the psychological changes of midlife, they begin to reconsider the qualities of life that make it worthwhile. Men often become more sensitive to the misfortunes of others. They no longer fear intimacy, and they begin to question the validity of doing, making, and having and never admitting weakness. Even more important, such ideas are no longer considered expressions of being queer.

In midlife, we are able to recognize that what we learned about being a man and what is expected of us may not be guidelines we must cling to. These expectations may not represent who we really are. Paul, a man I interviewed, is an excellent example. Paul was an identical twin and was a Lutheran minister until he was outed in 1991. At the age of forty-six, at a church leadership retreat, he disclosed that he experienced sexual attraction to other men.

From the age of thirteen Paul had felt called to the ministry, and the increasing struggle he felt about his sexuality led him to believe that if he were exposed, he would lose everything important to him. For him, coming out risked putting all of his familial, social, communal, and vocational relationships at risk. During the years before he came out, he dealt with suicidal feelings and fear of being exposed.

Although the group at the retreat had taken an oath of confidentiality, two colleagues went to his bishop. The bishop demanded his resignation. Losing his job meant coming out to his teenage children, an experience he anticipated would be devastating. Instead, it turned out to be a positive experience because each of his three children said that they still loved him. Paul began to accept that he was gay and believed that God accepted and affirmed him as a gay man.

Prior to coming out, Paul had only experienced limited, casual sexual encounters with other men. Paul and his twin brother had explored their sexuality with each other from the onset of puberty through high school. Paul's first date with a woman was for the homecoming dance his senior year in high school. He dated a woman in college, but when she wanted to have sex, he refused, rationalizing that it was because his moral standards were higher than hers. He had never had sex with a woman before his marriage. He felt his wife was a good choice for him, but even as he was getting married, he began to feel he was making a terrible mistake.

Paul describes his late-arriving gay "adolescence" in this way: "In 1984, after finally coming to terms with being gay and accepting my sexuality as a positive thing, as is common for gay men who are accepting their sexuality, I acted like a teenager. For me that mainly manifested itself as looking for a lot of sexual encounters and also shocking people by inappropriate revelations of my sexual adventures." Paul discovered in his coming out that his identical twin, who also had been married, was also gay and had a parallel sexual development. Paul legally married the man he had been with for nearly twenty years, and after that man passed, Paul began a new life with his second husband.

Eight of the men in my study came out in their eighties, four of them having been outed like Paul. Like Paul and me, they always felt very sexual, but acting on those feelings with women evoked considerable anxiety. We avoided heterosexual dating as much as possible, using justifications like morality, need to work, or Southern gentility to explain our restraint. What other young men were learning by trial and error with women, we never learned.

One older gay man I interviewed said about dating, "You eat, you laugh, and you cry. But mostly you just wait." The first task for many middle-aged men who have been concealing their sexuality is to spend some time alone, deciding how far to take this newly discovered truth about their sexual orientation. They must ask themselves, "Am I ready to forsake the life of heterosexual privilege to become a part of a stigmatized minority? Am I ready for a relationship? Do I believe that gay men are capable of long-term, monogamous relationships? Am I willing to give up a secret life of nonmonogamous sex?"

Romantic love is based on sex and passion, and it changes over time. Most men who come out in midlife are beginning a gay sexual adolescence, and they will spend much of their remaining life trying to integrate sex, romance, and love. Traditionally men have met their partners through family and work associates, but this is impossible when sexual orientation is concealed. Our deficiencies, however, began to be remediated when we began dating men. Each of us sought to tame the wild horse of Plato's allegory.

"Your Dad's a Faggot"

Men who are fathers can be attractive potential partners. They are often considered less self-oriented and better at compromise, but bringing kids into the mix adds a layer of complexity to a relationship. People underestimate the central role of children in the lives of gay men. For gay men, dating an older man with children is complicated because the children will always come first. The birth of Roberto's son permanently bumped me into a subordinate place in his affection.

In a nearly twenty-year-old study, researchers reported on a group of previously married gay men and women in Chicago. They found that people who have been heterosexually married tend to self-identify as gay an average of ten years later than those who never married. This is consistent with my experience and my survey results. Marriage also delays the age of coming out to both parents, although mothers were generally told earlier than fathers.[2] The difficulty of coming out to my mother far surpassed the difficulty I felt in telling her I wanted to be a psychiatrist.

One man I interviewed had retired from the military. Although he knew he was gay much earlier in his life, he had married and divorced twice. He said that his deployments for military combat enabled him to remove himself from the conflict he experienced about his sexual orientation while at home. He was the custodial father of his two daughters. Not yet out to his daughters, he was struggling to find a new life as a gay father.

Gay fathers have some unique problems. The image of the affluent gay man who hedonistically indulges himself doesn't fit most gay men I know, but it especially doesn't fit for most newly divorcing gay men. Many go through several years of legal and financial problems often compounded by a wife who feels deceived and cheated and in retaliation, may seek to contaminate the father's relationship with his children. Because of child support and alimony, these men may have very little discretionary income. Coparenting also makes significant demands on the time of gay fathers, which can be a big source of conflict for a partner who has never had children of his own.

People who have been heterosexually married tend to self-identify as gay an average of ten years later than those who never married.

Marital history and the timing of important life events significantly impact the coming-out trajectory. Because of their common struggle to balance being gay with the responsibilities of being fathers, men who have been in heterosexual marriages have much more in common with each other than they do with gay men who have different life histories. The development of gay men who have children is shaped in a much different way than the development of those who do not, because children are central in their lives. When I joined the gay fathers' support group, I felt an immediate sense of brotherhood with the other men in the group. Gay fathers have clusters of common experiences that make it easy to relate to each other, but those experiences may complicate relating to men who came out early in their lives and who have never heterosexually married.

Gay men who come out in later life, whether previously married or not, are rookies in a game they have never played before. Their lives are turned upside down. Some trade a comfortably familiar, heterosexual life in the suburbs for a new life in a gay urban environment. Their previous straight social network has been sidelined. They are out of sync with developmental tasks appropriate to their age. With little or no previous experience in the gay community, they battle with tasks that are typically associated with late adolescence and young adulthood rather than middle age. They lack certainty about their new world. Without a clear sense of their new identity, they compete in the game, but there is no rule book. Many are not prepared to begin life anew as a single man.

For many gay fathers, the biggest barrier to coming out is telling their children. Gay fathers know that they are different; they also know that their being different will define their kids as different. Fathers worry about how their being gay will impact their children's relationships with other kids. All parents want to buffer their children against the pain of being teased, accused, and rejected. Guilt stabs gay fathers when their kids hear slurs like "Your dad's a faggot." I worried that my daughters' boyfriends would be scared off when they said to them, "There's something important I need to tell you about my dad."

When I came out to my kids, they responded, "Oh, Dad, we've known that for a long time." Although coming out to their children occasionally sparks a wildfire, many gay fathers have had similar experiences of coming out to their children. One of the men I interviewed who has three adult sons said his children responded, "Pop, why didn't you tell us this ages ago?" They told him they loved and respected him even more because he demonstrated to them qualities he had been unable to see in himself. He regretted that he had been too afraid to tell them the truth when he first became confident that he was gay. Losses loom so much larger than gains.

Amity Pierce Buxton, who wrote *The Other Side of the Closet: The Coming-Out Crisis for Straight Spouses and Families*, offers this advice to fathers considering coming out to their children: "Most kids believe that the sooner a gay parent comes out to them the better for them it is. By the time the spouse has been told, children will already be aware of the tension in the household." Buxton suggests that children not be told at the time their parents separate; coming out should wait until both parents are somewhat comfortable with the revelation. Then both parents are in a better position to be supportive of the children when they are told. Depending upon their age, they may have already observed telltale signs of their parent's sexual orientation.[3]

Children should be told at a time when they can react, reflect, and ask questions. The goal is to lovingly help them understand. Unlike thirty years ago when I came out, with so many cultural changes and attention to same-sex relationships in the media, even very young children will already have some idea of what it means to be gay. Most children say that the divorce is a more difficult issue to accept than sexual orientation. But as my daughter said, "Children who have a gay parent must come out to our friends, too. Telling friends about a divorce is a one-shot thing, but coming out to our friends never ends." In some cases, estrangement may occur. It takes time, consistency, and work to reestablish damaged relationships.

I have never started an important venture feeling adequately prepared. No perfect way exists to come out to children. An acceptable job may be good enough. Everything that is painful is not necessarily dysfunctional. It may help to know that you're not in this alone, but it may not help much. Sometimes things are as bad as they seem, but often they are not.

Hating Adonis

As we age, both men and women experience a gradual decrease in the attributes that are culturally considered attractive. But from my research, women and gay men experience this decrease more dramatically and earlier than heterosexual men. For a while past the age of fifty, men get a free ride—age may even enhance some aspects of men's attractiveness and work to their advantage in some relationships. That said, the psychological impact of physical changes can be significant.

Central to the fear of middle age are attitudes about changes in the body. Those who are most deeply invested in their physical appearance encounter the greatest difficulty, fearing the loss of their external, youthful sexual attractiveness. As Rebecca Mead wrote in the *New Yorker*, "The new idea offered by the contemporary culture of cosmetic surgery is that it is the vessel itself that we must value, rather than the soul or spirit that it contains."[4] This physically attractive body is the person we present ourselves to be, and some have lived behind the façade of their bodies with little concern for relating to others in ways beyond the physical. Middle age, and the loss of that youthful body, can be shocking, and some gay men feel they've lost their former social self.

Stereotypes describe gay men as either limp-wristed and effeminate or obsessed with attaining the masculine body beautiful. In the article "Ageing Gay Men: Lessons from the Sociology of Embodiment," Julie Jones and Steve Pugh describe the relationship gay men have with their body image. While the extremes are captured by the exaggerated femininity in the form of drag and the exaggerated masculinity in the musculature of the gym rat, between these extremes an infinite variety of aesthetic preferences exist, but the unifying factor is the presentation of an attractive, attention-grabbing body.[5]

Some gay men consider their bodies their most significant asset, and they seek affirmation through admiration and envy from others. Rarely alone, but sometimes lonely, their bodies are their ticket to power and success, and the goal is perfection. When I was working out at the Iowa State gym years ago, some men would check their muscle definition several times during one workout. RuPaul, America's foremost drag queen whose show, *RuPaul's Drag Race*, has been nominated for an Emmy, said in her autobiography, "We are born naked and the rest is drag." What RuPaul is suggesting is that all of us use our bodies and the way we dress to influence others' opinions of us.[6]

Showering in a gym is surely as oppressive for a stocky, skinny, or aging gay man as it is for a woman trying on a new swimsuit. Chiseled good looks are achieved by very few and remain only a dream for the majority. Not being able to achieve those good looks is sometimes perceived as a lack of commitment to body maintenance or a lack of self-control. The body becomes a project, perpetually in need of development to prevent it from reverting to its natural, homely state. Continual fixation on body image sometimes means attempting to radically alter the way we look by "having a little work done," including the use of pectoral implants, steroids, and penile enlargers.

Our body image results from the difference between our ideal body and the way we see our current body. We are satisfied with our body image when we have a realistic expectation about what our body can be and we see it as it actually is. The saddest and angriest gay men are those who have failed to accept that their potential is limited and that perfection is unattainable. They feel as intimidated by beautiful gay men as they are by straight men. The enemy for these men is not their body; the enemy is their unrealistic expectation of what their body can be or must be.

Gay men's connection to physical attractiveness or preoccupation with fashion can be perceived as superficial or even threatening to heterosexual men. The American code of manhood dictates that real men must not be concerned about matters of style and taste, but all the while they are blasted by images of men reshaped by computers and wearing Calvin Klein briefs. The word *metrosexual* was created to describe American men who blend an interest in style, fashion, and culture while not letting go of balls-scratching, beer-guzzling masculinity. These men have always been a part of affluent groups, but now frosted hair and manicures have become accessible to the average man. In Europe, men don't need a special category to justify their emphasis on physical

The word metrosexual *was created to describe American men who blend an interest in style, fashion, and culture while not letting go of balls-scratching, beer-guzzling masculinity.*

grooming, but this crossover is something we are not yet comfortable with in the United States: being a metrosexual is just too queer.

Because of the importance of physical attractiveness in the gay community, middle age comes sooner to gay men than it does to heterosexual men. Pressure is put on gay men to work daily to maintain the appearance of youth, but the labor must also be hidden so no one knows how difficult it is to keep up. Harold Kooden wrote in *Golden Men: The Power of Gay Midlife* that the concept of a linear aging process is misleading. He suggested that gay men have four ages: chronological (clock age), biological (body age), experiential (heart age), and sexual (gay age). He proposed that we age in each of these four areas at different rates and times; chronological age represents only one portion of our authentic age.[7]

Another age might be added to Kooden's list: geographical age. Age functions quite differently in urban and rural communities. Because MSM may undergo conflict about their sexuality, their sexual age may lag behind their clock age, body age, and heart age. Geographical age may add another incongruity—men who grew up in the city may arrive at a gay identity at a much younger age.

The Spirit Is Willing

A midlife crisis is usually believed to involve a change in one's basic personality. Men are expected to go through this crisis as they begin to experience the physical and psychological changes of aging. In my research I examined the presence of stressful events in the lives of mature MSM. Although the loss of physical vitality can be stressful, the emotional stresses of midlife are far greater—loneliness; illness or death of parents, siblings, and contemporaries; marital discord, separation, or divorce; extramarital affairs; children leaving home; disappointment in children's achievements; or feeling caught between the demands of parents and children. However, I found evidence disputing the idea that midlife is a universally stressful time. Traditional beliefs about aging, in particular gay aging, overestimate the occurrence of midlife crises, and serious emotional disturbances are the exception rather than the rule.

Medical literature is not much help when one seeks to understand the midlife transition for gay men. Researchers ignore older people and are ignorant of the fact that they might still be having sex. Having been raised in an era when same-sex behavior was criminalized and pathologized, baby boomers are difficult to research because many gay men and women have never let go of their fear of exposure. Consequently they reject the labels that might sideline them from the general population. Many gay baby boomers have lived a heteronormative life, concealing their sexual orientation either by celibacy or by feigning disinterest in sex.

However, midlife can be liberating. Midlife is a time to stop living other people's values and start integrating that which is valuable from our roots and our later-life experiences. In midlife we shift away from using the external world as our main reference point and focus on what is correct for ourselves and our developing image of the future. Midlife has allowed me to realize that attractiveness is not measured by only one standard or from only one perspective; it includes a personal value system, a mature adult physical attractiveness, and a richness of personal history.

The Birth of Mortality

When I turned forty, a sense of urgency to deal with the parts of myself that I earlier had neglected, ignored, or put on hold swept over me. One of those was my sexual orientation. I had been committed to meeting obligations for family and career; a beautiful body, frequent sex, and dancing the night away were the least of my concerns. But I began to ask myself, "Am I too old to start over as a gay man?" I shuddered when I considered that one possible result from coming out might be a series of meaningless and clandestine sexual encounters with faceless men, the risk of disease, and eventual public humiliation.

The real result of my coming out was not that dire, but around that time I began to experience a series of losses: I lost my marriage, I lost the custody of my children, and I began to lose people I loved—my mother, my brother, my stepfather, and friends my own age were dying. Professionally, I had reached the apex of my career; I had to step aside as younger physicians filled with the energy and passion I once had passed me by. For the first time in my life, I had medical concerns. Erik Erikson wrote that "Despair expresses the feeling that the time is short, too short for the attempt to start another life and to try out alternate roads to integrity."[8] Was it possible for me to find integrity rather than despair in a new life as a gay man?

Coming out in midlife is characterized by deconstructing inherited values and reconstructing a value system of our own choosing. Deconstructing a value system does not mean destroying it. Although I needed to unlearn some things I had never questioned when I grew up in Wakefield, Nebraska, I still cherish a couple of things I learned there. One of those values is that no person is superior to another. We have all been given gifts—different gifts to be sure—and we have all used those gifts in different ways, but I abhor the idea that some people are superior to others because they were born into a different world. Another value I embrace that is rooted in my rural upbringing is that we don't own this earth; we are stewards of it.

I struggled for years with religion. Then I found a church that says, "We don't do dogma." This church has only two rules: love God and love one another. That's very basic—but not so simple. I wrestled for years with trying to understand God, but I came to the realization that if there is a God, he or she would not be understandable by the human mind. Loving one another isn't always easy, but I have no tolerance for any religious group—like the Westboro Baptist Church with their "God hates fags" tag line—whose members project their own hate of others onto their interpretation of God.

A mentor who can help a man examine his values around sexuality, someone who is further along in that process, is invaluable. Many MSM have lived for years in a heterosexual world where they passed as straight. Sometimes they have had only a partial or conditional acceptance of being gay, and their commitment to their sexual orientation was surpassed by their commitment to values of a heteronormative society. Because they have lived in a straight world and concealed their sexual orientation for so long, by coming out they risk losing their straight friends while they still only have underdeveloped relationships with gay people. Because their self-esteem is so damaged, people who do not undergo an internal transformation of their homonegativism may isolate themselves to a greater and greater degree. Isolated men who experience sexual attraction to other men don't need more sex; what they need is an emotional hug from men in a compassionate and understanding community.

One man I corresponded with online, a married father and Muslim from Egypt, said he cries himself to sleep each night, wishing some kind of treatment could make him stop wanting to have sex with a man so that he could go on with loving his wife and two children without those intrusive thoughts. He had no support in his community, and explained, "I am afraid I will be killed if my attraction is exposed." This is not an unrealistic fear in many parts of the world—and even in the United States. He hungered for a connection with like-minded men, and his only link was via the Internet, but Internet relationships are often with other emotionally starved men. Frequently these connections focus on sex to the exclusion of emotional intimacy. It saddens me to hear the stories from so many desperately lonely men, but their sheer number makes it impossible for me to maintain a connection with all of them.

Isolated men who experience sexual attraction to other men don't need more sex; what they need is an emotional hug from men in a compassionate and understanding community.

Regrets

The most common regrets people face in midlife are related to education, career, romance, family, and negative attitudes and behaviors. We are forced to make all of life's most important decisions without enough information—information that we receive only as our lives unfold. We should not regret a decision that we made in good faith, with the best information available at the time, even when we later receive information that proves the decision wrong. The decision about coming out can be just like that. Although few regret it, no one can know if the people they love will accept them. But not making a decision is a decision in itself—one that bears its own unpredictable consequences.

One man divorced his wife after he came out to her. Then he came out to his family, his friends, and his coworkers, but as a middle-aged man, a new gay life didn't immediately embrace him as he had anticipated, and he became quite depressed. He went to see his minister, who said the solution was to remarry his wife, and he did. He was no longer as depressed, but he was miserable living a pretense of a heterosexual life.

Some things we sacrifice with regret, some with relief. I do not regret the decision to leave my wife; I believed then—as I do now—that the consequences would have been worse for everyone if I had stayed. What I do regret is that I caused people I love so much pain.

Midlife: A Time to Grow

As we mature, we can begin to perceive that with loss comes an opportunity for personal growth, and failure to adapt to loss may lead to bigger losses. Our losses can strengthen us, and the losses experienced by people we love strengthen our capacity for compassion and empathy for others. We learn to accept that love and risk are inseparable. We finally realize that it is safe to openly express our pain and sorrow. We seek to age well, to be vibrant, well-adjusted, and involved in sexually intimate relationships.

In midlife, issues that once divided families can diminish in importance and be reconciled. A family of choice can be blended to include members of a family of origin. We are even able to reconcile with deceased family members with whom relationships were strained; we can learn to forgive them for some of the mistakes they made during their lives. As we mature in midlife, we can see the issues that our parents faced in midlife from a fresh vantage point. As Philip Larkin wrote in the poem "This Be the Verse,"

> They fuck you up, your mum and dad.
> They may not mean to, but they do.
> They fill you with the faults they had
> And add some extra, just for you.[9]

At some point in our lives we must stop blaming our parents for our failures. If we blame our parents for our failures, don't we also then have to give them the credit for our successes? We must also begin to accept that some of our choices have negatively affected our own children, too. But at some point we must stop blaming ourselves for that. Maturity allows us that freedom.

Each of us must direct our own development through midlife. The first step in helping a mature man in the coming out process is to help him understand his history in a new way, to help him understand decisions and choices he's made in the past. The process of development for gay men does not end with coming out, and as we age we must incorporate positive attitudes about aging. For a man to deal well with midlife, he must develop good relationships with others. He needs peers with whom he feels equal but from whom he also feels separate. He needs friends who accept and respect his individuality and are not just connected based on common activities or similarities. Maturity is a process of individuation, where a person changes in relationship to himself and to the world.

The formula for self-esteem is having confidence in what we think and feel and responding to our own perceptions in a positive way. We can move out from behind the mask of concealment and speak with our own voices, with confidence that our opinions, thoughts, and feelings are valid and worthwhile. We can stop living according to the expectations of others. To do so, we must observe and trust our own perceptions and develop our own vision for the future.

10

Accidental Sex: Never Pass Up a Hard-On

God gave men both a penis and a brain,
but unfortunately not enough blood supply
to run both at the same time.

—ROBIN WILLIAMS

When I was about sixty, I blew out my knee having sex. When I've told this story to groups, the looks I see in response suggest that the audience is thinking, "Man, I'd love to have sex like that!" I wish this story became more exciting but it doesn't. It was routine sex, the kind couples have after they have been together for a long time. Sex had grown predictable. It was Sunday-night-after-the-news sex. "I kinda want to but I have a full day tomorrow, so let's do it quickly." It was good sex, just not unusual or extraordinary. Let's face it: if I hadn't injured my knee, I wouldn't be writing about the sex at all. The most painful part of that experience, however, was recognizing that my body was becoming more fragile and vulnerable.

Shrinking time forces men who have passed the middle of their lives to take inventory. They begin to feel that not much time remains to catch up to where they might have expected to be by midlife. Social views, personal values, and ambitions evolve, and the focus changes from concern for self to concern for others. Men can no longer hide from the fact that they've made some bad choices and likely will do so again. The decision to come out in midlife causes others to accuse them of acting childishly, not dealing with reality, abandoning moral values, and most devastating of all, selfishly hurting their families. Some even shame these men for leaving the ones they love exposed and vulnerable. Helplessness, hopelessness, and a feeling of loss of control may lead to depression.

Victor Hugo said, "Forty is the old age of youth; fifty is the youth of old age." Is sixty, then, the midlife of old age? Developing pain in my arthritic right shoulder produced more of a crisis for me than coming out. I was hit with the emotional tsunami of being an old man. Old age began to dominate my thinking and influence everything I did. It resurrected my anxieties that had been dormant for many years about being fifteen years older than Doug. I tried Viagra, but it only made me feel as if my penis belonged to someone else; I had no pleasurable sexual sensation while using it. It helped me sustain an erection, but what's the point of an anesthetized erection? All I could think about was a body in decline. All around me I could hear doors of lost opportunities slamming shut, and I wasn't even sure that I wanted to open any of the few doors that were in front of me.

Attention to my minor medical problems precipitated an absorption in the other realities related to late life: fear of institutional living, financial insecurity, loss of family of origin and family of choice, lack of independence and mobility, and the possibility of discrimination in accessing social services and entitlements like Medicare. I have observed bizarre dynamics develop in families during times of grief, especially when families of origin and families of choice fight over end-of-life issues and inheritances. Although Doug and my family have always gotten along extremely well, I began to wonder how their grief following my death will alter their relationships and whether my family and our gay friends would be there to support Doug when I died.

As I pondered these things, I learned that the younger partner in a mixed generational gay couple in our social group was dying. Until I learned about their situation, I had never considered that I might be the one forced into the caregiving role. I could be the one left alone. Could I find the will and compassion to assume the role of Doug's care provider?

Was my love strong enough? Would I begin to resent him if his demands were very high?

The Hard Facts

Wrinkling and graying served as constant reminders that my body wasn't what it once was. The mature man begins to realize that he has fallen below earlier physical peaks of performance as his bodily powers decline. Aches and pains plague him and death asserts itself. Although fortunately I have never felt as old as my birth date tells me I truly am, situations remind me with increasing frequency that I am growing older. Once Doug and I were buying tickets for a movie, and the attendant very diplomatically asked, "Will either of you require the senior discount?" For a long time, I resisted accepting those discounts. Midlife punishes us for youthful indiscretions, and the punishments just keep coming.

As one ages, each physical problem cascades into a series of physical deteriorations. As an old injury to my shoulder grew more and more arthritic, I began to have more and more pain and an increasing loss of range of motion of my dominant right arm. Doug had to assist me to get my belt through the back loops of my trousers, and I had difficulty with those most intimate elements of personal hygiene. I learned to compensate for these problems, but one problem seemed to have no redress: during sexual activity, I would have pain.

Men who are seeking long-term relationships occasionally question how soon to introduce sex into a relationship. No answer is universally correct. Many gay relationships, both romantic and platonic, have been established following a casual sexual encounter. Doug and I spent the first night we met together, and we have spent almost every night together in the nearly thirty years since we met. Gay couples sometimes have difficulty in deciding what night to set as their anniversary. Doug once said, tongue in cheek, that gay couples should mark their anniversary as the second night they sleep together;

Midlife punishes us for youthful indiscretions, and the punishments just keep coming.

the first night is a hookup, but the second is the beginning of a new relationship.

After a couple has been together several years, sexual excitement ebbs. By then every new technique will have either been tried, or at a minimum, suggested. I don't mean to imply that sex is reduced to monotony, but as couples become more and more familiar with each other, sex doesn't hold many surprises. The dopamine rushes don't match those when the relationship was young. Sexual frequency declines as the length of the relationship extends. Whether gay or straight, the more time partners share a sexual relationship, the more perfunctory it can become.

Dan Ariely, who wrote *The Upside of Irrationality: The Unexpected Benefits of Defying Logic at Work and at Home,* addresses the issue of *emotional leveling.* He describes how pleasure can deviate in either a positive or negative direction from the baseline, but over time it always returns to the baseline.[1] About three months after I'd purchased my most recent new car, I began throwing empty Diet Coke cans in the backseat, just like I did with the old car. Neither the excitement of new romance nor the painful consequences of a broken relationship endure forever. The inability to accept the emotional leveling in relationships condemns a person to always chasing the high that comes with the next new man only to be disappointed when the high once again doesn't last.

Like a stone thrown into a pond, the effects of my knee injury rippled far beyond the point where it broke the surface. My body was aging. I thought about sex less frequently, and sometimes when I thought about sex, I tried to dismiss it. When there was a choice between sleep and sex, I opted for sleep. I had more difficulty achieving and maintaining an erection, and when I lost an erection during sex, I felt defeated and beat myself up about it severely. I became dissatisfied not only with my sex life but my life in general. According to a 2008 study by Carmita Abdo and her colleagues published in the *Journal of Sexual Medicine,* erectile dysfunction and reduced sexual satisfaction are linked to lower life satisfaction and a compromised quality of life. Sexual dysfunction lowers self-esteem and can lead to depression, anxiety, anger, and shame. It also results in obsessive concerns about performance.[2]

Scientists neglect the study of human sexuality. Funding isn't available, and subjects who will speak openly about their sexuality are difficult to find. We know very little about some of the fundamental questions related to sexual desire and arousal and how desire affects judgment. The origins of sexual identity are heatedly debated, and studies of homoerotic arousal, desire, and sexual activity make some people green around the gills. In particular, we know almost nothing about why people who understand sexual risks choose to act in ways that are potentially destructive. Freud and Kinsey both hypothesized that sex is a universal drive, and now neuroimaging has substantiated an anatomical location for that drive. But can science really answer the questions of who we are and why we do the things we do?

Sexuality exceeds the boundaries of a universal biological drive; cultural forces shape it, socialization modifies it, and environmental influences impact it. Ariely wrote, "In the same way that the chemical composition of broccoli or pecan pie is not going to help us better understand what the real thing tastes like, breaking people up into their individual attributes is not very helpful in figuring out what it might be like to spend time or live with them."[3]

Late-Blooming Boomers

Back in the days before reliable birth control existed, abstinence was promoted for all adolescents, as well as for adults, as a means to limit family size. When I was young, we were admonished, "Don't go getting some girl pregnant you would never want to be the mother of your children. Your life will be miserable." Abstinence-only programs became a political centerpiece during President George W. Bush's administration from 2001–2009 when funding for these programs tripled. Teens were asked to take an abstinence pledge, but from that expensive experiment we learned that despite such programs, teens were not only just as likely to have intercourse but ultimately were more likely to take part in sex without condoms, and rates of teen pregnancy and STDs increased.

While I was in medical school, the contraceptive pill was introduced, and women were finally released to have sex for pleasure, too. Now I had no reason to hold back, but in reality, I lost one more excuse for avoiding sex with women. For the first time, at age twenty-three, I began having sex with a woman. I struggled with putting on that first condom, thinking I should have practiced ahead of time. Real men should know how to condomize a penis.

As I was writing this chapter on sexuality, in the back of my mind were the accusations made by a young gay man. He had been quite harsh in his criticism, saying that it wasn't possible that I had no idea I was gay until I was forty. He went on to say that my marriage was a sham and that I had just been a hypocrite using my wife and kids to protect my secret. I began to wonder if he might have been right. I decided I needed to know from Lynn how she had experienced our sex life; basically I wanted to know if she felt I was totally present in our sexual relationship. I asked her if my lack of confidence about being a man was apparent to her during the years of our marriage. She responded, "When we were first married, we were both sexually inexperienced. I *know* you were an excellent lover." I was reassured that indeed we had loved each other—and in many ways we still do. She did not feel that I had used her to shield myself against the assaults from my own doubts. As my anxieties lifted, I could return to my writing.

As the Twig Is Bent

Men typically believe they know far more about their sexual functioning than they actually do, and they fail to admit when they don't know much. Drive, vigor, and performance form the core of men's sexuality. Society dictates that a man must always be ready, always be successful, and never leave a job half finished. A man fails with anything less. Although men learn the basics of sex experientially, they often do not understand some of the common explanations for failure and how their sexuality changes as they age. In order to understand sexual dysfunction, one must first grasp the fundamentals of normal sexual function. Four major domains constitute male sexual response: sex drive, erectile functioning, ejaculatory functioning, and general sexual satisfaction.

The Massachusetts Male Aging Study, a rare random sampling of ordinary men from a community in Massachusetts, studied a complex set of sexual variables, both physical (e.g., erections and masturbation) and emotional/cognitive (e.g., desires, fantasies, and satisfaction). The study, conducted from 1987 to 2004, found that older men reported lower erectile function, including less frequent erections, fewer morning erections, and trouble achieving and maintaining erections. The prevalence of erectile dysfunction (ED) increases with age, but ED is not an inevitable consequence of aging.[4]

Most of the age-related effects on drive, erections, and ejaculation begin past the age of fifty and increase over time. Although sexual function declines with age, sexual satisfaction often does not. Men do not seem to worry much about ejaculation, even though in older men ejaculation diminishes and sometimes may not occur at all during sexual activity. Men in their sixties reported levels of sexual satisfaction comparable to men in their forties.[5]

Aging brings on changes, but not necessarily for the worse. Body changes, hormonal changes, the need for medication, the onset of disability or illness, changes of sex partner, and changes in life respon-

Men in their sixties reported levels of sexual satisfaction comparable to men in their forties.

sibilities may all interfere with sexual function, but they do not eliminate sexual pleasure. In reporting on their work in *Sexuality across the Life Course*, John McKinlay and Henry Feldman cautioned that older men should not be held to a level of interest and performance more appropriate to younger men. Healthcare providers and therapists must be taught that older men are not only interested in sex but capable of having good sex. That said, goals must be set realistically.[6]

Many studies have shown that many men in their late seventies and eighties remain sexually active. For older men, frequency of sex diminishes, but when men learn that sensuality, touch, and emotional intimacy are all forms of sexual expression, they discover that sex can be satisfying and may even be better than it was when they were younger and equated good sex only with a powerful orgasm. The younger men I interviewed generally believed that older men emphasize emotional intimacy more than genital sex. They begin to cherish their relationships and put more time into them than younger men do. Although penetrating sex and ejaculation may become less frequent, kissing, caressing, and more prolonged sexual intimacy may contribute to greater sexual satisfaction and quality of life in old age. It may take a little longer to stoke the fire, but the flames may go higher.

For all men, sexual performance consists of a complex interaction of mood, health, thought, and physiological mechanisms. Sex drive is an innate force that motivates and impels a person toward sex partners and relationships. Often nudity, erotica, or the prospect of a willing partner facilitate the period of sexual excitement and provoke the thought "I need to have sex."

Sexual excitement taps into the memory banks of the amygdala and the hippocampus of the brain, producing arousal. If sex were purely a rational act, we would foresee all of the potential alternatives, analyze and calculate their value, and choose to respond in a way that maximizes our immediate and long-term interests. Instead, when these areas engage the prefrontal cortex to plan the appropriate response, our hormones often show an appalling lack of respect for the logic and reasoning of the prefrontal cortex.

As illustrated in figure 5, male sexual response includes five stages: excitement, plateau, climax, resolution, and refractory period. For the young male, progression through these stages often occurs rather quickly, and the resolution and refractory stages are often quite brief, leading to the possibility of multiple climaxes or ejaculations over a short period of time. As men age, the time it takes to progress through the stages extends and can be characterized by starts, stops, and even some reversals, and climax or ejaculation is not a guaranteed outcome.

During the excitement phase, a man experiences the sensation that his penis is beginning to swell. Physical touch to an erogenous area enhances arousal. Dopamine, the pleasure molecule, floods into the brain

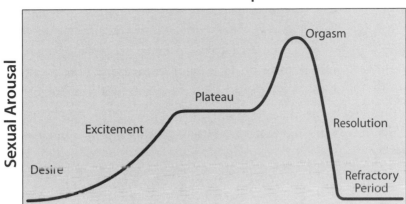

Figure 5: Diagram: Male sexual response

in anticipation of a pleasurable conclusion. As excitement intensifies and as prospects of success increase, the penis grows in size and firmness according to the degree of stimulation. Increased blood flow to the penis engorges the spongy tissue on the underside of the penis that contains the urethra, which leads from the bladder to the opening in the head of the penis. In response to touch and sometimes to arousal alone, the scrotum pulls the enlarging testicles toward the body. The tension of the muscles in the body increases, heart rate accelerates, and blood pressure rises.

During the plateau phase, the head of the penis continues to enlarge, and the testicles are drawn even closer to the body. A clear lubricating seminal fluid called preejaculate or precum begins to flow at varying rates from the head of the penis. A big price is paid for mechanical and indifferent sex because of a lack of dopamine buildup. Men who learn to prolong the plateau phase with extended periods of cuddling and body contact greatly increase their pleasure. At first, sexual pleasure does not insist on pushing one toward climax or orgasm, but similar to a tightening spring, the strength of the urge intensifies. Then, like a set mousetrap, the spring seeks to uncoil. This need to release the tension interferes with rational thought and has ensnared countless numbers of men.

As the plateau stage progresses, a man experiences a feeling deep within the pelvis that an orgasm is on its way and that ejaculation is inevitable, a feeling often celebrated with a verbal announcement. Almost immediately the genital muscles begin to contract, expelling semen with varying degrees of force through the urethra. During the resolution phase, blood leaves the penis in a process called detumescence. The penis shrinks to about half its erect size. Sexual activity concludes with a refractory period during which no amount of stimulation can produce an erection.

Aging modifies these stages. In adolescence, young men are in a perpetual state of excitement with an almost petrified erection. A young man might walk around most of the day with an erection, even when its evidence is quite embarrassing. As men mature, the excitement phase is longer and less intense; it generally requires richer fantasies and a higher degree of direct stimulation to the genital area. Unfortunately, the excitement phase is also more easily interrupted. One comedian joked that his wife wanted to have sex every day for thirty days to try to get pregnant. He responded, "I'm thirty-nine years old. The only way I could have sex thirty times in thirty days would be with thirty different women."

An older man, if distracted during the excitement phase, may lose some or all of his erection several times, only to regain it if he once again experiences a renewed sense of sexual excitement. Often, however, loss of an erection replaces excitement with despair. For an older man, orgasms shorten and they lack youthful insistence. Expulsive force and volume of seminal fluid decrease with age, and detumescence occurs more quickly. The refractory period, during which no erection can occur, lasts longer.

Fatigue, work, depression, finances, and illness also undermine excitement. Although at first I didn't recognize it, pain from my torn meniscus should have been only a temporary distraction. Instead, fears about failure displaced all sense of pleasure. My focus shifted from pleasure to ruminating about my performance failure.

The Blue Magic Bullet

Erectile difficulty happens to every man. Impotence is the persistent inability to get and hold an erection of adequate firmness to permit satisfactory sexual performance in the absence of any significant psychological problems. Although the term *impotence* remains in use outside of the United States, in America in the 1990s it was deemed pejorative. It connoted weakness rather than just dysfunction. Men dread this indictment because it hints at a permanent loss of all masculine capabilities. After former US senator Bob Dole became the pitchman for the blue, diamond-shaped Viagra pill, *ED* generally replaced the term *impotence*. ED implies reversibility, and the term has attenuated the emotional significance of erectile difficulties.

Erectile dysfunction can occur at any age, but it is more common in men that are older. *Mild and moderate* erectile dysfunction affects approximately 10 percent of men per decade of life (i.e., 50 percent of men in their fifties, 60 percent of men in their sixties). By the age of seventy, about 15 percent of men have *complete* erectile dysfunction.[7] While a man who fails to have an erection more than 50 percent of the time carries a clinical diagnosis of ED, a man who fails to have an erection less than 20 percent of the time does not. ED occurs when something interferes with the reflex activation of the system that enhances blood flow to the penis. These interferences are often physical changes in the body, such as vascular insufficiency, neurological problems, diabetes, high blood pressure, lack of exercise, medications, hormonal changes, alcohol and drugs, and cigarette smoking. Psychological problems rather than physical ones account for about two thirds of sexual dysfunction. The negative impact of ED on quality of life is independent of its explanation.

Some reports suggest that ED occurs in as high as 90 percent of depressed people, most commonly expressed as a lack of interest in anything that once gave them pleasure. Unfortunately, many of the medications used to treat depression also reduce libido. Other psychological factors that impact libido include a lack of good sexual information, negative attitudes toward sexual expression, low levels of general happiness, and low self-esteem. The length and the quality of a relationship are also important psychological factors. Unresolved anger, especially if directed at the partner, can lead to significant problems with ED. People who are passive also suffer more problems. Some struggle with ED mostly because of the lack of an available partner.

I dislike the term *sexual performance* because it suggests that an audience is there to offer a standing ovation. The outcome of sexual performance should be pleasure rather than applause. Performance anxiety complicates sexual functioning significantly. Men who are preoccupied with performance to the exclusion of emotional intimacy may be devastated by the loss of an erection during sex. Social messages browbeat men into believing that real men don't fail at sex. When performance is the primary criterion

The outcome of sexual performance should be pleasure rather than applause.

for judging success of male sexual functioning, erectile failure generates considerable anxiety. Anxiety, acting like an antiaphrodisiac, further blocks the spontaneous flow of sexual thoughts and feelings.

Men sometimes refer to their penises as tools. This is not surprising because in male sexuality the emphasis is on instrumentality. Functional measures and frequency dominate social ideals of masculinity and count more than intimacy and the bonds of sexual connectedness. Memories of earlier failures replace excitement with anxiety, causing men to avoid sex and another possible failure. After having erectile failure, men frequently begin to perform sexual autopsies on their performance and pleasurable sexual interaction becomes virtually impossible. Have you ever been afraid you were about to run out of gas so you drove faster and faster to get to your destination? Speedy sex is a counterproductive strategy. Sexual performance anxiety is like putting the pedal to the metal. Many men, after they have that fleeting fear of losing their erection, force sex faster and faster, further compounding the problem. Unless this emotional ambush is resisted, it can lead to loss of self-esteem, relationship discord, and greater sexual dysfunction.

After I tore up my knee having sex, a complex set of factors blunted my sexual functioning. A lack of confidence in being a man formed the bedrock of my difficulties. I experienced both the physical changes of aging and a preoccupation with the meaning of those changes. My worries expanded beyond the boundaries of reality. Instead of recognizing that my erections could be restored, fear of failure set in immediately. I obsessively analyzed my failures. I focused solely on the difficulty with my physical performance to the exclusion of the joy of emotional intimacy. Everything I did propelled me toward failure.

Preoccupation with erectile functioning has not gone unnoticed by the health products industry. One young man, writing on a health blog about the blue Viagra pill, praised it as a wonder drug. He said that it has brought about a change in sexual morality and sexual behavior throughout the world: "This isn't just another drug; it's the magic bullet we've been waiting for." Following its introduction, the brand name, Viagra, immediately became part of our sexual lexicon.

Viagra was a drug marketer's dream. With its promise to allow men to have sex anywhere, anytime, and with anyone, the use of Viagra exploded. With the iconic image of the Marlboro man fixed in our brains, men began to use the blue magic bullet not only for ED but to guarantee a world-class erection every time. The promotion of sexual enhancement products burgeoned as the pharmaceutical industry played upon our fears. Pharmaceutical companies added Cialis and Levitra to the formularies. The Food and Drug Administration mandated that product information contain a precaution about priapism, a continuous and painful erection. Priapism may seem like the answer to men's prayers, albeit not to those who have experienced it. Clever marketing converted what is seen as one of the risks of these products to an apparent strength. Men began to hope they might be the one to have an erection that lasted three hours and fifty-nine minutes. As use of Viagra expanded beyond ED to sexual enhancement, some men have conditioned themselves to believe they cannot have an acceptable erection without it.

The Renaissance Man

All gay men think and talk about is sex, or so some believe. Although we struggle to shed that stereotype, in some ways sex does define us. We are each quite unique, but we do have one thing in common: we want to have sex with someone of our own gender. Older men who are just beginning to explore man-on-man sex may experience sexual excitement much as they did in their adolescence and to a much greater degree than they did in their familiar heterosexual relationships. After I accepted my being gay, I experienced sexuality in a new and exciting way. I thought of sex constantly, and I began to feel as sexual as I did when I was a teenager. I was eager to make up for lost time. For men of all ages who come out, sexuality overshadows everything as they experience what has been referred to as a coming out crash. The penis is turned on autopilot as hormones erase all rational thought. In his role as Edward Cole in *The Bucket List*, Jack Nicholson advised older men of three things: "Never pass up a bathroom. Never pass up a hard-on. Never trust a fart."[8] Older men know precisely what he meant.

When I met Roberto, I had been married for sixteen years. Although my wife and I had a good sexual relationship, by then nothing surprised us. Aldous Huxley is quoted as saying, "Habit converts luxurious enjoyments into dull and daily necessities." Through the process of emotional leveling, the excitement of any new relationship returns to baseline. My relationship with Roberto was an entirely new sexual experience, with passion and intensity, but after my sexual relationship with Roberto I established an entirely new baseline.

The Antiaging Tonic

Popular culture equates testosterone with virility and a macho male physique. A doctor speaking at a medical conference I attended hyped testosterone replacement therapy (TRT) as "the amazing, medically proven" way to reverse aging. He promised that it would revitalize sexuality, strength, and stamina. He assured us that we would lose weight and gain muscle mass, and our memory and mental focus would improve. Apparently, TRT guarantees us that we will all bathe in the fountain of youth in the twenty-first century. But growth in its reputation and its increased use has outstripped scientific evidence of its potential benefits and risks.

Testosterone, sometimes referred to as androgen, is a hormone produced in large amounts in the testicles (testes), with smaller amounts produced in the distant adrenal glands. As anyone who has been an adolescent boy knows, production peaks in the teens and early twenties. Men don't run out of testosterone, but it does decline with age. Levels of testosterone continue to remain high between ages twenty and thirty, but somewhere around age thirty-five, levels begin to decline and continue to slide as we age. Diseases like diabetes and liver disease, chronic alcohol use, and some cancer treatments also reduce testosterone levels. Symptoms attributed to testosterone deficiency include decreased sexual function, lower vitality, loss of muscle mass and strength, increased fat, depression, anemia, and cardiovascular disease. These symptoms, however, can occur with normal levels of testosterone, and in some cases the symptoms may not occur even when testosterone levels are low.

Dr. Abraham Morgentaler, in his book *Testosterone for Life: Recharge Your Vitality, Sex Drive, Muscle Mass, and Overall Health*, writes, "Testosterone is critical, not only for how the brain responds to sexual thoughts and stimulation, but also for the proper function of the penis, by affecting its ability to get hard, to release the necessary chemical signals, and to maintain the proper types of cells that are essential for good erectile function."[9] Symptoms of testosterone deficiency include decreased sexual function, lower vitality, loss of muscle mass and strength, increased fat mass, and mood changes and depression. The possibility that TRT might be an antiaging tonic appeals particularly to older men, whose sexual functioning sags along with their muscles and energy.

Doctors debate the topic of male menopause. I don't like the term because the physiological changes that occur for men are distinctly different than they are for women. In women, menopause occurs when hormone production stops completely, ending their period of fertility. For men, hormone production falls, but it does not stop. Testosterone helps maintain sex drive and sperm production, but most men are capable of impregnating well into late life.

When we think about the characteristics of testosterone, we usually think about its sexual power rather than its potential impact on mental processes, but all of our body's attributes change with age. Unfortunately, mental functions are no exception. We can learn new truths; it just takes a little longer. New information is processed less carefully and details often slip away. Memory is the most fragile of mental functioning, and testosterone and memory begin their decline at about the same time.

In my sixth decade, I was hit by an emotional tsunami. The decline in my sexual performance resurrected all of my earlier fears about an unfinished masculinity. Men fix machines and they don't fail at sex, and worrying about failing at sex just about guaranteed that I would. I had never experienced a significant loss of sexual interest or satisfaction. Then I remembered the presentation on testosterone and began to consider that lowered testosterone levels might account for some of the problems I was having. My doctor ordered tests for testosterone level, thyroid function, and prostate specific antigen, which most men know of as PSA. After warning me of the risks, which include sleep apnea, acne, enlargement of the prostate, growth of any existing prostate cancer, testicle shrinkage, deep vein blood clots, breast enlargement, and possibly an increased risk of heart disease, my doctor recommend TRT. Remembering Jack Nicholson's advice about never passing up a hard-on, I readily agreed.

In many cases TRT helps relieve the symptoms of testosterone decline, whether it comes from aging or other causes, but it remains unclear whether or not restoring testosterone to youthful levels is of benefit. The primary impact of TRT on sexual function is related to increased sexual drive. Having more interest in sex has the added benefit of restoring some lost confidence in sexual functioning. A few studies have found some connection between higher testosterone levels and better performance on cognitive tests. Therapy can restore testosterone levels without improving the symptoms attributed to testosterone decline.

TRT can be administered through injections, patches, or a gel that is spread on the skin. One of the most effective forms of treatment is injection of long-acting testosterone pellets under the skin of the buttocks, but injections are inconvenient, and therapeutic levels and symptom relief may fluctuate between the injections. Patches are applied nightly. The gel in rubbed onto the skin of the abdomen, chest, arms, and shoulders. The gel is less irritating than the patches, but the TRT agent can be transferred through skin-to-skin contact to a sexual partner or even to a pet.

I opted for the TRT gel, and almost immediately I began to feel some improvement. How much of my response was placebo and how much was an effect of the TRT is hard to say. I knew that something convincing was happening. I thought more about sex, I was more successful at it, and the success restored my confidence. Even my aches and pains became more of a nuisance than a barrier to sex. I began to believe I could ride out the tsunami.

Just as Viagra is not a magic bullet, TRT is not the gunpowder for the problems of aging. Lifestyle changes that focus on diet and exercise must accompany TRT. When sexual dysfunction is primarily related to psychological factors, counseling may be required and in some cases antidepressants may be prescribed.

An entire industry has developed around TRT, but it will never return you to your sexual prime. TRT may cost several hundred dollars a month, and it may not be covered by all insurance plans. Claims for feeling sexier, stronger, and healthier are exaggerated, but claims about reversing low energy and improving muscle strength and libido have been proven. Improvement in sexual confidence creates an improved mood and a sense of well-being, which contributes to better sexual performance. TRT didn't fix my aging body, but awakening with morning wood still brings a smile to my face.

Thin Slicing

In a *New York Times* article, Benedict Carey wrote, "The nation that invented Viagra and 'Sex in the City' is still queasy about exploring sexual desire and arousal, even when this knowledge is central to protecting the public's health.... researchers say they still know precious little about fundamental questions, including how sexual desire affects judgment, how young people develop a sexual identity, why so many people take sexual risks, how personality and mood affect sexual health and how the explosion of sexual material on the Internet and trysts arranged online affect behavior."[10] Research on the subject of why people are attracted to a particular type of individual, however, has reached a consensus about a few things:

- Physical attractiveness is important for friendship, marriage, and financial success.

- Attractiveness begins at a very young age.

- Younger people are more attractive than older people.

- Age has a greater impact on women than men and a greater impact on gay men than straight men.

Even as we discover more about the biology of the brain, the concept of the unconscious is experiencing a renaissance. As Malcolm Gladwell suggests in *Blink: The Power of Thinking Without Thinking*, we always believe more data will lead to better decisions, but excessive analysis paralyzes us. We undervalue decisions based on feelings. Gladwell states that the unconscious finds patterns in situations and behaviors based on little information, something he calls "thin slicing." The unconscious leaps to conclusions much like a computer that processes a great deal of data quickly. Gladwell believes decisions made very quickly can be every bit as good as decisions made cautiously and deliberately.[11]

Most animals choose their mates in a nonrandom fashion through what is called assortative mating. Some animals favor mates with certain characteristics, such as traits that they possess themselves or, alternatively, traits they feel they lack. In this process, they reduce their field of selection of potential mates. Similarly, whether in a gay bar or Internet chat room, a gay man will scan his environment. Within a few seconds, he will unconsciously sort through all available men, narrowing his choices into his short list of prospects—without ever realizing he has been engaged in a selection process.

To impress a potential mate, male animals spread their feathers or puff up their chests to appear to be the strongest, most masculine, and most attractive they can be. In their mating rituals, men also exaggerate their virtues and minimize their weaknesses and vulnerabilities. They deceive others about those things that they feel make them unattractive. For gay men, cruising for casual sex frequently focuses on something sexually explicit such as a hand that lies on the crotch, moving ever so slightly. When the pursued man responds in a sexual way, sexual arousal is heightened. The interaction progressively focuses more and more on sex, dislocating any rational thought. Any search for information about who the two are as individuals is ignored. Those who are searching for a relationship that is more than just sex may be left feeling a little empty.

On a business trip to Washington DC, I left an O Street male strip club late at night to return to my hotel. A younger man who had left a little before me walked in the opposite direction. He looked over his shoulder at me, sensing that I was looking back at him. He walked a few more paces, stopped, and looked back at me again. I was still watching him. He then leaned against a car, lit a cigarette, and continued to look in my direction. In this brief nonverbal mating dance, we had communicated just enough.

Men with Rounded Corners

I am fifteen years older than my husband, Doug, but we rarely talk about it. When we first began seeing each other nearly thirty years ago, I felt insecure about the age difference, and I was quite certain that he would sooner or later dump me for a man closer to his own age. One day I mentioned my concerns to him, and he replied, "I've always been attracted to older men." At first I had trouble believing that, but I dismissed my concerns and we didn't talk about it, at least until I approached retirement.

My growing older seemed to expand the age difference because as my body sagged and wrinkled, I saw myself as increasingly undesirable.

Dormant and patched-over fears of abandonment crept back into my mind. Would Doug jump ship for a younger man? If I became physically unable to be his lover, would he find what genteel folks call a friend with benefits but what gay men often call a fuck buddy? Would his loyalty then shift to this new playmate? If my future includes needing a level of care that I cannot reciprocate, will he begin to resent me? When I retire, can he find a decent job in his midfifties?

I had always wanted to make sure he will be financially secure when I die. Then one day I was struck by the thought *What if he dies first? Am I prepared to live my life alone as an old man?*

In *The Upside of Irrationality: The Unexpected Benefits of Defying Logic at Work and at Home*, Dan Ariely writes, "To a large degree, beautiful people date other beautiful people, and 'aesthetically challenged' individuals date others like them." He goes on: "In terms of what they were looking for in a romantic partner, those who were more attractive cared more about attractiveness, while the less attractive people cared more about other characteristics (intelligence, sense of humor, and kindness).... The aesthetically challenged people were much more interested in going on another date with those they thought had a sense of humor or some other nonphysical characteristic, while the attractive people were much more likely to want to go on a date with someone they evaluated as good-looking."[12]

But Ariely's comments suggest that there is some universal definition of what constitutes a beautiful person. When I was in my midsixties, feeling old and fat, I was walking down the sidewalk in my swimsuit at a gay resort. Coming toward me was a man, probably in his midforties, who I thought was beautiful. As we met, he stopped, touched his index finger beneath my chin, slid his finger all the way down to the base of my happy trail, and said, "Delicious." Without any further conversation, we both kept walking in the opposite directions.

In that instant on the sidewalk, I began to understand that each of us has our own internalized idea of what makes someone delicious, what constitutes a beautiful person. He found beauty in my aging body with its sags and wrinkles, my white hair and protruding belly, while I found beauty in his youth, his masculinity, and his vigor. While I was feeling "aesthetically challenged," he did not see me as I saw myself; what I saw as a weakness, he saw as a strength. Ariely did admit that his observations had significant exceptions, and he added this disclaimer: "We are also a scent, a sparkle of the eye, a sweep of the hand, the sound of a laugh, and the knit of a brow—ineffable qualities that can't easily be captured in a database."

Intergenerational relationships (IGRs) are relationships between two people where the younger person is above the age of consent and where the older person is at least fifteen to twenty years older than the younger person. In writing the first edition of this book, I could not find any meaningful statistics about how often IGRs occur in relationships of gay men nor could I find any significant research on the nature of IGRs. Most in the straight world don't know gay IGRs exist, and many in the gay community don't understand them and even look upon them suspiciously.

Although I am now married to a man fifteen years younger than me, I had difficulty understanding IGRs. Why would a hard-bodied young man whose appearance approached that of the idealized gay man find himself physically attracted to someone who looks like Dick Cheney, politics aside? A young man I corresponded with said, "I am going through a kind of second coming out and have started psychoanalysis in order to understand my patterns of relationships and my choice of partners, who are always much older than me." Psychoanalysis is unlikely to reveal the answer.

We demand an explanation from these younger men who are drawn to older men, but why does it matter? Older men are rarely asked to defend their choice of a younger man. The older man has chosen up; the younger man chose down. The fact is that research hasn't determined why we are drawn to the people we're attracted to, and most likely, the explanations are very complex.

After speaking to a group of gay men, one tall, lean, and handsome young man told me about his sexual attractions. He said he is only attracted to heavier men with big bellies and hairy chests. Unconscious forces operating in his brain thin slice his sexual attractions to include only older men with mature bodies; younger men hold no appeal. When I asked another young man about his attraction to older men, he replied, "I like older men because they have all of their corners rounded off." It brought to my mind a class I'd taken on antiques. The instructor said that buying old furniture is a better investment than buying new furniture. "With new furniture, you hate to get it scratched, and its value goes down. But a mark on an old piece of furniture just adds more character."

When I was writing my blog, *MagneticFire*, it seemed as if, almost daily, younger men asked me, "Why do I find myself only attracted to men who are much older than I am?" Many of these young men don't understand their attraction and often feel backed into a corner to defend their choice.

"I like older men because they have all of their corners rounded off."

Frequently they have looked for an answer in their relationship with their father or their grandfather, just as I had done for an explanation of my attraction to men. Sometimes they say, "My relationship with my father [or grandfather] was so wonderful; I just want to try to recreate that with a partner." At other times, they say, "I had no relationship with a father figure, and I think my attraction to older men is to fill that void." When two contradictory hypotheses attempt to explain the same phenomenon, neither hypothesis is likely to be true. Explaining this attraction on the basis of their relationship with their fathers or grandfathers is far too simplistic.

Family and friends of men in IGRs may confront them with their belief that this relationship cannot be based on love but must be based on other motivations. Often these younger men protest, "I am fully capable of taking care of myself. I don't need a sugar daddy." As I talked with these young men, I repeatedly heard things like, "I don't need stuff! I want more than an orgasm. I want a relationship with someone who is sensitive, caring, and romantic—self-assured and satisfied with his life." They want relationships based on emotions rather than material things, something they feel they can only find with a mature man. One of my gay friends is in a relationship with a man who is forty years older than he is, and he's tired of defending his relationship. Although his family has come to accept their relationship, his gay friends are the most critical. One of his friends asked him, "What does a young, good-looking guy like you see in an old man who is well past his expiration date?"

Each of us has a chronological age, but we also have a physical age, a sexual age, and a psychological age. Older men who are attracted to younger men can't explain their choice either, although they often say that they feel much younger than their chronological age and emotionally in sync with the younger man. If an older man is attracted to a masculine man with ripped muscles, it's reasonable to assume that he would find it difficult to believe the claim that a muscular young man finds his too-fat, too-short, too-wrinkled body attractive. Some older men, loathing the impact of aging, resist the idea that younger men will find them attractive even to the point of being suspicious of the younger man's motives. One commented, "I do not need to raise another son. I don't need a helpless kid to protect." Other older men express fears of abandonment because they may be unable to satisfy the younger man's greater sexual appetites.

Each of us has a chronological age, but we also have a physical age, a sexual age, and a psychological age.

All stereotypes have validity for some but not all. While some young men may be seeking a sugar daddy, and some older men may wish for an Adonis-like trophy, often people mistakenly assume that all IGRs are based on one partner's exploitation of the other. What both the younger man and older man fail to recognize is that their own physical and psychological attributes may be exactly what will show up in the other's thin slices.

Almost all of the younger men I interviewed said they had never been attracted to men of their own age. One young gay man I interviewed explained, "All those guys who are under sixty years old might as well have vaginas because I have no interest in them." Another older man who had always been attracted to men older than he is said, "As I've grown older, the men I am attracted to are also older. Soon I will have no place to cruise but in a nursing home."

Young men describe older men they find physically attractive as lovely, gorgeous, possessing raw beauty, representing manliness, or more simply, "They just make me horny." For younger MSM who are attracted to older men, a big belly symbolizes sexuality in the same way that large breasts symbolize sexuality for some young heterosexual men. The younger men often respond, however, that they find other essential characteristics of the relationship to be even more important than sexual compatibility, and the words *wisdom* and life *experience* come up frequently.

Older men are sometimes described as daddies, a word that connotes the qualities of maturity, stability, and emotional safety. Daddies are seen as nonthreatening, while the sharp edges of their contemporaries are more menacing. When someone first referred to me as a daddy, I became very uncomfortable. I have two daughters who now call me Dad, but when they were young they called me Daddy. Using the word *daddy* in an erotic context seemed somewhat perverse. As my understanding of IGRs grew, I began to see the word *daddy* as a kind of metaphor for a wise and experienced man with white hair and rounded features. Later I learned that heterosexual couples also sometimes used *daddy* in an eroticized way. Although referring to a sexual partner as daddy makes some people uncomfortable, it is a term of endearment rather than suggestive of some deeply Freudian maladjustment.

We project our own attractions and expectations onto a prospective mate, expecting that the things they love and cherish are exactly the same as our own. If an aging man hates the changes in his body, he expects that any potential partner would abhor them just as much. If his sexual drive and potency have diminished, he may not trust that the younger man will find his interest in slow and sensual lovemaking desirable. Why would anyone want a fat and indolent man on a sexual decline?

In *Archives of Sexual Behavior*, Michael Seto writes, "We have an incomplete understanding of how human sexuality is oriented if we focus only on gender as the important dimension. . . . Age is important as well." Seto uses the term *chronophilia* to describe sexual attraction that targets specific age groups. He notes, however, that in addressing age, he is not talking only about chronological but also sexual and physical maturity. Sexual attraction is drawn from a person's level of sexual maturity, body size and shape, secondary sexual characteristics, and other visible features like gray or white hair, but Seto also includes psychological features that emphasize wisdom, maturity, and experience. Seto broadens the definition of sexual orientation to include age.[13]

What happens in our heads and how we behave are often not in alignment, but pornography provides a window into our culture's collective minds. Most porn is accessed through the Internet and is accessible to almost everyone, including those who might not otherwise be able to explore their erotic interests. Since my research has been skewed in the direction of exploring IGRs, I began to wonder just how common age might be a part of sexual orientation. Although not much is known about IGRs, gay or straight, I did a Google search for the rather crude but quite specific "DILF," defined in the Urban Dictionary as "Dad I'd like to fuck," with synonyms such as "who's your daddy?," "cradle robber," and "your friend's dad."[14] Within moments I had over 1.4 million references. Tumblr, a microblogging and social networking website, has an entire section devoted to DILF, and a search of "Silver Daddies," a popular chat site for MSM with intergenerational erotic interests found over 154,000 profiles. These sites cross geographic and cultural boundaries. For a topic of such broad popular interest, it is surprising how little we know about IGRs.

When we think of sexual orientation, we usually think of the continuum of gay, straight, and bisexual, but sexual orientation is a deep-seated attraction toward a certain kind of person. Erotic desire includes attention, attraction, fantasy, thoughts, urges, genital arousal, and behavior. Variations of sexual desire like dominance and submission, sadism and masochism, chubbies and chubby chasers, and bears and cubs complicate the idea of sexual orientation. Sexual desire may also include fetishes that extend from toes and noses to jocks and socks. These desires may manifest at different times and in different ways, and our decision whether or not to act on them can be influenced by a lack of opportunity or permissibility. Not all sexual behaviors are legal or morally acceptable.

The most studied aspect of sexual orientation is gender, with age being the second most studied, but age has been studied almost exclusively in the context of pedophilia. Huge gaps exist in our knowledge of maturity as it relates to sexual orientation. In Seto's thorough review of age as a sexual orientation, he wrote, "I am not aware of any empirical research on individuals attracted to middle-age [or older] persons."[15] But my interviews with younger men attracted to older men absolutely confirm Seto's claim that the erotic aspects of aging include wisdom, maturity, and experience. A person's chronological age tells us very little about him.

Huge gaps exist in our knowledge of maturity as it relates to sexual orientation.

Humans have a powerful need to attach to a spouse, family, friends, pets, and even objects. Physiological and environmental cues drive us to interact socially. Paul J. Zak, in an article called "The Neurobiology of Trust," reported that the hormone oxytocin enhances an individual's propensity to trust a stranger when that person exhibits nonthreatening signals. Oxytocin has been dubbed the cuddle hormone. It promotes social interaction, bonding, and romantic love in addition to its key procreative functions such as uterine contractions and lactation. As oxytocin rises, anxiety over interacting with strangers is reduced. A safe, nurturing environment may stimulate the release of more oxytocin.[16] Since nurturing is a recurring theme in IGRs, could variable levels of oxytocin account for younger men's attraction to older men? We know so little about what drives sexual attraction.

So what is the relationship between sexual orientation and sexual identity? Sexual orientation is more fluid and multidimensional; sexual identity is narrower and more fixed, develops at an early age, and is more stable over time. How then can I say I have a gay identity if I didn't come out until age forty? How can young men attracted to older men incorporate that they are gay and attracted to older men? First of all, although we all have a fairly well-defined sexual orientation—defined in the broadest sense—we may choose to act outside of that orientation. My story and many stories of other mature MSM are about men who have chosen to act outside of how their erotic attractions are directed. When all of the elements of our sexuality come together and become fixed and stable over time, we develop our sexual identity. When I finally accepted that I am attracted to men, learned what kind of men I am attracted to, and knew what I liked and didn't like sexually, it was as if I had come home to a reality where I wanted to stay. But saying "I am gay" does not define all of who I am as a person, nor does it even define all of who I am sexually.

We obsessively analyze the reasons for our choices, emphasizing categorization rather than accepting the great diversity of same-sex attractions. Explanations for all the elements of our sexual attractions are complex and probably unknowable. All research runs the risk of reductionism. When it focuses on genital sexual activity alone without considering attraction, affection, and affiliation, it falls short in identifying our sexual orientation and our sexual identity.

In *Sexual Behavior in the Human Male*, Alfred Kinsey wrote:

> Males do not represent two discrete populations, heterosexual and homosexual. The world is not to be divided into sheep and goats. Not all things are black nor all things white. Nature rarely deals with discrete categories. Only the human mind invents categories and tries to force facts into separated pigeon-holes. The living world is a continuum in each and every one of its aspects. The sooner we learn this concerning human sexual behavior, the sooner we shall reach a sound understanding of the realities of sex.[17]

Emotions always accompany behavior. Concentrating exclusively on genital sex causes us to miss the real significance in relationships. Sex is a nice, momentary pleasure, but having someone who cares about you and is there to support you, even if it is just a close friendship, is much more valuable in any long-term view. One wise young man that I interviewed summed it up nicely when he said, "Don't question the whys. They will be answered in the growth of the relationship. Decisions will be made as we grow together or apart. He likes you, you like him, and you're both legal. Go for it. Life experience is the issue, not age."

11

The Urgency of Time: The Unbucket List

I am now face to face with dying, but I am not finished with living.
— OLIVER SACKS, *GRATITUDE*

Although our culture as it relates to the LGBTQ community began to evolve slowly following Stonewall, the rate of change has accelerated since the first edition of this book was published. In a hard-fought victory for the gay rights movement, on June 26, 2015, the United States Supreme Court ruled 5–4 that the Constitution guarantees the right to marry for all same-sex couples in all fifty states and that all states must recognize these unions wherever the marriages took place.[1] In an article in the *New York Times* on the day the decision was announced, Adam Liptak noted that Justice Anthony M. Kennedy, who wrote the majority opinion, stated, "No longer may this liberty be denied.... No union is more profound than marriage, for it embodies the highest ideals of love, fidelity, devotion, sacrifice and family. In forming a marital union, two people become something greater than once they were." Kennedy added that the plaintiffs in the case were seeking "equal dignity in the eyes of the law...The Constitution grants them that right."[2]

This ruling by the Supreme Court overturned the bans on same-sex marriage that were being passed by individual states with increasing frequency. The ruling was a bit anticlimactic in Iowa, as Raygun, Iowa's snarky T-shirt company, announced on one of its shirts, "26 June 2015:

America is now FINALLY as gay as Iowa." Iowa was the third state to legalize same-sex marriage by a unanimous and emphatic decision of the Iowa Supreme Court in April 2009, and by the time of the US Supreme Court ruling, Doug and I had already been married for six years. A sense of complacency had set in as people began to say things like "Now we have equal rights."

This complacency was fed by a series of decisions that had gone favorably for the LGBTQ community preceding the decision on marriage equality. On September 20, 2011, the United States military's Don't Ask, Don't Tell policy was removed, lifting the military's eighteen-year ban on openly gay and lesbian service personnel. As Dave Philipps noted in a *New York Times* article, as many as one hundred thousand service members were discharged for being gay between World War II and the 2011 repeal of Don't Ask, Don't Tell policy. Many were given less-than-honorable discharges barring them from veterans' benefits, costing them government jobs and other employment, and leaving many grappling with shame for decades.

According to Philipps, the United States military's punishment of homosexuality dates back to the Revolutionary War when historians report that General George Washington personally ordered that a young officer be dismissed.[3] Starting in World War II, the military treated homosexuality as a mental defect rather than a crime, but still purged gays with quick discharges. As a physician serving as a flight surgeon in the US Navy, I signed several of those discharge papers. During the time I was in the service, military investigators employed long interrogations and threats of public humiliation to coerce the service members to confess and name names.

When Don't Ask, Don't Tell was repealed, President Obama said, "As of today, patriotic Americans in uniform will no longer have to lie about who they are in order to serve the country they love ... Today, every American can be proud that we have taken another great step toward keeping our military the finest in the world and toward fulfilling our nation's founding ideals."[4]

Another major change preceded the decision on marriage equality by exactly two years when on June 26, 2013, the United States Supreme Court in *United States v. Windsor* struck down parts of the Defense of Marriage Act, giving full federal recognition of legally married gay couples. In addition, it turned away a case involving California's prohibition of same-sex marriage, known as Proposition 8, restoring the rights of same-sex couples to marry in California.

In the ten years preceding these decisions on marriage equality, public opinion had increasingly swung in support of marriage equality, more than doubling. Although the issue remains politically divisive, support for same-sex marriage has increased among all political stripes. As Justice Kennedy wrote in the court's opinion after *Obergefell v. Hodges*, "The nature of injustice is that we may not always see it in our own times."[5]

And Yet—

On Sunday morning, June 12, 2016, I woke up planning to spend the morning writing more about how much social progress has been made for the LGBTQ community in the forty-seven years since Stonewall. After I settled in with my coffee, I opened my laptop and read that a lone-wolf shooter had killed twenty young men and women during last call on Latin night at Pulse, a gay bar that was the epicenter of gay life in Orlando, Florida. As the day progressed, I was unable to concentrate on anything else as I watched the number of dead climb to forty-nine with fifty-three others wounded—the largest mass shooting in United States history, the deadliest attack on a gay target ever, and the worst act of terrorism on American soil since the World Trade Towers were brought down in New York City on September 11, 2001.[6]

The scene at Pulse was described as an unimaginable slaughter, many survivors lying in blood amidst their dead and dying friends, some feigning death for hours because they believed that if they moved they would surely be shot. During the night, the victims' families and friends helplessly received cell phone messages from those in the club who texted that they were about to die. The following morning those same friends and family members paced around in a daze waiting for the names of who was alive and who had not survived the deadly attack. Some parents first learned of their son's or daughter's sexual orientation when they learned that their child was present in the massacre at that gay nightclub.

Investigators reported the motive as undetermined, but in all likelihood a single cause can never explain something so complex, as President Obama suggested when he described it as "an act of terror and an act of hate."[7] Some jumped quickly to the familiar narrative that because the shooter patronized the bar previously—in fact, he had been in the bar earlier in the evening of the attack—and had posted selfies on gay dating sites, that this was a case of suicide-by-cops by a self-loathing, homophobic young man.[8] One question may never be satisfactorily answered: Had he been there as an ambivalent wannabe of the LGBTQ community, or was he just scoping it out for his planned attack? Could both be true? At the time of this writing, none of that is clear, and since the shooter died in the massacre, I believe the truth will never be known.

Many of the perpetrators of hate crimes against the LGBTQ community have a history of domestic violence, and parallel factors seem to drive hate crimes and domestic violence. The shooter in the massacre in Orlando showed evidence of preoccupation with sex and violence as early as the third grade.[9] Many mass killers are men who feel aggrieved by someone who has done them wrong either on a personal or on a political level. In domestic abuse the abuser seeks to control the victim's life through violence. This same dynamic of asserting control through provoking fear appears to apply on a grander scale in the hate crimes against LGBTQ people (not only in the United States but throughout the world) as the perpetrators attempt to restore traditional norms of heterosexual-male dominance.

Hate crimes against the LGBTQ community are depressingly familiar. On June 24, 1973, an arsonist splashed lighter fluid on the stairs of the UpStairs Lounge in New Orleans, set it on fire, and rang the doorbell. When someone answered the door, it detonated a conflagration inside the bar. The fire consumed the lives of thirty-two people. Some considered this tragedy a joke, and authorities, lacking motivation to solve the crime, poorly investigated the incident or ignored it altogether. No one was ever brought to justice.[10]

While attending the APA convention in New Orleans, I had visited a gay bar that had an upstairs lounge. Had I known about the earlier tragedy, I might have thought twice about climbing those stairs, and I definitely would have located the exits. For most of us, gay bars have been a sanctuary, and at the time I visited the bar in New Orleans I was just taking a peek out of the closet door. I saw gay bars as a safe place to have a trial run at being a gay man. For most of us these bars were judgment-free zones, safe places to shed our defenses. As an old man I have not always found them welcoming, but when I first entered those gay bars as a younger man, I had a feeling of coming home. I could shed the loneliness I had felt as I struggled to live the life of a straight man. Although I felt protected from a world that was often hostile to gay men and women, these places were not always safe.

Hate crimes in America target LGBTQ people more than anyone else. According to the Federal Bureau of Investigation in 2015, 18.6 percent of hate crimes against people were based on sexual orientation, plus an additional 1.8 percent based on gender identity, taking the number two spot behind racially based hate crimes.[11] These crimes are undoubtedly underreported because some fear outing themselves and some police departments don't classify them as hate crimes. The majority of hate crime victims are racially based, and it must be recognized that the Orlando massacre was also an attack not only on the LGBTQ community but on the Hispanic community as well.

Ignorance as a Weapon

Many in the LGBTQ community viewed *Obergefell v. Hodges*, which made marriage a right for gay men and women nationwide, as the crowning achievement in the struggle for LGBTQ civil rights. Although social evolution converted some wary politicians from opponents to allies of marriage equality, these cultural shifts radicalized others into becoming increasingly aggressive opponents of LGBTQ rights. As we gay people began to live more openly and proudly within a society that was beginning to accept us, our opponents felt more and more threatened and searched for new ways to oppose us. The pushback began immediately after the Supreme Court ruling on marriage equality under the cleverly chosen label of religious freedom, a term that does not lend itself to opposition—if you don't support laws under the rubric of religious freedom are you then by definition in favor of religious oppression? In the United States, we increasingly see every issue in terms of black and white, right or wrong; ambiguity and nuance don't exist.

Some civil authorities refused to issue marriage licenses to same-sex couples, invoking religious freedom and claiming that following the law ran counter to their religious beliefs; however, signs of a counter-pushback are emerging. US district judge Carlton Reeves ruled that clerks are required to provide equal treatment for all couples, gay or straight. Judge Reeves said, "Mississippi's elected officials may disagree with *Obergefell*, of course, and may express that disagreement as they see fit—by advocating for a constitutional amendment to overturn the decision, for example. But the marriage license issue will not be adjudicated anew after every legislative session."[12] The ruling establishes some precedent but applies only in Mississippi; individual states are expected to continue trying to pass laws based on religious freedom that resist issuing marriage licenses to gay couples.

In a *Washington Post* article, Everdeen Mason, Aaron Williams, and Kennedy Elliott write:

> While the lesbian, gay, bisexual, and transgender community has become more visible and won more legal protections in recent years, state lawmakers have increased attempts to pass legislation that could restrict civil rights for LGBTQ people. Since 2013, legislatures have introduced 254 bills, 20 of which became law. According to data collected by the American Civil Liberties Union and analyzed by the Washington Post, the number of bills introduced has increased steadily each year. In the first half

of 2016 alone, 87 bills that could limit LGBTQ rights have been introduced, a steep increase from previous years.[13]

According to ACLU data, legislation focusing on transgender people, particularly those known as bathroom bills, didn't appear until 2015, when four bills were introduced in state legislatures; by the middle of 2016, thirty such bills had been introduced in state legislatures.[14] North Carolina redoubled its fight against increasing LGBTQ legal protections when the state legislature hastily passed a bill limiting access to bathrooms to the gender listed on a birth certificate. Texas, along with several additional states, filed a lawsuit against the Obama administration after schools and colleges were told to allow transgender students to use the bathroom that matches their gender identity rather than their birth gender. Essentially claiming that you can't house wolves with rabbits, the states made the spurious claim that transgender men were potential rapists and child molesters. In 2015 more transgender people were killed than in any previous year, the majority being people of color.[15] The fact that laws were already on the books that protected against all of the predicted criminal behaviors demonstrates the purely political motivations of this legislation.

The exploitation of fears based on stereotypes and misinformation worked as a motivator to draw the conservative political base to the polls, but this exploitation did not begin with the US Supreme Court's decision about marriage equality; it only exacerbated it. Karl Rove, President George W. Bush's chief strategist, along with Ken Mehlman, the Republican National Committee chairman (who has since come out as gay), worked together with other Republicans to make sure that anti-gay initiatives appeared on ballots in 2004 and 2006.[16] These legislative issues were designed to stir up fear about God, gays, and guns and motivate social conservatives to vote. For decades the Republican party has used a "we'll protect you" narrative. Prior to President Bush's election in 2004, I was speaking with a family member who said, "I have to vote for Bush; I'm too afraid not to." The campaign's deliberate attempt to stir up his fear captured his vote, as it likely did for many others.

These tactics are operating once again in the 2016 presidential election cycle. Capitalizing on the politics of fear, James Dobson, an American evangelical Christian who founded Focus on the Family, wrote: "Would you remain passive after knowing that a strange-looking man, dressed like a woman, has been peering over toilet cubicles to watch your wife in a private moment?... If this had happened 100 years ago, someone might have been shot. Where is today's manhood? God help us!"[17]

In Orlando, smoldering bigotry, marginalization, denigration of minorities, and politicians bent upon scapegoating created a culture that collided with a national crisis of violence. Some preachers responded to the killings in Orlando by saying it was divine justice and the real tragedy was that more people didn't die. A Texas politician said, "God cannot be mocked. A man reaps what he sows."[18] People who sought to cling to white-heterosexual-male dominance tightened their grip by exploiting rather than extinguishing prejudice. The amount of hatred is jaw dropping and appears to be on the rise.

When ignorance becomes a weapon, violence tragically and inevitably follows. Violence appeals to those who feel that it is the only answer to their concerns about social issues. Evidence of this retaliatory violence was made apparent

When ignorance becomes a weapon, violence tragically and inevitably follows.

again on July 8, 2016, with the killing of five police officers in Dallas, Texas, converting a peaceful demonstration focused on violence committed by police into an act of bloodshed targeting them.[19] The mass shootings in Orlando and Dallas are only two in a series of violent events on a global level growing out of hate and hysteria in our political and cultural climate of violence.

I feel guilty for times in the past when I didn't speak up, when I rightly or wrongly thought that I risked too much; those are things I cannot change but from which I must learn. One of the advantages of age is that I have little to lose now and I have a perspective I could not have had when I was younger. Statistics don't change minds, but stories do. My coming out at age forty was spurred by the 1978 murder of Harvey Milk, who said, "Rights are won only by those who make their voices heard."[20] The killings in Orlando have inspired others to come out, just as the AIDS crisis did in the 1980s. It would be easy for me as a septuagenarian to say this is unmanageable; leave it to the next generation. I am tempted to put activism on my unbucket list. But as a septuagenarian I have an advantage. I can speak out without the fear of consequences I feared when I was a younger man. I don't have as much to lose. I may not have the answers, but I do have a voice.

Doffing My Hat to Don

Other advantages come with growing old. When I speak to groups about what I think I know, in the process I always learn so much that I didn't know, and I learned a lot from a man named Don. After the release of the first edition of *Finally Out*, I spoke to the Houston Prime Timers, a social group for gay and bisexual men, and after I finished Don raised his hands in the air and said, "I'm eighty-two, and this is the best time in my life." Don had been married to his deceased wife for thirty-eight years before he had the courage to step into a gay bar where he met the next great love of his life. Don was on the far side of his life, and yet his perspective was that his life was expanding rather than shrinking, while I, on the other hand, had been focusing on wrapping things up. When I met Don again about five years later, he still felt the same way. I began to wonder what Don knew that I needed to try to understand.

Death had been a reality to me ever since my father died when I was three years old and my grandfather shot himself when I was six, but I began thinking about death more seriously when I was thirteen years old. With the immaturity of early adolescence, I thought, Thirteen is an unlucky number; this will probably be my unlucky year. From the time my brother had an accident that left him paralyzed when I was nine years old, I held the idea that our bodies and minds are fragile and that we grasp life with a soft grip. As I turned thirty-two, the age of my father when he died, I wondered, "Is this my time, too?" Now in my eighth decade I can see that I had lived each moment as if I were dying instead of just living and enjoying each moment. Don's comment challenged me to ask myself, How can I make the most of whatever time remains?

What I had arrived at without realizing it was the concept of mindfulness, a significant element of some Buddhist traditions. Earlier in my life I had thought of Buddhism as donning a saffron robe, shaving my head, begging for alms, and living with other like-minded men in some mountainous Buddhist retreat. Mindfulness, however, is simply a state of active and open attention to the internal and external experiences of each moment of the present. It means living in the moment instead of worrying and ruminating about the past or the future.[21] Mindfulness tells me that instead of worrying about the deadline for finishing this chapter and the subsequent lengthy process of editing this second edition, wondering if the book will find an audience, and stressing about the reviews, I need to concentrate on the joy of discovering just the right word to complete a thought or finding a story or creative metaphor to illustrate a point.

William Faulkner said, "The past isn't dead; it isn't even past." In other words, our past is always with us. Throughout this book I have examined my history to understand how I got to where I am today, hoping that relating my experience might help others understand their own, and the feedback I received from those who read the earlier edition confirmed that to be true. But we can spend too much time examining our past—even using it as an excuse to explain away mistakes we're making in the present—because that history has already been written. I've often been asked if I regret not coming out sooner because I "missed all the fun of being young and gay," but I try to live my life without regret, believing that the decisions I've made were the best I could make with the information I had available to me at the time. Coming out later provided me with different opportunities to experience things I would not have if I had come out earlier in my life. My past is immutable; my future is unknowable. Why should I worry about them?

But we're confronted by a paradox: we remember our lives backward but must live our lives forward. The past is problematic because it is set, fixed in stone, immutable. We cannot change our past but only our relationship to it. The future is problematic, too. We can make plans for some of the contingencies of the future—and we should—but ultimately the outcome will be determined by fate; we can influence it but not control it. One of the concepts that comes from those recovering from addictions is to look at our lives in terms of manageables and unmanageables, a simple but not simplistic approach to sorting out what is or isn't worth worrying ourselves about. Our history is unmanageable, so why get stuck ruminating about it? Our intentions can influence the direction of our future but not control it; worrying about things over which we have no control is wasted energy.

The source of the following saying is debated, but its truth is not: "Pain is inevitable; suffering is optional." Pain is something that happens to us; it is out of our control, unmanageable. My father's death, my grandfather's suicide, my brother's injury, and the deaths of my mother and stepfather were painful but unmanageable. Suffering is how we choose to deal with those pains inflicted upon us. Pain is losing a relationship, being diagnosed with bipolar disorder, or realizing we're gay; suffering is failing to accept those truths. But many of us suffer unnecessarily when faced with pain. Life will always have pain, but we have choices, we can make changes, and we can take action.

I once met a married man who was struggling with his attraction to men. In considering coming out, he wondered, Am I moving from one life of regret to another life of regret? Those same doubts bore down on me as I considered my decision to come out. It was in 1980 near the beginning of the AIDS crisis, when little was known about HIV and when I was still unsure if it was even safe to shake hands with an HIV patient. The rational side of my brain told me what I needed to do, but the more irrational side flashed warning signs about what might lie ahead. Being gay is unmanageable; I didn't choose it. I could, however, choose to live authentically, to stop denying it.

My age is also unmanageable; no amount of Botox or Viagra is going to change the fact that I am seventy-three, almost seventy-four. I can choose to spend what remains of my life worrying about how it will end, or I can live the best way I can in the present moment. When I turned seventy-three I found myself rounding up rather than down, just as I did as a child: I'm going on seventy-four. When asked how long Doug and I have been together, I answer, "Almost thirty years," even though we are just beginning our twenty-ninth year together. One of us will inevitably die first, or our relationship might end in other ways, but if I obsess about how it will come to a close, I will miss the joy of the moments right in front of me.

Even though I didn't yet have a label for it when I discovered the concept of mindfulness, I subsequently learned that studies show that the practice of mindfulness relieves depressive symptoms and reduces stress and anxiety.[22] Discovering mindfulness also led me to explore some other concepts from the Buddhist tradition that have changed my attitudes about aging.

"You Look Good...for Seventy-Three"

It's strange the things I hear when I tell people how old I am. The most frequent response is "You look good...for seventy-three." I restrain myself from asking, "What were you expecting?" It's as if they are saying to me, "You don't sweat much...for a fat person." I know they mean it as a compliment, but it just doesn't *feel* like one. I hear another response frequently—"Age is only a number"—but I hear it as a partially expressed thought: age is only a number—but it's a really big number. But the truth is that although the marks of decay are visible, I don't feel like I'm seventy-three; or perhaps I should say I don't think or feel as I expected to think or feel at this age. For example, I still think about sex. Frequently. And when I say I *think* about it, I don't mean that I *reminisce* about it; I think about it as in I anticipate it. But this entire conversation about my age reveals that I am responding to internalized stereotypes of what aging must mean, just as those who've commented upon it. When I say, "I don't feel seventy-three," what I'm really expressing is that my experience of aging doesn't match the stereotypes I internalized sixty-five years ago when I rightly or wrongly interpreted seventy-three years old as much older than it seems today.

Ageism is a form of discrimination and prejudice experienced by seniors. Most seniors are mentally and physically active regardless of age and have a great deal to contribute. However, societal norms marginalize seniors, treat them with disrespect, make them feel unwelcome, and otherwise generalize about them as if they are all the same. Ageism robs seniors of choice, independence, and dignity and negatively impacts the quality of their lives.

Although many of our politicians are past their own best-if-used-by date, they often see the years past sixty as a time of low or no productivity, as if all seniors do is stand in line to collect entitlements like Medicare and Social Security. That attitude is both disabling and disempowering. Many of these politicians are of my own generation, and they have internalized the same outdated stereotypes that lump those of us over sixty together as if we are a millstone around the neck of society. Few in my generation knew anyone old and gay at the time we incorporated the stereotype of old age into our psyches, so we didn't assimilate semblances of older gay men and women who are filled with vitality. Older gay men and women are in double jeopardy: many people see us old people as a drain on society's resources, and since we're largely invisible, the idea that old gay people might have special needs is impalpable.

Younger generations cannot imagine the world in which we grew up, where we had no role models who lived openly as gay men and women. On the other hand, the stigma of homosexuality—the belief that homosexuality was sinful, evil, criminal, or pathological—surrounded us. Without obvious gay role models to challenge those images, we had to unlearn all that we thought we knew, and some of us succeeded more than others in reeducating ourselves.

As I researched the first edition of this book, I questioned the accuracy of my memories of what it was like when I grew up, but they proved to be as accurate as memories can be. Growing up in Nebraska and small-town America led to a great deal of naiveté and lack of sophistication. But even those who were raised in urban areas and who understood their sexual orientation at a much earlier age were forced to live in an underground society, the only place they could be semisafe from harassment and police entrapment. The African American civil rights movement began in 1955, and the feminist movement really took hold in the 1960s and '70s, paving the way for the Stonewall uprising on June 28, 1969. Stonewall kicked off the gay rights movement, precisely at the time I was entering the gay-unfriendly world of the US Navy. I did not know anyone who lived openly as a gay man or woman until 1975 when I was thirty-two years old, and that contributed to my confusion about my sexual feelings.

This separation of the worlds of the gay and straight reinforced the stereotypes and in turn the stereotypes helped keep those worlds apart. For me the gay world wasn't just unexplored, it was undiscovered.

Many of the men in my era came out between the ages of thirty-five to forty years old, and we couldn't come out until after we shattered some of those internalized stereotypes of what it means to be both gay and gray.

Many of the men in my era came out between the ages of thirty-five to forty years old, and we couldn't come out until after we shattered some of those internalized stereotypes of what it means to be both gay and gray. Those of us who came out at an older age find it difficult to conceive that today an elementary-school-age child can come out as gay or transgender. For young people to understand what took us so long to come to that same realization is equally difficult.

Just as internalized stereotypes of being gay keep us from accepting we're gay, internalized stereotypes of aging cause us to resist the idea that we are getting old. If ageism is a form of prejudice against old people, we have developed a prejudice against ourselves, another form of self-hatred. We are then not only the victims of discrimination but we are also the perpetrators of it. For me to age successfully, I needed to shed the stereotypes of aging in the same way I shed the stereotypes of homosexuality. Meeting Don in Houston and hearing him say "I'm eighty-two and this is the best time in my life" upended my negative mindset about getting older.

Slow Time

For too much of my life I lived with to-do lists and schedules. I lived through the stresses of getting into medical school, examinations, starting a practice, and making my professional life successful. We're always trying to bust through another ceiling instead of realizing that sometimes roofs are over heads to protect us. It seemed that no matter what mountain I climbed I was then faced with another even higher one to climb. I never learned to play very well. I gained a different perspective of play as I traveled around the world. I discovered that other cultures value their playtime much more than we do in our American culture.

I straddle between the traditionalist and the boomer generations. The traditionalist generation, born prior to 1945, tends to follow the rules, delay rewards, and value duty and hard work before pleasure. Baby boomers, born between 1946 and 1964, bought into the American dream, so they are sometimes seen as greedy, materialistic and ambitious. Many of them have seen the workplace transformed from being an environment where employers and employees were loyal to each other to one where workers are treated as commodities. Many boomers have a strong work ethic and have experienced working many years in a job only to find they are being laid off shortly before their retirement age; to achieve the American dream, they have lived to work. Another part of the explanation for my committing myself to work comes from my Germanic heritage. I can explain another part of it by my need to demonstrate I was worthy of approval.

Generation X, born between 1965 and 1980, includes latchkey kids who grew up having to take care of themselves and seeing their parents get laid off. It is the first generation not to do as well financially as the preceding generation. Because of this Gen Xers tend to balance work and play more effectively and place a higher priority on fun. They think more globally and are suspicious of the values of those more senior to them. As children, Millennials, who were born after 1981, were overscheduled and overprotected. They never lived without computers. They are hotly competitive but often more competitive in their fun than in their work, and they earn money to spend it.

Any time we put people in these kinds of boxes, we hear an outcry: "But I'm not like that!" Yet these descriptions have value, particularly in understanding intergenerational conflicts. They also help us to understand why traditionalists might have delayed their coming out until later in their lives and why the younger generations have been more open about their sexual orientation at a much earlier age. Perhaps cultural changes aren't entirely responsible for allowing this to happen; perhaps generational differences created the cultural changes.

The ancient Greeks had two words for time: *kairos*, meaning the right time or the opportune moment, and *chronos*, meaning sequential time or time as it is measured. *Chronos* is quantitative; *kairos* has a qualitative nature. Another way to characterize the generations would be to suggest that the older generations lived by *chronos* or quantitative time, and the younger generations live by *kairos* or qualitative time. As I've grown older I have discovered that life is not shrinking but expanding, and this has given me a greater appreciation for the quality of time. We can either measure time or experience time. We measure time when we say "I'll meet you for a coffee at ten a.m." or "How will I get all this done by five o'clock?" I learned from Don in Houston that life is about savoring slow time, and I look forward to opportunities to experience time with people from whom I want nothing and who expect nothing from me. Don—with limited and diminishing time— focused on experiencing time.

A few years ago, I went out to dinner with some men I had just met. The eight of us sat outside at the restaurant on a night that was so perfect it could have been created for outdoor dining. The service was good and efficient but not rushed. We inhabited that patio table for about three hours, eating and drinking, but mostly talking. As we paid our checks, one of the men commented, "This has been so much fun, I hate to see the evening end." It was an evening of unmeasured time, slow time, nothing-to-rush-off-to time. It contrasted sharply with those times I had sat at my desk eating a sandwich while doing paperwork and returning phone calls. I don't remember what I ate; I only remember the men with whom I ate that evening. I began to see that with whom you eat dinner is far more important than what's on the menu.

I have an old White Mountain hand-cranked ice-cream freezer that I bring out when we have guests. Making ice cream was a family tradition, and our unspoken rule was that if you didn't turn the crank, you couldn't eat the ice cream. In my childhood the women prepared the mixture—a tradition that has long since disappeared—and placed it in the stainless steel cylindrical tank, but then the men took over. The cylinder is placed in a wooden bucket, the churn is fastened into place, and it's all covered with ice. Salt is added to melt the ice and draw the heat from the liquid ice-cream mix. I always remind guests of the crank-turning rule, but I'm struggling to hang on to that tradition. Making ice cream is about spending slow time with people you care about; making memories is more important than making ice cream.

With whom you eat dinner is far more important than what's on the menu.

Once when my daughters and their families were visiting, I brought out the freezer. I explained the rule to everyone and I heard things like "Breyers makes very good ice cream," or the truly blasphemous comment "Loren, you know they make freezers with electric motors now." I languished on the porch, turning the crank and growing slightly irritated that I was out there alone, when my oldest granddaughter came out and turned the crank until it started growing solid. Then she sat on the freezer as I finished it off. She said with insight beyond her years, "Grandpa, I get it. It's not about the ice cream. It's about making the ice cream together." I'm leaving the White Mountain freezer to her in my will. During a visit in 2016, the same daughter's family visited and we made ice cream. Without having to mention the rule, every member of the family turned the crank. Everyone understood that we weren't just making ice cream; we were creating memories of joyful times together.

The Wisdom of Elephants

A myth about wild and domesticated animals is that if they're not being reproductive they're useless; perhaps to a lesser degree, that myth carries over to humans. A recent study investigated the decision-making and cognition effects of culling the post–breeding age females in herds of elephants. Graeme Shannon and his fellow researchers found that without the ability to learn from the matriarch and other group elders, the young elephants suffered a profound loss of social knowledge that affected their ability to make informed decisions, eat, find water, and breed successfully. When the older animals were culled, the herd did not thrive.[23]

When Doug and I raised cattle, we found the same thing. An older cow would babysit the young calves while the other mothers wandered off to graze. The older cows protected the young calves and knew where to look for the best grass and sources of water. The herd was more easily managed with the leadership of the experienced herd elders. Although the economic success of the operation depended upon successful herd reproduction, it also depended upon making difficult decisions about culling the nonproducers.

Erik Erikson writes that aging is just another step in personal development and cannot be understood in isolation from the rest of our lives because each stage builds on the developmental changes of previous stages.[24] In this context, each family member and each generation of the family must be understood in relation to developmental changes within the others. We expect parents to structure the development of their children, but we fail to realize that children also mold the development of their parents.

In elephants and cattle, in our development as individuals and tribes, and in the history of gay culture, the elders are the seat of active wisdom that leads to the thrift and survival of future generations. Marginalizing old people within our society and then marginalizing gay old people within that subgroup might undermine the fitness of our entire society. Elephants transfer their wisdom through sophisticated communication; humans have an even more sophisticated system of communication, but when we attempt to communicate with each other, we often get a busy signal.

The Urgency of Time

Doug and I are what is described as a mixed-generational couple because fifteen years separate us in age. Although sociologists classify him as a boomer and me as a traditionalist, his values are enough traditionalist and mine are enough baby boomer that we rarely give much thought to the number of years that separate us. We've made it work, after all, for nearly thirty years. At my age about a third of my contemporaries have died, which leads me to ponder the urgency of how best to live the time I have remaining. In three mixed-generational gay couples among our friends, the younger partners have died. Pain is learning our friends were dying; suffering is ruminating about how this might play out in our lives.

If I apply what I've learned about mindfulness, I will not spend time regretting time I might have wasted, and I will accept that how the next ten years unfolds is an unknowable. I will realize that I am healthy today; with some luck I'll feel good tomorrow. Sigmund Freud said, "Love and work are the cornerstones of our humanness," and I will continue to love and to work, the two most important things in life according to Freud. Yet I am aware that my time is limited and with each day it grows shorter. Death is no longer an abstract concept. I have little time left for anything inessential. Pain is being realistic about my age; suffering is being defeated by it.

Bucket and Unbucket Lists

Being present in the moment is not always easy to do. I still have bills to pay, I have some health issues, and if I want to continue to practice psychiatry, I must meet all the licensing requirements. I want to read more and write more, and I want to travel and immerse myself in other cultures, but even more than that I want to deepen my relationships with the people I love. I want to live richly and deeply in every corner of my life so that on that last day I can say I have completed it successfully.

Erikson's perception of aging reassured me; this wasn't the decline of my life, it was another part of my development. For my sense of well-being, aging demands a robust and active lifestyle. I was determined that I was not going to become a depressed, lonely, prematurely aged queen who was oversexed but incapable of making love. I was not going to waste whatever time remained. I stopped wearing neckties. I decided I would never attend at a cocktail party where I was sure there would be no one there I really liked. I decided I would never finish a book I didn't like, nor would I ever sit through a bad lecture or a boring movie. I warned my minister that his sermons had better be good. This was the beginning of a new sense of freedom. I intended to trust my own judgment; I would take charge of my own thoughts. I began to search for ways to approach this time in my life as the beginning of the next part of my life rather than the beginning of the end of it.

I once bought a book about one thousand places to visit before you die. As I glanced through the book I realized that even the wish to read the book was something I could take off my bucket list. Although I love to travel, I would rather make a list of the ten people I'd like to meet before I die. As I started the research on this book I began to communicate with and love people that live across the globe in places I would love to visit but will never be able to. I have immersed myself in their worlds via the Internet. We have touched and changed each other's lives. I realize now that my thoughts and feelings do not separate me from but profoundly connect me to the universe.

Our bucket lists are all the things we wish to do before we die. My bucket list has grown shorter, much shorter, but my unbucket list, the things that once seemed important but matter far less to me now, grows longer and longer by the day. Even some of the causes I have always felt and still do feel passionate about have been transferred; they belong to the future. Doug and I have deep roots in the soil of our small farm in Iowa, but as I worked on this book, I realized that sooner or later—probably sooner—our declining bodies would force us to make the decision to sell the farm and move to something more easily managed.

We have lived here on the farm for twenty years, longer than either of us has lived anywhere before. We've planted seven thousand trees and created a prairie restoration without using chemicals and poisons. Every spade of once-depleted soil is now filled with earthworms. The silence of our morning coffee on the porch is only broken by the cacophony of songbirds; our evening cocktails, by the thunder of bullfrogs. The night sky is powdered with stars and lightning bugs. Will the next owner cherish the bass we stocked in the pond we built, the asparagus bed we started, the fruit trees in the orchard that are just coming into full production? That is uncertain. I only allow myself to think about that now as I write, to describe how these decisions burden us. I must be content to know that tonight, this night, I can sip a cocktail and watch the lightning bugs and listen to the bullfrogs. And tonight, before I go to bed, I will once again experience the pleasure that every farm boy understands: I will pee off my porch.

But I know as the evening draws late I must climb the stairs to our bedroom on the second floor of our 125-year-old farmhouse, and they seem steeper now. Somehow we must come to believe that we are moving toward something instead of away from something.

Striving for Emptiness

In contemporary American society, winning is everything. The consumer culture has created a demand for a mountain of stuff, stuff we never had and yet think we cannot live without. We have products that are supposed to make us happy, change our lives, and keep us young. We worship a youth culture of Botox and Viagra. George Orwell is said to have written, "At fifty, everyone has the face he deserves." Martin Amis modified it to say that now everyone gets the face he can afford. Generations of marketing culture have drained a sense of meaning from our lives. We are told to climb the ladder of success but not to be careful against which wall we place the ladder. We network in a quest that asks, "What can you do for me?"

I was suffering when I turned sixty, but much of that was my own making. As I passed through that sixtieth birthday, I began to realize that

I had been caught in a culture of ambition and concept of forever-young. Striving is the hallmark for men in the prime of their lives. As I completed one goal, I replaced it with another. I wanted to climb one step higher on the ladder of success, and I had courted relationships with people who would assist me in my climb. I collected stoneware bowls, and I have so many I could break one a week and the collection would outlive me. I have a junk drawer full of brass rings I thought I had to collect on the way up. We have come to believe that our value as humans and the proof of our success depend on designer clothing labels or the number of square feet in our houses rather than see those things as the temporary fulfillment of ultimate materialism.

I climbed the ladder of success until I discovered there was no more "up" up there. I looked for a life of meaning "out there" and "up there"—I pursued social status, adopting an ideology that would satisfy my need for meaning, and in the process I adopted other people's values. But all of this was a delusion, albeit a pervasive and seductive one. I was imprisoned by it and felt estranged from my soul. But I didn't see an alternative. Meanwhile, of course, the clock was ticking—quite loudly, in fact. I became breathless. I had no time left for a calm and reflective appreciation of my twilight years, no deliciously long afternoons sitting with friends that I might not ever get another chance to idle with. What I discovered as I grew older was that I had made two false assumptions—that I am powerless, and that others had unlimited power over me. I discovered that the meaning I was looking for was in fact within me.

When I chose to go into psychiatry, my mother wasn't happy about it. She didn't tell me I shouldn't, but she couldn't understand it.

I discovered that the meaning I was looking for was in fact within me.

What I found in psychiatry was a sense of meaning, something that enriched my soul. It was the place where I felt that there was something big within me that was separated by only a thin space from something bigger out there. I felt it when each of my children and grandchildren were born. I felt it when I married my wife and later when I met and married Doug.

One of the common threads among the patients that I see is a lack of meaning. They have no idea what will fill their soul. I see many drug addicted people, and during their addiction their only goal is to find meaningful relief from their pain in the short time that follows the entry of the needle into their vein. For some, it is their only sense of meaning, for which they sacrifice their jobs, their marriages, and their children. Others search for meaning by attaching themselves to a strong personality who defines their meaning for them. They seek approval of another who rarely gives it in order to keep his or her victims always a bit hungry, trying harder and harder to find that approval that is withheld.

I have a gay cousin who believes that he can find happiness if he just finds the right husband who loves him unconditionally and has sex with him whenever he wants it. Gradually he is beginning to understand that no perfect soul mate can bestow happiness upon him; he must find it for himself. It has been difficult for him to discover that passion has a definite shelf life and that all relationships have some measure of disappointment.

U-Turns

All relationships are U-shaped. If one thing exists that is fundamental to the social meaning of marriage, it's monogamy, but passion in a relationship has a finite shelf life. Each relationship begins with the magic of romance, a blending of lust and love. Then an aura of disappointment sets in, and try as we might, the original, unsullied attraction that drew us into the relationship is impossible to recapture. All three of the major relationships in my life have followed this course. When I was married to my wife, Lynn, we started with a strong connection and a high degree of commitment to the traditional values of marriage. Falling in love with Roberto corrupted that relationship with Lynn and it fell to the

If one thing exists that is fundamental to the social meaning of marriage, it's monogamy, but passion in a relationship has a finite shelf life.

bottom of the U. Because I could not let go of my sexual orientation, our relationship just lay there at the bottom of the curve, and we could not slog our way out of it.

When I fell in love with Roberto, the relationship started off at a point even higher than my relationship with Lynn. I believed he was my perfect soul mate, but I had created him to fill the empty spots in my life. The illusion of the perfect soul mate was ripped away rather quickly and culminated with his beating me, excising any interest I had in trying to form a new and different relationship with him.

Doug and I have followed the U-shaped curve to a different place than I did in my relationships with Lynn and Roberto. After about twenty-five years in the relationship we came to a point of considering dissolving it. We fell into a pattern of blaming each other for all the problems in our relationship without examining our own contribution to those problems. Both of us avoid conflict whenever we can so many of the little sparks conflagrated into a large wildfire. We lost trust in each other.

But at the bottom of the curve, when we were both thinking that perhaps there was someone else out there that might make us happier, we came to realize that what we had was worth hanging on to. We began to ask whether we could begin afresh and build a second relationship based on the same values we had when we originally committed to one another. Our choice was either to move on or accept that the person we loved was imperfect—but even more, to admit that we also were imperfect.

In her TED talk "Rethinking Infidelity," Esther Perel said that relationships can achieve no higher level of development than the level of each partner's maturity. She said that people who cheat often believe in monogamy, but they find their values and behavior in conflict when they actually have an affair.[25] But instead of changing partners for that last dance, Doug and I decided to find in our last dance some of the magic we had found in our first dance so that we wouldn't have to sacrifice all of the memories, all of the relationships, all of the life we had shared for the previous twenty-five years.

Chocolate or Vanilla?

When I speak to groups I often ask the audience to raise their hands if they prefer chocolate ice cream or vanilla. Puzzled looks cross their faces as the chocolate lovers raise their hands followed by the vanilla lovers. Then I ask, "Who's right?" Obviously neither answer is correct, but so often we believe that our own opinion outweighs the opinion of others. In insisting on the correctness of our preference, we deny the humanity of others and their right to have an opinion that differs from our own. We often make that mistake in our intimate personal relationships, as Doug and I had in ours. The more we insist that our partners satisfy our needs in a relationship, the more dissatisfied we become. Loving another is giving him the freedom to love chocolate or vanilla, and being loved is being accepted for our own choices.

As Doug and I gained control over the wildfire in our relationship, we focused on both mindfulness and meaningfulness. We began to focus on the joy of each day we shared without wondering if someone better would come along to rescue us when some days were darker. We also began to realize that the most meaningful aspect of our lives was the relationship we had with each other as well as those relationships with families and friends that we shared. The food at the family reunion potluck is not what brings us all together.

Loving another is giving him the freedom to love chocolate or vanilla, and being loved is being accepted for our own choices.

If we were to thrive in our relationship rather than just survive, Doug and I needed to make some changes. We had to begin talking with each other instead of someone else about things that weren't working in our relationship and accepting responsibility rather than blaming. We had to let go of our anger because, as the saying goes, "Holding onto anger is like drinking poison and expecting the other person to die." Trust, once damaged, can be difficult to reestablish but being more honest with each other than we had been allowed the trust to return. Trustworthiness in ourselves and each other was a value we shared. When Doug and I first began dating, I told him I worried that he would leave. His response was, "If I'm still here in the morning, you'll know I'm still committed." Another interpretation of that is to be mindful of the present and stop worrying about tomorrow. One way or another, all relationships end. Love and risk are inseparable. Tonight we'll go to bed together, and I hope that he's still there in the morning.

Fidelity, Cheating, and Polyamory

Gay men frequently have different expectations about monogamy in their relationships than heterosexual couples do. Some monogamous gay couples experience a relationship that feels too narrow, with no room even for male platonic friendships. In a *New York Times* article, Scott James reported that about 50 percent of gay couples surveyed have sex outside their relationships with the knowledge and approval of their partners.[26] Statistics like these have been used as evidence that gay men are incapable of long-term, committed relationships. As romance and passion diminish, love may exist without desire. New attractions cause excitement to build, judgment to fail, and trouble to begin.

Our culture socializes men to be independent, and some male couples seek to reduce their dependence on each other by seeking sex outside the relationship. Some couples consider their relationships open but run into problems when the members of the couple lack agreement about how nonexclusiveness will be managed. Nonmonogamous sex can interfere with sexual desire for the spouse, and if adventures become regular, they can become destructive in the relationship. Couples sometimes introduce a third person into their sexual relationship to add excitement, but problems result if the primary spousal relationship is already strained and one of the pair feels left out.

Cheating can be an occasional indiscretion or it can become habitual. It can lead to lying about sexual exclusivity and undermining trust in a relationship. Cheating can also become the preferred way of getting needs met or a way of acting out anger. Although gay male couples may be sexually nonmonogamous, most will remain emotionally monogamous; the emotional commitment to their partner binds them together more than the nonexclusive sex pulls them apart.

While I was seeing Roberto, we were both married. We both understood that we were cheating on our wives. We each justified our behavior with our own personal rationalizations, however weak. Attaching oneself to more than one person emotionally is possible, but loving more than one person is very difficult to do. The question "Did you have sex with that person?" is what most people who've been betrayed insist upon asking, but emotional infidelity is far more damaging to a relationship than sexual infidelity. Once loyalty shifts and trust is broken, it can be very difficult, though not impossible, to reestablish a solid relationship. In seeking resolution, the individuals in the relationship lock themselves into conflict if they focus only on how the other person could have betrayed them without asking what they might have done to contribute to the weakening of the relationship.

Emotional infidelity is far more damaging to a relationship than sexual infidelity.

Some people, both gay and straight, are turning to what they call responsible nonmonogamy or polyamory. *Polyamory* literally means many loves. No statistics are available for how common polyamory is. Proponents of polyamory believe that humans experience varying degrees of loving others. They see the barrier between friends and lovers as permeable. Polyamory follows rules of polyfidelity, or fidelity within a closed system. In polyamory, the primary relationship takes on the characteristics of a spousal relationship with a high degree of commitment; all other relationships are subordinate. Secondary relationships involve both emotional and sexual intimacy and are enduring, but the secondary relationship does not carry the power or authority of the primary relationship.

One man spoke of his twenty-five-year relationship with his partner, who became impotent after surgery for cancer of the prostate. Although he continues to love his partner, he also loves another man with whom he has engaged in a daily, long-term Internet relationship that includes webcam sex, as sexually intimate as it can be in two dimensions.

Variations are seemingly endless. Many find it difficult to comprehend that a man can love a woman while preferring to have sex with another man. Many of these men claim to have a good sex life with women, all the while knowing that for them sex with a man is more satisfying. I know of several pairs of heterosexually married couples in which the two men have developed ongoing, long-term sexual relationships with each other. They sought these relationships as a way of dealing with their same-sex attractions with their other foot planted in a heteronormative world. The families are friends, travel together, and seem content. Others I know have been open with their wives about their male sexual partners; their wives have agreed to share their spouse with a man rather than accept a divorce. Even in those situations where they do divorce, these men may never define themselves as gay.

The most common problems in these relationships are predictable. When someone new is brought into the system, sexual interest focuses intensely on the newest member, and triangulation of relationships results in possessiveness and jealousy. Frequency of sexual intimacy between the primary spousal partners may diminish. Schedules and an overriding commitment to children complicate these relationships. To be successful, all relationships within the system must be respected. They must be based on honesty and authenticity rather than sex alone. Members must also be assertive to get their own needs met and boundaries and limits must be respected.

Nothing Is Too Late

In "Morituri Salutamus," a poem for the class of 1825 at Bowdoin College in Brunswick, Maine, Henry Wadsworth Longfellow wrote:

> But why, you ask me, should this tale be told
> To men grown old, or who are growing old?
> It is too late! Ah, nothing is too late
> Till the tired heart shall cease to palpitate.[27]

The words *opportunity* and *aging* are rarely used in the same sentence, but as we age we have extraordinary opportunities we've never had before and will never have again. We have gained wisdom from the experience of making good and sometimes bad choices. Aging tames the limbic system, the part of our brain that controls our emotions and is the source of the dopamine that makes us crazy. We are free to think more rationally. Testosterone levels drop and lower our sex drive to more manageable levels. We can think more rationally than we've ever thought before and from a substantially different perspective than we did earlier in our lives. We reexamine our value system and make it our own.

We can understand our history in new ways. We can examine the value system we were given and make one of our own, keeping the best parts and discarding those that don't work. We can learn to value the gifts we were given instead of envying the gifts of others. We can value our friends for who they are, not what they can do for us. We can make ourselves vulnerable and let others know us deeply. We can learn to make love in slow time, not because we have to but because we want to. We can be the first to say "I love you."

We can learn to play and take a leap into the world of imagination. We have the freedom of time and the freedom from our overscheduled lives, but we must stop being frightened by the limited amount of time we have left. We can appreciate time as an experience rather than a measurement. We can establish new priorities. The clock is ticking, and as I inventory my bucket list, I'm checking some things off knowing I will never do them. What continues to rise to the top of that list is sharing deliciously long afternoons sitting with friends I love and sharing the stories of our lives. When I get ready to move to that assisted living place in my future, the stoneware bowls that I collected for years will go in the tag sale, but that hand-cranked ice-cream freezer will go to my granddaughter.

You have one possible life composed of a chain of connected moments. Savor each moment. Nurture important relationships. Be authentic. Do the things that give your life meaning. Let your past become history and the future be a surprise. Make this day the best time in your life.

12

Outed at Eighty: The Infancy of Old Age

Try to keep your soul young and quivering right up to old age,
and to imagine right up to the brink of death
that life is only beginning.

—GEORGE SAND

It was a perfect day to die, if such a thing exists. Spring of 1999 had delivered a dazzlingly beautiful morning for my mother's last day. The sun that burst through the window spotlighted the three dozen multicolored tulips on her bedside table. Doug, who loved my mother almost as much as I did, had sent the tulips with me as I made the seemingly endless trip from Des Moines to my hometown in Nebraska. A few days before, my mother had suffered a debilitating stroke that left her speechless, unable to swallow, and paralyzed on one side, but as much as we could tell, until near the very end her mind remained clear.

As a physician, I assumed the role of the family's spokesperson with the doctor. When I first consulted him after the stroke, the doctor told me that my mother would not recover from this stroke as she had from her earlier ones. He asked, "Do you want a feeding tube?"

"No," I responded immediately. She had been a strong and vibrant woman, fully engaged in her life, and she had a strong belief in an afterlife. I was confident I spoke for her and my siblings: "No feeding tube."

"Intubation and resuscitation?" I assured the doctor she would not have wanted either.

"How about antibiotics?"

Again I said no.

"Then what about IVs?" I hesitated. The questions had gotten progressively more difficult. I was torn between knowing what could be done medically and what should not be done ethically. Even without those life-saving interventions, she died more slowly than any of us had hoped.

Early one morning a few weeks after my mother's death, the ringing of the phone startled me from a sound sleep. It was my sister-in-law. My brother, age sixty-two, had died in his sleep. He was a quadriplegic, and for many years before he married, my mother had cared for him. Even after he married, he spoke with my mother daily. He died of pneumonia and a broken heart.

The grass on my brother's grave had scarcely sprouted before I received another call announcing that my ninety-year-old stepfather had died. After my mother died, he had lived alone in the home he had shared with her, but he didn't know how to live alone. Following her death, he had lost his will to live. After his burial, my capacity to grieve was exhausted. I could not have squeezed one more tear out of my eyes.

For older men and women, losing emotionally important family and friends harbors life's most difficult challenges, but midlife frees us to express our pain and sorrow more openly. We gain strength through our own losses, and we grow in compassion for others through their losses. By facing the reality of death, we learn to accept that love and loss are inseparably joined.

During the late summer of 2009, Congress debated the Affordable Care Act. Sarah Palin, who had been the Republican vice-presidential nominee, popularized false but intractable rumors that the bill contained provisions for "death panels." In a town hall meeting in Iowa, Iowa's veteran Republican senator Charles Grassley spoke of "pulling the plug on Grandma."[1] In an attempt to derail the real issues of the debate, social conservatives had twisted the bill's proposed optional consultations for end-of-life care to suggest that committees would decide who was worthy of living and who would die. Tragically, Medicare payment for the optional end-of-life counseling was stripped from the legislation as a compromise to move it forward. Doctors were to be paid for keeping people alive, not for helping them die with dignity.

I was incensed with what I considered to be immoral propaganda. I had personally experienced the importance of discussions about end-of-life care. Families wrestle painfully with decisions about when to stop care. End-of-life counseling can give serenity to patients, families, and physicians knowing that the wishes of the dying are being respected. I pulled the plug on my mother, Senator Grassley, but only to allow my mother to die as she wished.

I've Fallen and I Can't Get Up

A growing tidal wave of aging LGBTQ baby boomers is reaching retirement age. This group is the first post-Stonewall group to have experienced a high LGBTQ visibility. About 40 percent have previously been married in heterosexual marriages, something that is much more common in the senior cohort group than in younger ones.[2]

I am still troubled by a report I received of a preoperative male-to-female transgender person in her seventies who had Alzheimer's disease. Her social worker was unable to find placement for her within one hundred miles of her hometown in Nebraska. Transgender people often face the question, "Which bathroom will she use?" In late life they must also confront the question, "Who would want to be her roommate?"

Little thought has been given to the special needs of elderly LGBTQ people. Researchers have failed to include questions about sexual orientation in their studies. In the research that has been done, affluent white gay men from urban areas have been overrepresented. Women, people of color, and those with low incomes have virtually been ignored. No one seems to know about the existence of straight-identified MSM. Gay elderly people are a much more diverse group than was once thought; they are diverse in culture, ethnicity, physical ability, income, education, marital and child-rearing histories, places of residence, and the importance they place on an LGBTQ identity.

In 2006, MetLife published "Out and Aging: The MetLife Study of Lesbian and Gay Baby Boomers" and in 2010 followed up with a report called, "Still Out, Still Aging." The latter report credits LGBTQ boomers for advancing the US gay rights movement and within one generation changing social attitudes from seeing homosexuality as a psychiatric condition to supporting same-sex marriage rights. It also suggests that boomers have the ability to change the face of aging as much as they have changed attitudes about sexual orientation and gender identity. The updated study reports that LGBTQ boomers aren't much different from non-LGBTQ boomers; they have the same fears about aging, are similarly struggling to finance their retirement, have similar desires for end-of-life care at home, and have similar patterns of caregiving.[3]

Although many of the concerns about couples' relationships are now resolved with marriage equality, other differences between LGBTQ and non-LGBTQ seniors remain. LGBTQ boomers are twice as likely to be living with a parent and are far more reliant on close friends they consider their chosen family. LGBTQ boomers have more close friends, are more likely to get emotional support from those friends, more often live with friends, and are twice as likely to have discussed their end-of-life preferences with close friends. Since the earlier MetLife study, LGBTQ boomers have increasing confidence that they will be treated with dignity and respect by healthcare professionals, perhaps because they have more experience in demanding respect when it is not forthcoming.[4]

Gay, bisexual, and transgender men provide many more hours of care each week to another adult than the comparison groups.

One striking difference is that gay, bisexual, and transgender men provide many more hours of care each week to another adult than the comparison groups, but they are also care recipients. In this study, more LGBTQ people had received care on a regular basis from a friend or family member because of a health problem. The vast majority of elder caregiving is done by unpaid family members and others with whom the elder person has longstanding ties. LGBTQ boomers are four times as likely to depend on a friend as a caregiver, but a significant number of LGBTQ boomers felt they had no one to rely on in an emergency or serve as their long-term caregiver.[5]

All caregiving produces stress. As we leave midlife and move into our senior years, we progress closer either to requiring care or being a caregiver for someone else. One of the great challenges for a caregiver is to find ways to replenish emotional reserves consumed by the caregiving role. During caregiving, emotional energy flows only in one direction, away from the caregiver. When caregiving depletes emotional reserves, care and compassion can be transformed into anger and resentment.

Bisexuals in this MetLife study had significantly different experiences than do lesbians, gay men, or transgender people. They have significantly fewer friends, have by far the lowest rates of being out and finding acceptance, are twice as guarded with other people as any other LGBTQ subpopulation, and are far less likely to say that being LGBTQ was an important part of their identity.[6]

With aging comes a need to access social services. Aging service providers are not ready to face this flood of gay boomers. Although a wide variety of social programs and services support the elderly, few of these programs recognize or support the families of LGBTQ seniors. Social service agencies almost always operate with a presumption of heterosexuality; to access services of social agencies, many elderly gay men and lesbians have felt forced to recloset themselves. Retreating back into the closet reinforces isolation.

Because of widespread homophobia, the agencies and institutions entrusted with the care of seniors have been oblivious and alienating to the LGBTQ community. Caregivers often do not understand the nature of the informal support groups that many gay people have. They expect children and extended families to provide for the needs of the elderly. Families of choice often are not afforded many legal protections. Until April 2010, when President Obama asked the Department of Health and

Human Services to establish a rule that would prevent it, hospitals could deny visitation privileges to gay and lesbian partners.

"Woody" Baldwin, who founded Prime Timers Worldwide, an international social organization for mature gay and bisexual men, lived in an assisted living situation in Austin, Texas, until the time of his death in 2016 at the age of ninety-six. Woody had twenty-four-hour nursing assistance but he was fearful that his care would be compromised if he was open about being gay. When I visited him in 2015, he complained about his total lack of privacy, and he laughed as he said, "I can't even make a dirty phone call if I want to." This remarkable man who began an organization that gave renewed life to thousands of gay and bisexual men was incarcerated in his last days in a life of secrecy and isolation.

Shortly after Doug and I were married, I had shoulder replacement surgery. When I went to register prior to the surgery, the computer would not accept Doug's name as my spouse. A male patient could not have a male listed in that box. Since that time, attitudes have changed considerably, and each time we've accessed medical care, our relationship has been respected and accepted.

Two or Three Times Hidden

Gay elderly have been a mostly invisible demographic. Except for those who represent the extremes of the LGBTQ community (and the ones most often shown in the media), most gay men are indistinguishable from their heterosexual contemporaries. The media tend to represent gay men as quite young and physically buff. The rest of us disappear like smoke. Mature gay men and women have been called twice hidden because of both their age and their sexual orientation. Those men who have chosen not to reveal their same-sex attractions or prefer not to be labeled gay are buried even deeper. I was shocked when after seeing a woman for thirty years to treat her depression, as she stood to leave after her final visit, she shook my hand and said, "I've always thought I was a lesbian." Then she darted for the door.

Now when I interview a new patient, I confirm his or her gender by saying "You appear to be male/female." The next question is, "Are you gay, straight, or other?" Patients frequently respond, "No one has ever asked me these questions before," and I did not address any of these issues in my examinations until recently. Many times the answers aren't predictable.

Gay men who come out in midlife or later not only lose the favored status of the heterosexual life they've been living but also must face compounded ageism from the youth culture of our society. Youth bias in the broader culture and among LGBTQ people in particular is reflected in our standards of beauty. This emphasis on youth accelerates the effects of aging for gay men.

Gay elders are often segregated from the LGBTQ community. Until recently, gay seniors have frequently been excluded from community discussions, and senior issues have been absent from the LGBTQ political agenda. Older gay men and women do not advocate for their own interests very well and outreach to them is lacking. Some who grew up prior to Stonewall simply have never learned to be comfortable expressing their sexual orientation publicly. Older people in general have less fire in their bellies; they have fought the good fights and now have political fatigue.

Although gay men are said to experience themselves as older than their chronological age, perhaps this is changing. During a visit to Las Vegas, I rode in a beautiful vintage Cadillac with a group of men from the Las Vegas Prime Timers. As the car edged its way through the crowd, the streets were lined with young gay men and women and LGBTQ supporters who with thumbs up shouted their support to us. This sense of separation between the older and younger members of the LGBTQ community wasn't apparent at that Pride event. These seniors were applauded because they were there to say, "We're here. We're queer, too."

The MetLife study found that LGBTQ boomers expect more dignity and respect in old age from their health providers than do others, and a large majority feel better prepared for their own aging. LGBTQ boomers may have self-advocacy and resilience skills that would be useful to other boomers and elders as they face many similar challenges of age.

These findings offer support for what Douglas Kimmel described in a 1978 paper as crisis competence. Kimmel suggested that coming out serves as a training ground for successful future crisis management, suggesting that working through the conflicts of coming out creates a buffer against later traumas and a capacity to deal with the stresses of midlife with a higher degree of skill: "If I survived that, I can survive anything." Crisis competence consists of our innate ability to recover from adversities and our coping mechanisms learned from earlier life experience. It can mitigate feelings of loss, help us develop some immunity to traumatic events, and hasten our recovery from losses.[7] Gay people may age in a more positive way because living through the crisis of coming out facilitates resolving crises that lie in our future.

"Doctor, Meet My Friend"

I once cared for an aging lesbian who began to have memory problems. She went to a neurologist who said bluntly, "Get your affairs in order. You have Alzheimer's disease." My patient was confused, devastated, and depressed. She asked a companion to accompany her on her return visit. This time the neurologist said, even more bluntly, "I never told you that you have Alzheimer's disease!" Enraged, her companion suggested that she get a second opinion. The second neurologist compassionately confirmed the diagnosis of Alzheimer's disease. Taking a companion to visits with a physician will improve both quality and satisfaction with the medical care received.

Most Americans worry about quality, access, and affordability of healthcare, especially those past sixty. In general, the sicker you are, the less satisfied you are with the care you receive. Writing in the *Archives of Internal Medicine* in 2008, Jennifer Wolff and Deborah Roter suggested that being accompanied by a companion to doctors' visits will improve both quality and satisfaction with the medical care. A companion allows even the frailest and most vulnerable people to have more confidence in their doctors' skills, to feel better about the information they receive, and to have a better relationship with their doctors. According to the study, patients' companions facilitated communication, recorded physicians' instructions, provided medical history, asked questions, and explained instructions to patients. In addition, they offered moral support, provided transportation, and handled details like appointments and paperwork. The more functions the companion performed, the higher the patient's satisfaction was for the services received.[8]

Aging well without a social support system is difficult, and families often act as a protective buffer. For many LGBTQ seniors, prejudice disrupted their lives and their connections with their families of origin. When LGBTQ people become estranged from their family, that buffer is removed. They are also less likely to have children of their own. The MetLife "Still Out, Still Aging" study found that nearly two-thirds of LGBTQ boomers have a chosen family, defined by the survey as "a group of people to whom you are emotionally close and consider 'family' even though you are not biologically or legally related."[9]

Those who are partnered have a greater sense of well-being. They tend to have fewer sexual problems, lower levels of regret about their sexual orientation, and less depression. Because gay relationships are misunderstood, when caregiving decisions are made, the roles of the family of origin trump those of the family of choice. Kristijan, whom I wrote about in chapter 7, told me that as his partner lay dying, his partner's sister —from whom his partner had been estranged since learning he was gay several years prior—pushed Kristijan aside during his partner's final days when she rushed back into his life.

So here is the dilemma for gay people: medical care improves when you have a companion, but over half of gay men between sixty and seventy-nine years of age live alone. Aging gay seniors also must become assertive about developing a good support system and a family of choice when no family of origin is available. But the LGBTQ community must also begin to recognize the needs of those gay people who are isolated and alone and unable to advocate for themselves. This is an increasingly serious challenge for our LGBTQ community.

Many of the men who responded to my survey are quite healthy and active. Many have been married and have children, but many have friends who have become a family of choice. But a significant number are in poor health, live alone, and have no one to drive the car to the hospital or doctor's office.

Come Out, Come Out

To many older gay men, coming out seems almost routine for young people today. The life of pre-Stonewall men and women is nearly unimaginable to the young. Those who grew up in the pre-Stonewall era were accustomed to being considered sick, sinful, perverse, or arrested in their development. They lied to their parents, teachers, coworkers, and the military. They often denounced other gay men and women. They risked loss of stature, employment, social and economic standing, housing, friends, and family. Religion condemned them. Law enforcement brutalized them. Society stripped them of their dignity. Their social lives were disguised and addressed only in secret code. They found safety in marriages and in the priesthood while secretly having sex with men outside those relationships. They hid their identity, their relationships, and the depth of their sexual intimacy with their same-sex partners.

In general, the older one is, the more reticent one is to reveal sexual orientation. However, greater awareness of LGBTQ culture and increasing civil rights protection along with fewer repressive social constraints have all created new opportunities for older men to come out in the latter half of life. In addition, as men age, they have greater financial independence, are further along in their education and career, and have greater access to social options. Unfortunately, older gay men may have lacked access to positive gay role models. Or they may have been actively blocked in the process of identity development by societal messages about the validity of their same-sex attachments. Mature gay men have had less capacity to resist the internalized negative societal messages about their sexual identity.

Men who come out in midlife or later often were well adjusted and lived lives more consistent with heterosexual development sequences. Their social associations have been heterosexual, and their lives have been concealed. Remaining closeted later in life (or being forced back into the closet because of homophobic social services) leads to lower self-esteem and greater feelings of isolation. Having said that, ultimately having friends who accept one's being gay is more important than whether those friends are gay or straight.

It Ain't All Bad News

Not all elderly people, gay or straight, are depressed and lonely. We live our older years in much the same way as we lived our younger years, and late life reflects all the stages that came before it. Prior life experiences such as education, occupational experiences, and social class influence how people experience their declining years. A piece by Kirk Johnson in the *New York Times* described how some older people view old age as a never-ending adventure. Some senior adrenaline junkies hike in South Africa, travel to Antarctica, walk on the wings of planes, skydive, and tour New England on bicycles. For them, getting old is just the next stage of exploration of their lives. Entrepreneurs are developing businesses based on sensation, education, adventure, and culture that cater to these active elderly.[10]

It's a Wrap

I was speaking to someone at the Services and Advocacy for LGBTQ Elders office in New York City where I had gone to discuss my book. She said that during a discussion of older LGBTQ who are just coming out one of their young male staffers had asked, "Why would a forty-year-old man come out, anyhow? He's too old to have sex." The young staffer was unaware of three things:

1. Forty is the infancy of old age.

2. Men and women have sex well into late life.

3. Being gay is about far more than just having sex.

Over and over through the years, I have said to my patients, "All of life's most important decisions are made without enough information." As I have reflected on the two questions I'm often asked—"How could you not know you were gay?" and "Wasn't your marriage just a sham to protect yourself?"—I can say confidently that my marriage was not a sham. I did not use my wife and children as a shield from the possible consequences of my being gay. I loved her as much as I was capable— just not enough for either of us. I simply didn't have all the information I needed to make a different decision. I do not regret my marriage or my children; my only regret is the pain my being gay has caused them. I do not wish I had done it all differently, nor could have I done it differently. Many aspects of the heterosexual life I left behind brought me great joy.

Those of us who enter midlife before coming out have only begun to confront the cognitive complexities of paradox, ambiguity, and uncertainty in our lives. We discover the world is no longer black and white as we once believed. Mortality has become personal as we experience the liver spots and erectile changes. By midlife we have discovered that loving someone and bereavement are two sides of the same coin. Social status and religious support may be threatened while one seeks the emotional freedom and release of coming out. The depths of sexual intimacy may appear elusive. They must tack their ship in heavy winds and high seas, sailing from port to port as they offload the straight world they lived.

In his book about the life of Samuel Steward, Justin Spring wrote:

> Each generation of writers reinvents its perception of sexuality through novels, poetry, and autobiographical writing, and in the process rebels against the perceptions and experiences of the generation before. For male homosexuals in the twentieth-century United States, these shifts in perception have up to now been largely described merely as "pre-Stonewall" and "post-Stonewall." But clearly there have been other equally significant generational breaks between pre–World War II and post–World War II; pre-Kinsey and post-Kinsey; pre-McCarthy and post-McCarthy; pre-AIDS and post-AIDS; and, most recently, pre-Internet and post-Internet.[11]

I have lived through all of that and more. I would add to Spring's list pre-DNA and post-DNA and pre–brain imagining and post–brain imaging. We now know that DNA and the human genome function as a GPS that guides development in universal ways from the point of conception until our return to dust. On a global level, our brains are all alike; and yet the intricate networks that develop in our brains make us all unique. Little by little, scientists uncover secrets about our brains, and more will be revealed as the study of the brain dominates science in the twenty-first century. But will they answer the question, Why do some stars shine brighter when I see an attractive man and not as brightly when I see an equally attractive woman? Life cannot be defined by genetic codes, neurotransmitter substances, or hormones. We do not connect with the entirety of humanity on a purely biological level.

Pre-Freud and post-Freud might also be added to Spring's list. Sigmund Freud was an extremely good biologist, but the embryonic nature of biology constrained his exploration of the mind. A fear of familial and societal disapproval and observance of the canons of religious establishments helps to explain why some gay people live straight, even though compliance to the dictates of family and religion make them feel guilty and worthless. Studying Freud, much like studying the Lutheran catechism, served me well. But it served me better when I became mature enough to understand that I could challenge the dogma and unlearn some of what I had been taught. Not all truths have been revealed. Perhaps the unconscious is simply all of the truths about the brain that are yet to be revealed.

Perhaps the unconscious is simply all of the truths about the brain that are yet to be revealed.

I have grieved my father's death and I have sought out male mentors to understand how to be a man. But I now understand that it wasn't my father's death that made me gay. Of course his death was a tremendous loss for my family and impacted each of us in various ways, but I no longer feel I need to try to be a better man than he was just to feel as if I am his equal. I can also understand that my mother held me close after he died because she needed someone to touch and hold on to, especially after my grandfather took his own life. And it took me a while, but I finally learned that I would never lose her love simply by making choices for my life that were different than the ones she would have made for me.

The question, How could you not know you were gay until you were forty? is much easier to answer now. I was a child in an era when the Nazis were performing experiments on homosexuals in Germany. I was an adolescent when our own government associated homosexuality with communism and believed that gay men and women needed to be exposed and eliminated. I had a therapist who suggested my being gay might lead to jumping off a bridge, as it did so tragically for Tyler Clementi, a young Rutgers student. I have experienced the AIDS epidemic and hearing people say that my friends deserved to die because God was punishing them for their abominations. I have had a friend murdered by someone who felt that killing a gay person might bring power to his powerless existence. Living in a world so hostile to being gay or bisexual inhibits development and creates contradictions and dissonance that demand repression. In fact, it seems almost surprising—even heroic—that anyone comes out at all.

Mature MSM who have not yet come out have asked me, "Is it too late for me?" I respond with something Carlos Castaneda wrote: "The trick is in what one emphasizes. We either make ourselves miserable, or we make ourselves happy. The amount of work is the same." In my lifetime, older gay men were once thought to be poor, to live in the Bowery, to seek oblivion in cheap alcohol, and to regress to a point where they prey on small children. But a new image of mature gay men is emerging. Having confidence in what we think and feel and responding to our own perceptions in a positive way allows us to move out from behind the mask of concealment and to live life authentically.

Some older men resent the push by gay activists for them to openly and fully acknowledge their sexual orientation. Degrees of outness are not predictors of happiness in old age. As men become older they often distance themselves from an all-encompassing gay identity. Sex

These are the essential coming out tasks for mature MSM:

- Finding a stable acceptance of yourself
- Constructing a new reality
- Assertively meeting your needs
- Seeking a satisfactory sexual and social life
- Publicly acknowledging your same-sex attractions except where it might interfere with access to resources

diminishes as the central organizing force of one's life, and these men may choose to come out only to the point of self-acceptance.

Several months after Doug and I got married, I spoke with my favorite uncle, the one man I believe is most like how my dad would have been. Speaking about our marriage he said, "What you did almost broke my heart." For a while I felt sad for having caused him pain, but it did not undermine my confidence that what I had done was right. I am confident that my opinions are valid and worthwhile, and I know that he will continue to love me even though he may never approve of my marriage. Hugo von Hofmannsthal said, "To grow mature is to separate more distinctly, to connect more closely." For years I thought that I was not a man because I was gay. Now I know that being a man means accepting that I am gay and knowing that I am the person I want to be.

Dr. Mihaly Csikszentmihalyi, a psychology professor at the University of Chicago, wrote, "Happiness is not something that happens. It is not the result of good fortune or random chance...Happiness, in fact, is a condition that must be prepared for, cultivated, and defended privately by each person."[12] Your future can be different from your past, but you have a role in making that happen. What is stopping you from moving ahead? What do you want that future to be? What have you tried? What worked? What didn't work? What are you willing to sacrifice for it? We might pay a price for taking action, but we risk paying a significantly higher price for not taking any action.

I was sixty-seven when I first wrote this book, and I am seventy-three as I revise it for the second edition. I haven't started feeling old, but I now can see old age lurking like a predator in the shadows. Aging has compelled me to ponder what I value most. But it also allows me the freedom to discard what I least value. The transition from living straight to becoming gay began by unlearning things that I once thought were true and discovering an entirely new reality. I had to shed my old images of what it means to grow old to discover that this is the best time in my life. Life is but a series of connected moments, and this moment is all that I have. I cannot relive my past nor predict my future. I don't expect to ever confront having to start another lawn mower. I can choose to practice only those parts of psychiatry that I continue to love. I will focus my energy on the people I love. I've written my first book and now revised it. I may start another.

"Would you tell me, please, which way I ought to go from here?"

"That depends a good deal on where you want to get to," said the Cat.

"I don't much care where—" said Alice.

"Then it doesn't matter which way you go," said the Cat.

"—so long as I get somewhere," Alice added as an explanation.

"Oh, you're sure to do that," said the Cat, "if you only walk long enough."

—LEWIS CARROLL, *ALICE'S ADVENTURES IN WONDERLAND*

Notes

Preface

1. John Schwartz, "Highlights From the Supreme Court Decision on Same-Sex Marriage," *New York Times*, June 26, 2015, http://www.nytimes.com/interactive/2015/us/2014-term-supreme-court-decision-same-sex-marriage.html, accessed August 29, 2016.

2. "Changing Attitudes on Gay Marriage," Pew Research Center, May 12, 2016, http://www.pewforum.org/2016/05/12/changing-attitudes-on-gay-marriage/, accessed August 29, 2016.

3. Justin McCarthy, "Same-Sex Marriage Support Reaches New High at 55%," Gallup Politics, May 21, 2014, http://www.gallup.com/poll/169640/sex-marriage-support-reaches-new-high.aspx, accessed August 29, 2016.

4. "Varnum v. Brien," Lambda Legal, http://www.lambdalegal.org/in-court/cases/varnum-v-brien, accessed August 29, 2016.

5. GLAAD, *Reporting on the Bisexual Community*, April 2016, https://issuu.com/glaad/docs/bimediaresourceguide/1?e=6038659/34933376, accessed September 12, 2016.

6. Matt Goodman, "GLAAD's 'Accelerating Acceptance' Report Provides Snapshot of Americans' Feelings about LGBT Issues," *GLAAD* (blog), January 20, 2016, http://www.glaad.org/blog/glaads-accelerating-acceptance-report-provides-snapshot-americans-feelings-about-lgbt-issues, accessed August 29, 2016.

7. Mona Chalabi, "Killings of LGBT and HIV-Affected People Rose 20% in 2015, Report Finds," *Guardian*, June 13, 2016, https://www.theguardian.com/world/2016/jun/13/lgbt-hiv-killings-rose-20-percent-2015-orlando-nightclub-shooting-doubles-2016, accessed August 29, 2016.

8. Gary J. Gates, The Williams Institute, *LGBT Adult Immigrants in the United States*, March 2013, http://williamsinstitute.law.ucla.edu/wp-content/uploads/LGBTImmigrants-Gates-Mar-2013.pdf, accessed September 12, 2016.

9. James Ball, "More than 2.7 Billion People Live in Countries Where Being Gay Is a Crime," *Guardian*, May 16, 2014, https://www.theguardian.com/world/2014/may/16/countries-where-being-gay-is-a-crime, accessed August 29, 2016.

Introduction

1. Jane Gross, "Aging and Gay, and Facing Prejudice in Twilight," *New York Times*, October 9, 2007, http://www.nytimes.com/2007/10/09/us/09aged.html, accessed August 29, 2016.

2. "Pneumocystis Pneumonia—Los Angeles," Centers for Disease Control and Prevention, June 5, 1981 http://www.cdc.gov/mmwr/preview/mmwrhtml/june_5.htm, accessed August 29, 2016.

3. Harry Levinson (lecture, Physician Executives Conference, Phoenix, Arizona, 1988).

4. "Gay and Bisexual Men's Health: Suicide and Violence Prevention," Centers for Disease Control and Prevention, http://www.cdc.gov/msmhealth/suicide-violence-prevention.htm, accessed August 29, 2016.

5. "Suicides Among Adults Aged 35–64—United States, 1999–2010," Centers for Disease Control and Prevention, May 3, 2013, https://stacks.cdc.gov/view/cdc/29179, accessed August 29, 2016.

6. Joel Paris, *Prescriptions for the Mind: A Critical View of Contemporary Psychiatry*, (New York: Oxford University Press, 2008).

Chapter 1

1. *Bringing Up Baby*, directed by Howard Hawks (RKO Pictures, 1938).

2. Simon Maloy, "NY Times, Networks Ignored Sen. Craig's Record on Gay and Lesbian Issues," Media Matters, August 28, 2007, http://mediamatters.org/research /2007/08/28/ny-times-networks-ignored-sen-craigs-record-on/139701, accessed August 29, 2016.

3. Preeti Pathela et al, "Discordance between Sexual Behavior and Self-Reported Sexual Identity: A Population-Based Survey of New York City Men," *Annals of Internal Medicine*, September 19, 2006, http://annals.org/article.aspx?articleid=728543, accessed July 10, 2016.

4. Mandy Oaklander, "Same-Sex Hookup Rates Have Doubled in the U.S.," *Time*, June 1, 2016, http://time.com/4352899/sex-relationships-hookups, accessed August 29, 2016.

5. "HIV Among Gay and Bisexual Men," Centers for Disease Control and Prevention, http://www.cdc.gov/hiv/group/msm/index.html, accessed August 29, 2016.

6. "HIV among Women," Centers for Disease Control and Prevention, http://www .cdc.gov/hiv/group/gender/women/index.html, accessed September 11, 2016.

7. Rebecca M. Young and Ilan H. Meyer, "The Trouble With 'MSM' and 'WSW': Erasure of the Sexual-Minority Person in Public Health Discourse," *American Journal of Public Health* 95, no. 7 (2005): 1144–1149, doi: 10.2105/AJPH.2004.046714.

8. Brad Allen et al, "Former Ex-Gay Leaders Unite in Opposition to Conversion Therapy," National Center for Lesbian Rights, http://www.nclrights.org/former-ex-gay -leaders-unite-in-opposition-to-conversion-therapy, accessed August 29, 2016.

9. Justin Spring, *Secret Historian: The Life and Times of Samuel Steward, Professor, Tattoo Artist, and Sexual Renegade* (New York: Farrar, Straus and Giroux, 2010).

10. John Howard, *Men Like That: A Southern Queer History* (Chicago: University of Chicago Press, 2001).

11. George Chauncey, *Gay New York: Gender, Urban Culture, and the Making of the Gay Male World 1890–1940* (New York: Basic Books, 1994).

12. Colin Johnson, *Just Queer Folks: Gender and Sexuality in Rural America (Sexuality Studies)*(Philadelphia: Temple University Press, 2013), Kindle edition.

13. Chauncey, *Gay New York*.

14. Alfred Kinsey, *Sexual Behavior in the Human Male*, reprint ed. (Bloomington: Indiana University Press, 1998).

15. Spring, *Secret Historian*.

16. "Position Statement on Therapies Focused on Attempts to Change Sexual Orientation (Reparative or Conversion Therapies)," American Psychiatric Association, March/May 2000, http://www.psychiatry.org/File%20Library/About-APA/ Organization-Documents-Policies/Policies/Position-2000-Therapies-Change-Sexual -Orientation.pdf, accessed August 29, 2016.

17. Katy Steinmetz, "California Ban on Gay Conversion Therapy Stands," *Time*, June 30, 2014, http://time.com/2940790/california-ban-on-gay-conversion-therapy-stands/, accessed August 29, 2016.

Chapter 2

1. Plato, *Phaedrus*, trans. Robin Waterfield, Oxford World's Classics (New York: Oxford University Press, 2009).

2. Greg Botelho, "From Police Officer's Son to Pope: The Life of Benedict XVI," CNN, last modified February 12, 2013, http://www.cnn.com/2013/02/11/world/europe/pope-benedict-profile/index.html, accessed August 29, 2016.

3. Rachel Donadio, "On Gay Priests, Pope Francis Asks, 'Who Am I to Judge?,'" *New York Times*, July 29, 2013, http://www.nytimes.com/2013/07/30/world/europe/pope-francis-gay-priests.html, accessed August 29, 2016.

4. Ibid., accessed September 11, 2016.

5. Charles Darwin, *The Works of Charles Darwin, Volume 21: The Descent of Man, and Selection in Relation to Sex (Part 1)* (New York: NYU Press, 2010).

6. Stella Hu et al, "Linkage between Sexual Orientation and Chromosome XQ28 in Males but Not in Females," *Nature Genetics* 11 (1995): 248–256.

7. J. Michael Bailey and Richard Pillard, "A Genetic Study of Male Sexual Orientation," *Archives of General Psychiatry* 48 (1991): 1089–1096.

8. Barbara Natterson-Horowitz and Kathryn Bowers, *Zoobiquity: What Animals Can Teach Us About Health and the Science of Healing* (Visalia: Vintage Press, 2012), Kindle edition.

9. Ibid.

10. Spring, *Secret Historian*.

11. Felix Warneken and Michael Tomasello, "The Roots of Human Altruism," *Science* 100 (2009): 455–471.

12. David Masci, "Americans Are Still Divided on Why People Are Gay," Pew Research Center, March 6, 2015, http://www.pewresearch.org/fact-tank/2015/03/06/americans-are-still-divided-on-why-people-are-gay, accessed August 29, 2016.

13. Jonathan Haidt, Silvia Koller, and Maria Dias, "Is It Wrong to Eat Your Dog?," *Journal of Personality and Social Psychology* 65, no. 4 (1993): 613–628.

Chapter 3

1. Westboro Baptist Church, http://godhatesfags.com/, accessed August 30, 2016.

2. Marcus Borg, *Meeting Jesus Again for the First Time: The Historical Jesus and the Heart of Contemporary Faith* (New York: HarperCollins, 1998).

3. Karen Leigh and Asa Fitch, "Islam's Punitive Line on Homosexuality," *Wall Street Journal*, last modified June 14, 2016, http://www.wsj.com/articles/islams-punitive-line-on-homosexuality-1465859532, accessed August 30, 2016.

4. Douglas Haldeman, "Gay Rights, Patient Rights: The Implications of Sexual Conversion Therapy," *Professional Psychology: Research and Practice* 33, no. 3 (2002): 260–264, http://www.drdoughaldeman.com/doc/GayRightsPatientRights.pdf, accessed July 10, 2016.

5. Reza Aslan, *No god but God: The Origins, Evolution, and Future of Islam* (London: William Heinemann, 2005).

6. *The Trials of Ted Haggard*, directed by Alexandra Pelosi (HBO, 2009).

7. Candace Chellew-Hodge, *Bulletproof Faith: A Spiritual Survival Guide for Gay and Lesbian Christians* (San Francisco: Jossey-Bass, 2008).

Chapter 4

1. James Fowler and Nicholas Christakis, "Dynamic Spread of Happiness in a Large Social Network: Longitudinal Analysis Over 20 Years in the Framingham Heart Study," *BMJ* 337, a2338 (2008): 1–9.

2. Rakesh Satyal, *Blue Boy* (New York: Kensington, 2009).

3. Tumaini Coker, S. Bryn Austin, and Mark Schuster, "The Health and Health Care of Lesbian, Gay, and Bisexual Adolescents," *Annual Review of Public Health*, http://www.ncbi.nlm.nih.gov/pubmed/20070195, accessed August 30, 2016.

4. "CDC Finds Suicide Rates among Middle-Aged Adults Increased from 1999–2010," Centers for Disease Control and Prevention, May 2, 2013, http://www.cdc.gov/media/releases/2013/p0502-suicide-rates.html, accessed August 29, 2016.

5. Ibid.

6. Arnold Grossman, Anthony D'Augelli, and Scott Hershberger, "Social Support Networks of Lesbian, Gay and Bisexual Adults 60 Years of Age or Older," *Journal of Gerontology Psychological Sciences* 55, no. 3 (2000): 171–179.

7. Vivienne Cass, "Homosexual Identity Formation: A Theoretical Model," *Journal of Homosexuality* 4 (1979): 219–235.

8. Seth Stephens-Davidowitz, "How Many American Men Are Gay?," *New York Times*, December 7, 2013, http://www.nytimes.com/2013/12/08/opinion/sunday/how-many -american-men-are-gay.html, accessed October 19, 2016.

9. Richard Russo, *Bridge of Sighs* (New York: Random House, 2007).

10. "Non-Discrimination Laws," Movement Advancement Project, http://www .lgbtmap.org/equality-maps/non_discrimination_laws, accessed August 30, 2016.

11. HRC Staff, "HRC Study Shows Majority of LGBT Workers Closeted at the Workplace," *Human Rights Campaign* (blog), http://www.hrc.org/blog/hrc-study-shows -majority-of-lgbt-workers-closeted-on-the-job, accessed August 30, 2016.

12. Spring, *Secret Historian*.

13. Harold Kooden, *Golden Men: The Power of Gay Midlife* (New York: Avon Books, 2000).

Chapter 5

1. Gary Titus, "Replacing a Heart of Hate," *Christianity Today* International, January 1, 2005, http://www.crosswalk.com/11622581/, accessed August 30, 2016.

2. Daniel Kahneman and Amos Tversky, "Prospect Theory: An Analysis of Decision Under Risk." *Econometrica* 47, no. 2 (1979): 263–292.

3. John Gottman, *The Seven Principles for Making Marriage Work: A Practical Guide from the Country's Foremost Relationship Expert* (New York: Crown, 1999).

4. *Wikipedia*, s.v. "Karl-Maria Kertbeny," last modified March 29, 2016, https://en .wikipedia.org/wiki/Karl-Maria_Kertbeny.

5. *Wikipedia*, s.v. "Paragraph 175," last modified July 25, 2016, https://en.wikipedia .org/wiki/Paragraph_175.

6. Steven Petrow, "The Changing Rules of Outing," *New York Times*, November 5, 2013, http://www.nytimes.com/2013/11/05/booming/the-changing-rules-of-outing .html?_r=0, accessed September 1, 2016.

7. Marilynn Brewer, "The Psychology of Prejudice: Ingroup Love or Outgroup Hate?," *Journal of Social Issues* 55, no. 3 (1999): 429–444.

8. Jason DeParle, "Rude, Rash, Effective, Act-Up Shifts AIDS Policy," *New York Times*, January 3, 1990, http://www.nytimes.com/1990/01/03/nyregion/rude-rash-effective-act -up-shifts-aids-policy.html, accessed August 30, 2016.

9. Andrew Tobias, *The Best Little Boy in the World* (New York: G. P. Putnam's Sons, 1973).

10. Levinson (lecture).

Chapter 6

1. John Gerassi, *The Boys of Boise: Furor, Vice & Folly in an American City*, reprint ed. (Seattle: University of Washington Press, 2001).

2. Ibid.

3. Ibid.

4. Indiemcemopants, "A Group of Homosexual American Citizens...Is Picketing the White House Today...," *Daily Kos*, December 28, 2010, http://www.dailykos.com/story /2010/12/28/932045/-A-group-of-homosexual-American-citizens-is-picketing-the -White-House-today, accessed August 31, 2016.

5. Randolph Baxter, "'Homo-Hunting' in the Early Cold War: Senator Kenneth Wherry and the Homophobic Side of McCarthyism," *Nebraska History* 84 (2003):119– 132, January 20, 2010, http://www.nebraskahistory.org/publish/publicat/history/full-text /2003-Homo_Hunting.pdf accessed August 31, 2016.

6. Ibid.

7. *Wikipedia*, s.v. "Mattachine Society," last modified July 7, 2016, https://en .wikipedia.org/wiki/Mattachine_Society.

8. Mike Wallace, "CBS Reports: The Homosexuals," *60 Minutes*, CBS, March 7, 1967, http://www.towleroad.com/2010/02/1967/.

9. Vito Russo, *The Celluloid Closet: Homosexuality in the Movies*, rev. ed. (New York: Harper & Row, 1987).

10. *Making Love*, directed by Arthur Hiller (Twentieth Century Fox, 1982).

11. *Wikipedia*, s.v. "Homosexuality: A Psychoanalytic Study of Male Homosexuals," last modified August 6, 2016, https://en.wikipedia.org/wiki/Homosexuality:_A _Psychoanalytic_Study_of_Male_Homosexuals.

12. Steven Lee Myers, "Irving Bieber, 80, a Psychoanalyst Who Studied Homo-sexuality, Dies," *New York Times*, August 28, 1991, http://www.nytimes.com/1991 /08/28/nyregion/irving-bieber-80-a-psychoanalyst-who-studied-homosexuality-dies .html, accessed August 31, 2016

13. Margalit Fox, "Charles W. Socarides, Psychiatrist and Psychoanalyst, Is Dead at 83," *New York Times*, December 28, 2005, http://www.nytimes.com/2005/12/28 /nyregion/charles-w-socarides-psychiatrist-and-psychoanalyst-is-dead-at-83.html?_r=0, accessed August 31, 2016.

14. George Engel, "The Need for a New Medical Model: A Challenge for Biomedicine," *Science*, April 8, 1977, www.ncbi.nlm.nih.gov/pubmed/847460, accessed August 31, 2016.

15. Joel Watts, "Plato—Homosexuality and Philosophy," *Unsettled Christianity*, January 14, 2011, http://unsettledchristianity.com/plato-homosexuality-and-philosophy, accessed August 31, 2016.

16. *Wikipedia*, s.v. "Homosexuality in ancient Rome," last modified August 30, 2016, https://en.wikipedia.org/wiki/Homosexuality_in_ancient_Rome.

17. Walter Williams, *The Spirit and the Flesh: Sexual Diversity in American Indian Culture* (Boston: Beacon Press, 1986).

18. Shirley Oliver-Miller, "CCIES at The Kinsey Institute: Papua New Guinea," *International Encyclopedia of Sexuality*, https://kinseyinstitute.org/pdf/ccies -papuanewguinea.pdf, 813–823, accessed July 10, 2016.

19. Ginny Dougary, "Lord Browne: 'I'm Much Happier Now Than I've Ever Been,'" *Times* (London), February 6, 2010, http://www.thetimes.co.uk/tto/business /moversshakers/article1891575.ece, accessed August 31, 2016.

20. Ibid.

21. "'We Don't Have Any Gays in Iran,' Iranian President Tells Ivy League Audience," *Daily Mail*, last updated September 25, 2007, http://www.dailymail.co.uk/news/article -483746/We-dont-gays-Iran-Iranian-president-tells-Ivy-League-audience.html, accessed August 31, 2016.

22. Faith Karimi and Nick Thompson, "Uganda's President Museveni Signs Controversial Anti-Gay Bill into Law," *CNN*, last modified February 25, 2014, http://www .cnn.com/2014/02/24/world/africa/uganda-anti-gay-bill/index.html, accessed August 31, 2016.

23. "Ugandan MPs Pass Life in Jail Anti-Homosexual Law," *BBC News*, December 20, 2013, http://www.bbc.com/news/world-africa-25463942, accessed August 31, 2016.

24. Paul Semugoma, Chris Beyrer, and Stefan Baral, "Assessing the Effects of Anti-Homosexuality Legislation in Uganda on HIV Prevention, Treatment, and Care Services," *SAHARA-J: Journal of Social Aspects of HIV/AIDS* 9, no. 3 (2012): 173–176, doi: 10.1080/17290376.2012.744177.

25. "Museveni Responds to Obama on Anti-Gay bill," *New Vision*, February 12, 2014, http://www.newvision.co.ug/new_vision/news/1337946/museveni-responds-obama -anti-gay#sthash.pWfkcrKW.dpuf, accessed August 31, 2016.

26. Patrick Kurth, "LGBT Rights in Kenya: A Conversation with David Kuria," *World Policy Blog*, July 28, 2015, http://www.worldpolicy.org/blog/2015/07/28/lgbt-rights -kenya-conversation-david-kuria, accessed August 31, 2016.

27. Nimisha Jaiswal, "India's Gay Rights Activists Start All Over Again," *USA Today*, February 5, 2016, http://www.usatoday.com/story/news/world/2016/02/05/india-gay-rights-globalpost/79864224, accessed August 31, 2016.

28. Amnesty International, "Japan 2015/2016 Annual Report," https://www.amnesty.org/en/countries/asia-and-the-pacific/japan/report-japan, accessed August 31, 2016.

29. Andrew Francis and Hugo Mialon, *Tolerance and HIV*, March 10, 2009, http://www.natap.org/2009/newsUpdates/Tolerance.pdf, accessed August 31, 2016.

Chapter 7

1. "The Brain Series: Brain Development," interviews with Charlie Rose, PBS, February 23, 2010.

2. Satyal, *Blue Boy*.

3. *Wikipedia*, s.v. "Two-Factor Theory of Emotion," last modified August 9, 2016, https://en.wikipedia.org/wiki/Two-factor_theory_of_emotion.

4. Hilary Whiteman, "Gay outrage over cardinal's child abuse comment," *CNN*, April 15, 2010, http://www.cnn.com/2010/WORLD/europe/04/14/vatican.homosexuality.pedophilia/index.html, accessed August 31, 2016.

5. James Cantor, "Is there a link between homosexuality and Church abuse?" *CNN*, April 22, 2010, http://www.cnn.com/2010/OPINION/04/22/cantor.homosexuality.church.abuse/index.html, accessed August 31, 2016.

6. American Psychiatric Association, *Diagnostic and Statistical Manual of Mental Disorders*, 5th ed. (Washington, DC: American Psychiatric Publishing, 2013).

7. Gregory Herek, "Facts about Homosexuality and Child Molestation," retrieved from http://facultysites.dss.ucdavis.edu/~gmherek/rainbow/html/facts_molestation.html, accessed September 1, 2016.

8. Penn Bullock and Brandon Thorp, "Christian Right Leader George Rekers Takes Vacation with 'Rent Boy,'" *Miami New Times*, May 6, 2010, http://www.miaminewtimes.com/news/christian-right-leader-george-rekers-takes-vacation-with-rent-boy-6377933, accessed July 8, 2016.

9. Rachel Slajda, "Rekers, in Resignation, 'I Am Not Gay,'" *Talking Points Memo*, May 12, 2010, http://talkingpointsmemo.com/muckraker/rekers-in-resignation-i-am-not-gay, accessed July 8, 2016.

10. Stuart Timmons, *The Trouble with Harry Hay: Founder of the Modern Gay Rights Movement* (New York: White Crane Books, 2012), Kindle edition.

11. *Wikipedia*, s.v. "Sexual Offences (Amendment) Act 2000," last modified March 10, 2016, https://en.wikipedia.org/wiki/Sexual_Offences_(Amendment)_Act_2000.

12. Gladys Martinez and Joyce Abma, "Sexual Activity, Contraceptive Use, and Childbearing of Teenagers Aged 15–19 in the United States," Centers for Disease Control and Prevention, July 2015, http://www.cdc.gov/nchs/products/databriefs/db209.htm, accessed August 31, 2016.

13. Bruce Lambert, "Case Highlights Sex Abuse at Church, Beyond Priests," *New York Times*, May 15, 2007, http://www.nytimes.com/2007/05/15/nyregion/15church.html?_r=0, accessed September 1, 2016.

14. Dennis Coday, "Pope's remarks Sunday on sexual abuse," *National Catholic Reporter*, September 27, 2015, https://www.ncronline.org/blogs/ncr-today/pope-s-remarks-sunday-sexual-abuse, accessed September 1, 2016.

15. Reuters, "Pope Francis: Church Should Ask Forgiveness from Gays for Past Treatment," June 17, 2016, http://www.gospelherald.com/articles/64929/20160627/pope-francis-church-ask-forgiveness-gays-past-treatment.htm, accessed September 1, 2016.

16. *Wikipedia*, s.v. "Two-Factor Theory of Emotion."

17. Paris, *Prescriptions for the Mind*.

Chapter 8

1. Trevor Hart et al, "Sexual Behavior among HIV-Positive Men Who Have Sex with Men: What's in a Label?" *Journal of Sex Research* 40, no. 2 (2003), 179–188, https://www.researchgate.net/publication/10622205_Sexual_behavior_among_HIV-positive_men_who_have_sex_with_men_What%27s_in_a_label, accessed September 1, 2016.

2. Ibid.

3. Ibid.

4. Keith Boykin, *Beyond the Down Low: Sex, Lies, and Denial in Black America* (New York: Da Capo Press, 2006).

5. J. L. King and Karen Hunter, *On the Down Low: A Journey into the Lives of "Straight" Black Men Who Sleep with Men* (New York: Harmony, 2007), Kindle edition.

6. Spring, *Secret Historian.*

7. *Wikipedia,* s.v. "Klein Sexual Orientation Grid," last modified June 29, 2016, https://en.wikipedia.org/wiki/Klein_Sexual_Orientation_Grid.

8. Gerulf Rieger, Meredith Chivers, and Michael Bailey, "Sexual Arousal Patterns of Bisexual Men," *Psychological Science* 16, no. 8 (2005), 579–584.

9. James Surowiecki, "Unlikely Alliances: When North Carolina's Legislators Tried to Limit L.G.B.T. Rights, Big Business Was Their Toughest Opponent," *New Yorker,* April 25, 2016, www.newyorker.com/magazine/2016/04/25/the-corporate-fight-for-social-justice, accessed September 1, 2016.

10. "Social Networking Fact Sheet," Pew Research Center, December 27, 2013, http://www.pewinternet.org/fact-sheets/social-networking-fact-sheet/, accessed September 1, 2016.

11. Julie VerHage, "Baby Boomers Flock to Facebook While Teens Exit En Masse," *Fox Business,* January 22, 2014, http://www.foxbusiness.com/markets/2014/01/22/baby-boomers-flock-to-facebook-while-teens-exit-en-masse.html, accessed September 1, 2016.

12. L. A. Eaton et al, "Online Sex Partner Meeting Venues as a Risk Factor for Testing HIV Positive Among a Community-Based Sample of Black Men Who Have Sex With Men," *Sexually Transmitted Diseases* 46, no. 6 (2016): 360, http://www.ncbi.nlm.nih.gov/pubmed/27200520, accessed September 1, 2016.

13. "Pornography Study That Was Doomed to Fail after Scientists Couldn't Find a Single Man Who Hadn't Viewed X-Rated Material," *Daily Mail,* last modified December 3, 2009, http://www.dailymail.co.uk/news/article-1232787/Pornography-study-doomed-fail-scientists-single-man-hadnt-viewed-x-rated-material.html#ixzz4J0In9Svt, accessed September 1, 2016.

14. *AARP,* "Sex, Romance, and Relationships: AARP Survey of Midlife and Older Adults," April 2010, http://asscts.aarp.org/rgcenter/general/srr_09.pdf, accessed September 1, 2016.

15. "The Stories Behind Sex Addiction," *CBS News,* November 16, 2008, http://www.cbsnews.com/news/the-stories-behind-sex-addiction-16-11-2008, accessed September 1, 2016.

16. Richard Wike, "French More Accepting of Infidelity Than People in Other Countries," Pew Research Center, January 14, 2014, http://www.pewresearch.org/fact-tank/2014/01/14/french-more-accepting-of-infidelity-than-people-in-other-countries/, accessed February 8, 2016.

17. Scott James, "Many Successful Gay Marriages Share an Open Secret," *New York Times,* January 28, 2010, http://www.nytimes.com/2010/01/29/us/29sfmetro.html, accessed September 1, 2016.

18. William Sloane Coffin, *Credo* (Louisville: Westminster John Knox Press, 2004).

19. Pamela Druckerman, *Lust in Translation: Infidelity from Tokyo to Tennessee* (New York: Penguin Books, 2008).

20. AARP, "Sex, Romance, and Relationships."

21. M. V. Lee Badgett, *When Gay People Get Married: What Happens When Societies Legalize Same-Sex Marriage* (New York: NYU Press, 2010).

22. "HIV among Gay and Bisexual Men," Centers for Disease Control and Prevention, http://www.cdc.gov/hiv/group/msm/index.html, accessed September 1, 2016.

23. Francis and Mialon, "Tolerance and HIV."

24. Centers for Disease Control and Prevention, "Viral Hepatitis—Hepatitis B Information: Hepatitis B FAQs for the Public," last updated May 23, 2016, http://www.cdc.gov/hepatitis/hbv/bfaq.htm.

Chapter 9

1. "Social Security Life Expectancy Calculator," Social Security Administration, https://www.ssa.gov/cgi-bin/longevity.cgi, accessed September 1, 2016.

2. Gilbert Herdt, Jeff Beeler, and Todd Rawls, "Life Course Diversity Among Older Lesbians and Gay Men: A Study in Chicago," *Journal of Gay, Lesbian, and Bisexual Identity* 2 (1997): 231–246.

3. Amity Pierce Buxton, *The Other Side of the Closet: The Coming-Out Crisis for Straight Spouses and Families*, rev. ed. (New York: Wiley, 1994).

4. Rebecca Mead, "Proud Flesh: The Cult of Cosmetic Surgery," *New Yorker*, November 13, 2006.

5. Julie Jones and Steve Pugh, "Ageing Gay Men: Lessons from the Sociology of Embodiment," *Men and Masculinities* 7, no. 3 (2005): 248–260.

6. RuPaul, *Letting it All Hang Out: An Autobiography* (New York: Hyperion, 1996).

7. Kooden, *Golden Men*.

8. Erik Erikson, *Identity and the Life Cycle*, reissue ed. (New York: W. W. Norton, 1994).

9. Philip Larkin, "This Be the Verse," *New Humanist*, August 1971.

Chapter 10

1. Dan Ariely, *The Upside of Irrationality: The Unexpected Benefits of Defying Logic at Work and at Home* (New York: Harper Collins, 2010).

2. Carmita Abdo et al, "Sexual Satisfaction among Patients with Erectile Dysfunction Treated with Counseling, Sildenafil, or Both," *Journal of Sexual Medicine* 5, no. 7 (2008): 1720–1726.

3. Ariely, *The Upside of Irrationality*.

4. Michael O'Leary et al, "Distribution of the Brief Male Sexual Inventory in Community Men," *International Journal of Impotence Research* 15 (2003): 185–191.

5. Arnstein Mykletun et al, "Assessment of Male Sexual Function by the Brief Sexual Function Inventory," *BJU International* 97 (2005): 316–323.

6. John McKinlay and Henry Feldman, "Age-Related Variation in Sexual Activity and Interest in Normal Men: Results from the Massachusetts Male Aging Study," in *Sexuality across the Life Course*, ed. Alice Rossi (Chicago: University of Chicago Press, 1994).

7. Dan Williams, "Erectile Dysfunction," http://www.uwhealth.org/urology/erectile-dysfunction-ed/20537, n.d., accessed September 1, 2016.

8. *The Bucket List*, directed by Rob Reiner (Warner Brothers, 2007).

9. Abraham Morgentaler, *Testosterone for Life: Recharge Your Vitality, Sex Drive, Muscle Mass, and Overall Health* (New York: McGraw-Hill, 2008).

10. Benedict Carey, "Long After Kinsey, Only the Brave Study Sex," *New York Times*, November 9, 2004.

11. Malcom Gladwell, *Blink: The Power of Thinking Without Thinking* (New York: Back Bay Books, 2007).

12. Ariely, *The Upside of Irrationality*.

13. Michael Seto, "The Puzzle of Male Chronophilias," *Archives of Sexual Behavior*, August 22, 2016 (copy obtained from author).

14. Urban Dictionary, s.v. "DILF," http://www.urbandictionary.com/define.php?term=DILF, accessed September 8, 2016.

15. Seto, "The Puzzle of Male Chronophilias."

16. Paul Zak, "The Neurobiology of Trust," *Annals of New York Academy of Science* 1032 (2004): 224–227.

17. Alfred Kinsey, *Sexual Behavior in the Human Male*, reprint ed. (Bloomington: Indiana University Press, 1998).

Chapter 11

1. Adam Liptak, "Supreme Court Ruling Makes Same-Sex Marriage a Right Nationwide," *New York Times*, June 26, 2015, http://www.nytimes.com/2015/06/27/us /supreme-court-same-sex-marriage.html, accessed June 26, 2015.

2. Ibid.

3. Dave Philipps, "Ousted as Gay, Aging Veterans Are Battling Again for Honorable Discharges," *New York Times*, September 6, 2015, http://www.nytimes.com/2015/09/07 /us/gay-veterans-push-for-honorable-discharges-they-were-denied.html, accessed September 1, 2016.

4. President Barack Obama, "Statement by the President on the Repeal of Don't Ask, Don't Tell," September 20, 2011, https://www.whitehouse.gov/the-press-office/2011 /09/20/statement-president-repeal-dont-ask-dont-tell, accessed September 1, 2016.

5. Debra Cassens Weiss, "Gay Marriage Is a Constitutional Right, Supreme Court Rules," *ABA Journal*, June 26, 2015, http://www.abajournal.com/news/article/gay _marriage_is_a_constitutional_right_supreme_court_rules/, accessed September 1, 2016.

6. Marc Santora, "Last Call at Pulse Nightclub, and Then Shots Rang Out," *New York Times*, June 12, 2016, http://www.nytimes.com/2016/06/13/us/last-call-at-orlando-club -and-then-the-shots-rang-out.html, accessed September 1, 2016.

7. Juliet Eilperin, "Obama: 'We Know Enough to Say That This Was an Act of Terror, and an Act of Hate,'" *Washington Post*, June 12, 2016, https://www.washingtonpost.com /news/post-politics/wp/2016/06/12/obama-we-know-enough-to-say-that-this-was-an -act-of-terror-and-an-act-of-hate/, accessed June 12, 2016.

8. *Wikipedia*, s.v. "Omar Mateen," last modified August 25, 2016, https://en .wikipedia.org/wiki/Omar_Mateen.

9. "Orlando Shooter Was Kicked Out of Jail Guard Training," *CBS News*, last modified June 17, 2016, http://www.cbsnews.com/news/orlando-shooting-omar-mateen -florida-department-of-corrections/.

10. Liam Stack, "Before Orlando Shooting, an Anti-Gay Massacre in New Orleans Was Largely Forgotten," *New York Times*, June 14, 2016, http://www.nytimes.com/2016 /06/15/us/upstairs-lounge-new-orleans-fire-orlando-gay-bar.html, accessed June 12, 2016.

11. "Latest Hate Crime Statistics Available," FBI, November 16, 2015, https://www .fbi.gov/news/stories/latest-hate-crime-statistics-available, accessed September 1, 2016.

12. Reuters, "Judge Rules Mississippi Clerks Can't Use Religious Beliefs To Deny Same-Sex Marriage Licenses," *Huffington Post*, last modified June 27, 2016, http://www .huffingtonpost.com/entry/gay-marriage-religious-beliefs_us_5771c8b8e4b0f168323abac4.

13. Everdeen Mason, Aaron Williams, and Kennedy Elliott, "The Dramatic Rise in State Efforts to Limit LGBT Rights," *Washington Post*, https://www.washingtonpost.com /graphics/national/lgbt-legislation, last updated July 1, 2016.

14. "Anti-LGBT Religious Exemption Legislation Across the Country," ACLU, https://www.aclu.org/anti-lgbt-religious-exemption-legislation-across-country?redirect =anti-lgbt-religious-refusals-legislation-across-country, accessed September 2, 2016. This website is updated weekly.

15. "Violence Against the Transgender Community in 2016," HRC, http://www.hrc .org/resources/violence-against-the-transgender-community-in-2016, accessed September 2, 2016.

16. Marc Ambinder, "Bush Campaign Chief and Former RNC Chair Ken Mehlman: I'm Gay," *Atlantic*, August 25, 2010, http://www.theatlantic.com/politics/archive/2010/08

/bush-campaign-chief-and-former-rnc-chair-ken-mehlman-im-gay/62065, accessed September 2, 2016.

17. James Dobson, "Dr. Dobson Addresses the Transgender Bathroom Debate," *Dr. James Dobson's Family Talk, July 2016,* https://drjamesdobson.org/news/commentaries /archives/2016-newsletters/july-newsletter-2016, accessed September 2, 2016.

18. Reuters, Jon Herskovitz, "Texas Politician Slammed for Tweet Sent after Florida Shooting," June 12, 2016, http://www.reuters.com/article/us-florida-shooting-texas -idUSKCN0YY0TA, accessed September 2, 2016.

19. Manny Fernandez, Richard Perez-Pena, and Jonah Engel, "Five Dallas Officers Were Killed as Payback, Police Chief Says," *New York Times,* July 8, 2016, http://www .nytimes.com/2016/07/09/us/dallas-police-shooting.html?_r=0, accessed September 2, 2016.

20. Lizeth Martinez, "Rights Are Won Only by Those Who Make Their Voices Heard," *International Exchange Alumni,* July 2014, https://alumni.state.gov/alumni-story /rights-are-won-only-those-who-make-their-voices-heard, accessed September 2, 2016.

21. *Wikipedia,* s.v. "Mindfulness," last modified September 2, 2016, https://en .wikipedia.org/wiki/Mindfulness.

22. "Stress, Anxiety and Depression," NHS Choices, http://www.nhs.uk/Conditions /stress-anxiety-depression/Pages/mindfulness.aspx, accessed June 1, 2016.

23. Graeme Shannon et al, "Effects of Social Disruption in Elephants Persist Decades after Culling," *Frontiers in Zoology* 10, no. 62 (2013), http://frontiersinzoology .biomedcentral.com/articles/10.1186/1742-9994-10-62, accessed September 2, 2016.

24. Erikson, *Identity and the Life Cycle.*

25. Esther Perel, "Rethinking Infidelity: A Talk for Anyone Who Has Ever Loved," *TED,* March 2015, http://www.ted.com/talks/esther_perel_rethinking_infidelity_a _talk_for_anyone_who_has_ever_loved, accessed September 2, 2016.

26. Scott James, "Many Successful Gay Marriages Share an Open Secret."

27. Henry Wadsworth Longfellow, "Morituri Salutamus," Maine Historical Society, http://www.hwlongfellow.org/poems_poem.php?pid=275, accessed September 2, 2016.

Chapter 12

1. Brian Montopoli, "Iowa's Veteran Republican Senator Charles Grassley Spoke of 'Pulling the Plug on Grandma,'" *CBS News,* August 12, 2009, http://www.cbsnews.com /news/grassley-warns-of-government-pulling-plug-on-grandma, accessed September 2, 2016.

2. MetLife, "Still Out, Still Aging: The MetLife Study of Lesbian, Gay, Bisexual, and Transgender Baby Boomers," March 2010, https://www.metlife.com/assets/cao/mmi /publications/studies/2010/mmi-still-out-still-aging.pdf, accessed September 2, 2016.

3. Ibid.

4. Ibid.

5. Ibid.

6. Ibid.

7. Douglas Kimmel, "Adult Development and Aging: A Gay Perspective," *Journal of Social Issues* 34, no. 3 (1978): 113–130.

8. Jennifer Wolff and Debra L. Roter, "Hidden in Plain Sight: Medical Visit Companions as a Resource for Vulnerable Older Adults," *Archives of Internal Medicine* 168 (2008): 1409–1415.

9. MetLife, "Still Out, Still Aging."

10. Kirk Johnson, "Seeing Old Age as a Never-Ending Adventure," *New York Times,* January 8, 2010, http://www.nytimes.com/2010/01/08/us/08aging.html, accessed September 2, 2016.

11. Spring, *Secret Historian.*

12. Mihaly Csikszentmihalyi, *Flow: The Psychology of Optimal Experience* (New York: Harper & Row, 1990).

Index

About the Author

Loren A. Olson, MD, is a board-certified psychiatrist with over forty years of experience. He is a Distinguished Life Fellow of the American Psychiatric Association and has been named an Exemplary Psychiatrist by the National Alliance for Mental Illness.

Dr. Olson has spent his professional life treating and advocating for those who suffer from mental illness. He has served as a medical executive, working to improve the quality care in psychiatric programs. He has taught psychiatry to a wide variety of healthcare professionals. He is an award-winning writer. Prior to becoming a psychiatrist, he served four years as a flight surgeon with the US Navy.

Dr. Olson has been a consultant to the media and has been interviewed numerous times on television and the radio, including on *Good Morning America*. He is a popular speaker on a variety of subjects, most recently on the subject of the opportunities of aging.

As Dr. Olson began his coming out at age forty, he researched the literature and found very little in both the lay and professional press about why some men come out later in life and how that process is different from coming out for younger men. He then conducted independent research of a nonclinical population of mature men who have sex with men, leading him to writing the first edition of *Finally Out*.

Dr. Olson was married to his former wife, Lynn, for eighteen years, and together they have two children and six grandchildren. The marriage ended in divorce when he finally came to terms with his being gay. His experience as a father has given him very personal insight into the centrality of children in the lives of gay men who are also fathers.

Dr. Olson has been with his partner, Doug Mortimer, for thirty years. They were married after the Iowa Supreme Court found, in a unanimous decision, that the Iowa statute limiting marriage to a man and a woman violated the equal protection clause of the Iowa Constitution.

With his husband, Doug, Dr. Olson lived until recently on a farm in Madison County, Iowa, where they raised Belted Galloway cattle that they sold throughout the United States. Dr. Olson was featured on national television on the subject of raising grass-fed cattle.

You can reach Dr. Olson via the following:

Website: www.lorenaolson.com
LinkedIn: https://www.linkedin.com/in/lorenaolsonmd
Facebook: http://bit.ly/2g1FjUL
Twitter: https://twitter.com/LorenAOlsonMD